Modern Critics
in Practice

By the same author:

A Concise Chronology of English Literature, Croom Helm, 1985
Johnson's Preface to Shakespeare edited with introduction and commentary, Bristol Classical Press, 1985

Modern Critics in Practice

Critical Portraits of British Literary Critics

Philip Smallwood

Department of English and Communication Studies, Birmingham Polytechnic

HARVESTER WHEATSHEAF

New York   London   Toronto   Sydney   Tokyo   Singapore

First published 1990 by
Harvester Wheatsheaf
66 Wood Lane End, Hemel Hempstead
Hertfordshire HP2 4RG
A division of
Simon & Schuster International Group

© Philip Smallwood 1990

All rights reserved. No part of this publication may be reproduced, stored in a retrieval system, or transmitted, in any form or by any means, electronic, mechanical, photocopying, recording or otherwise, without prior permission, in writing, from the publisher.

Typeset in 10/12pt Baskerville by
Eager Typesetting Company, Hove

Printed and bound in Great Britain by
Billing and Sons Limited, Worcester

British Library Cataloguing in Publication Data

Smallwood, P. J.
  Modern critics in practice: critical portraits of British literary critics.
  1. Literature. English criticism
  I. Title
  801'.95'09942

ISBN 0–7108–1252–3

1 2 3 4 5 94 93 92 91 90

Unbiass'd, or by *Favour* or by *Spite*;
Not *dully prepossest*, nor *blindly right*;
Tho' Learn'd, well-bred; and tho' well-bred, sincere;
Modestly bold, and Humanly severe[?]
Who to a *Friend* his Faults can freely show,
And gladly praise the Merit of a *Foe*[?]
Blest with a *Taste* exact, yet unconfin'd;
A *Knowledge* both of *Books* and *Humankind;*
Gen'rous Converse; a *Soul* exempt from *Pride;*
And *Love to Praise*, with *Reason* on his Side[?]
    Such once were *Criticks* . . .
(Alexander Pope, *An Essay on Criticism* [1711])

Whither then shall we turn for that union of qualifications which must necessarily exist before the decisions of a critic can be of absolute value? For a mind at once poetical and philosophical; for a critic whose affections are as free and kindly as the spirit of society, and whose understanding is severe as that of dispassionate government? Where are we to look for that initiatory composure of mind which no selfishness can disturb? For a natural sensibility that has been tutored into correctness without losing any thing of its quickness; and for active faculties capable of answering the demands which an Author of original imagination shall make on them . . . .
(William Wordsworth, 'Essay Supplementary to the Preface [to *Lyrical Ballads*]' [1815])

The critic of poetry should have the finest tact, the nicest moderation, the most free, flexible, and elastic spirit imaginable; he should be indeed the *ondoyant and diverse* being of Montaigne.
(Matthew Arnold, 'On Translating Homer' [1861])

The only judge, the only just literary critic, is Christ.
(Gerard Manley Hopkins, Letter to Dixon, 13 June 1878)

Contents

Introduction   1

1   Radical Theorists I: Terry Eagleton   7

2   Radical Theorists II: Catherine Belsey   41

3   Media Dons I: John Carey   72

4   Media Dons II: Christopher Ricks   101

5   Liberal Humanists I: H. A. Mason   130

6   Liberal Humanists II: W. W. Robson   161

7   Creators as Critics I: Ted Hughes   192

8   Creators as Critics II: David Lodge   222

Index   253

Introduction

I wish to keep my Reader in the company of flesh and blood, persuaded that by so doing I shall interest him.[1]

Criticism of criticism is an inherently tricky affair. In some people's view, it ought not to happen at all, since it is too many stages removed from what matters most in literary studies: the literature. But this attitude is now in decline. In proportion to the growth of interest that has occurred in recent years in the theory of literature, criticising the critic is increasingly the thing: in some quarters, it seems almost to have taken over from criticising literature altogether. And yet with the expansion of the empire of Critical Theory, the hazards of discussing literary criticism have in no way declined. This is because, as enthusiasm for theory has grown, so correspondingly has a powerful belief in the existence of a modern 'crisis in literary studies' (a phrase which has become the almost unchallenged short-hand way of introducing discussions of the modern critical condition). In its turn, this belief has helped to justify the inclusion of the study of theory (if only of one particular kind), while propagating the view that debate about literary criticism has reached an exceptionally lively pitch. The appearance that may therefore be given is that, in as far as critical discussion has undergone an institutionalisation in recent years, it follows (since this is where the crisis is) that the fundamentals of literature and of criticism are now at last getting discussed – thanks to the theory of those who have put forward the idea, in the first place, that there is a crisis. This being so, it may then be reasonably enough argued that

1

Critical Theory, by its very institutionalisation, has effectively advanced literary criticism.

It is therefore very much in the interests of the institutions in which the academic study of criticism and literature takes place to be seen in crisis, just as it is equally in the interests of those institutions that the source of crisis should be regarded as theory. The one is served by the other. Two things, at least, would seem to question the reality of the idea of a crisis. The first is the fact that, with the growth, in those same institutions, of an international 'market' in critical ideas, the opportunities for misunderstanding in critical discourse have never been greater. The second is that, with the advance of particular linguistic communities within the academic world, each devising a critical vocabulary of its own, critical antagonists are often using different terms when what they are talking about is the same. It is nevertheless a consequence of believing in the idea of a 'crisis in literary studies' that a sense of division, if nothing else, should be real, and is felt to be so (even if some people are excited and delighted by the splits in opinion that appear to occur while others seem only to regret that consensus – if it ever existed – is no longer to be had). Yet within this sense of division, one thing still seems to be largely agreed: that a major source of the perceived divide rests on different understandings of the term 'literary criticism' itself. According to the framework of what has become an almost universally accepted interpretation, or model, of the 'crisis in literary studies', there are two groups. For one, criticism *is* theory. For another, theoretical approaches to literature are seen as inherently reductive, a further move away from the literary models which criticism, if it is anything, must be about. Therefore, the idea is now firmly established that the modern crisis in literary studies has two sides (and two only).

The case, in both directions, has been powerfully argued in recent years, both in Britain and in the United States (where the nature of academic life has meant that, compared with Britain, academic critics have been under less pressure to address themselves to the actual tastes and reading experience of the students they teach). However the dominant group to emerge is the one that has been most vocal in promoting the idea that a crisis exists, and that the crisis results from a conflict of two sides. This is despite the fact that, as a 'side', it is, in various ways, divided against itself: into a complex of Marxist, feminist, structuralist, poststructuralist and deconstructive approaches. Sometimes these approaches operate together in loose alliance. Sometimes they compete one with another, Marxist with feminist criticism, for example. At other times, they may be chronologically conceived, as poststructuralist follows structuralist, in which case they appear in onward progress, inexorable succession, as a March of Theory. But although the picture is complicated by the fact that the boundaries of these sub-divisions are constantly being re-drawn, the views of this 'side' have affected, and to many intents and purposes have determined, both 'sides' ' understanding of what literary criticism is perceived to be: schismatic, doctrinal and ideologically based. Even those who do not explicitly subscribe to a doctrine or ideology must now – according to this conception of the conflict – accept that they have one. Concern about feelings, for instance (or the complexity and intangibility of literary 'effects' in general), is therefore, within this view, just another theory. In this way, disagreement about the nature of criticism has come to be explained in terms of how political conflict tends to be viewed from a position that, in Britain at least, is situated on the political Left. In a sense, it is a political conflict, even if we may regard some of the tensions as more characteristic of the birth pangs of a minor religion, and thus little to do with politics, and even less to do with the 'scientific' criticism which the movement aspires to advance.

It would be therefore a mistake to regard this 'crisis' (any more than theory itself) as new, or to suppose that what is happening in the world of criticism today has never happened before. But it is not however a mistake to regard the definition of criticism as itself a critical problem, if not a new one, and one that cannot be reduced to two, polar opposite, sets of ideas. For although we cannot realistically expect a single dictionary definition of literary criticism, the process of isolating some of its available or optional meanings suggests that, rather than two, there are many; and that by no means all of these are controlled by the terms of the academic debate in which talk of a crisis in literary studies has been exclusively framed. The meaning (and value) of the term 'criticism' differs depending on who happens to use it. Its meanings are not dual but protean, comparable in their complexity of relations and oppositions to those of literature itself. Like all truly useful terms, 'literature' and 'criticism' are necessarily vague, valuable in proportion to the extent that the threads of meaning they comprise are not easily disentangled from the fabric of language itself. Those who believe that the literary critic is necessarily a theorist (whether he likes it or not) will be happy to accept by the same theory that the meaning of the term is socially constructed; that it is determined by the people who use it, and to whom we may collectively agree to apply it, at any one time.

To this end, this book aims to sketch within available limits contributions to the variety of the modern, British, *communis criticorum*. For if saying what literary criticism is is going always to be a matter of valuing certain examples of discourse (written or spoken), not all valuations are simply personal. There is such a thing as a social or public valuation, regardless of the popularity of the idea of a 'crisis'. This is because the disagreements are only apparent because they are stated – by critics. Even though there may be extreme disagreement over which are critics, and which are not, the fact remains that a number of writers still succeed in reaching an audience of readers prepared to confer on them the title of 'critic', just as the public confers the title 'poet' on some writers and not upon others. We may therefore conclude that a consensus exists in the attribution of the term critic to persons who characteristically and sufficiently produce writing of the kind that literate society, whatever its other divisions, recognises as literary criticism (as far as it is capable of recognising and through the means available for it to do so). This does not mean that writers who are known widely as critics today are always correctly described, since their status as critics is always contestable. It is simply to point, without fear of serious disagreement, except on the level of particular inclusions, to a spectrum of *persons* to whom the title critic may be applied as a *prima facie* indication of modern society's current valuation of their activity as writers. A collection of such writers is the starting point and organising principle of this book. Wordsworth wanted to keep his readers in touch with flesh and blood and the aim of this book is the same. The 'theory' behind it is that while there are many varieties of theory, there are also varieties of critic (whose relation to theory is itself varied), and that the variety of criticism, like that of art (or for that matter science), exists on several simultaneous planes. The portraits of eight British literary critics are presented in pairs in order to convey some of the various domains, or socio-critical contexts, of modern British criticism and to suggest as far as possible the representative status of each of the critics discussed. But the types are not completely distinct, because different individuals stand in different relationships to their social or professional role, and add individually to the modern sense of the 'critic'. In contributing to construction of a collective meaning for this term, this study can treat only a small number of representative groups.

1. It only discusses British critics, while many important modern critics writing in English are American, or of other nationalities.
2. Though the critics are modern critics, they are only critics of literature. (Some of the best recent criticism is criticism of other arts, film for example.)
3. The critics discussed are 'modern' in a very restricted sense. At the time of writing, all were active as critics. It therefore follows that only a provisional judgement of their work can be made; a judgement to date. But this is a defect in all commentary on living authors. It is not peculiar to criticism of critics.
4. A further objection might be that some of the critics chosen are a rather obvious choice. Some, on the other hand, will seem not obvious. If so, their inclusion is open to criticism for the opposite reason.

The consensus this book relies on is the recognition that most of the critics chosen are familiar, if only as names, and that all have won public acceptance, often in different ways, as literary critics. But if the diversity of views represented suggests a widening of the idea of the critic in recent years, all the critics have a common feature central to the purpose of the book: they all write about authors that readers of English are likely to read. This is the sense in which they are all to be seen as critics in practice. The objection to this way of discussing criticism rests on the view that criticism, at least modern criticism, is really the same as theory. In this book, they are not *just* two words for the same thing. For while we may feel that theory is what makes modern criticism as interesting as it is, that, too, is a critical judgement.

Notes

1. William Wordsworth, Preface to *Lyrical Ballads* (1800), *Poetry and Prose*, selected by W. M. Merchant (Hart-Davis: London, 1967), p. 226.

1
Radical Theorists I: Terry Eagleton

'The first thing', said the third [of R. L. Stevenson's *The Three Reformers*], 'is to abolish mankind.'[1]

Terry Eagleton exemplifies a category of critic increasingly popular in Britain in recent years, particularly among students in Higher Education. His works are likely to appear on most course reading lists in English studies. Eagleton, like important critics from the past, is an Oxbridge don. From 1964 to 1969 Eagleton was attached to a Cambridge college, as Research Fellow in English. This appointment was followed by a lengthy period as Fellow in English at Wadham College, Oxford. Then, in 1988, Eagleton moved from Wadham to Linacre College, where at the time of writing he was Oxford University's Lecturer in Critical Theory. Despite his traditional background, Eagleton marches under a 'radical' banner. In the widest political sense of the term, though not the historically British one, Eagleton is intentionally radical: he joins literary study with interest in political ideals of the Left. For many readers this stance has sufficed to make Eagleton's criticism a welcome relief from tired traditions of (in Eagleton's own terms reactionary) 'liberal humanist' thought. It has placed him at the centre of a currently vigorous movement in modern British criticism. Eagleton's 'pull' at conferences on English and English teaching is strong, and lately he has attracted admirers who have helped to disseminate Eagletonian thought through works of their own. Eagleton is General Editor of the popular Blackwell's 'Re-Reading Literature' series, designed largely for students. So placed, he is confirmed as *chef d'école* of the 'new, excitingly revolutionary' critical doctrine believed to be mainly responsible for the present 'crisis' in literary studies. Eagleton, a leading rebel in the critical 'revolution', sets out to cut powerfully 'against the grain', to offer a critique of establishment culture and to annihilate assumptions of a monopolistic, fundamentally bourgeois, concept of 'Eng. Lit.' Those are his aims. They should not be confused with his achievements as critic. Nor should they cause us to lose sight of the occasion and context of Eagleton's work, or his value as literary, as distinct from political, critic. In an obvious respect Eagleton is a representative voice of the contemporary critical vogue, speaking to the provincial backwaters of critical life with a special authority (political and literary) that Oxbridge has always enjoyed.

But Eagleton deserves his notoriety. He is outwardly a bolder, more combative, truculent and outspoken critic than almost any literary academic author of his generation writing in English. He aims to provoke, and in this he has succeeded; partly no doubt because his writing, if only at best, is marvellously clear. It is for this reason as attractive to students as it is irritating to colleagues. But Eagleton's appeal is not just, at first sight, a matter of style: Eagleton's mind offers a genuinely dazzling constellation of complementary and conflicting ideologies and ideas. From his popular study of literary theory published in 1983, it is clear that his knowledge of theory, above all, is wide, if not historically far-reaching. Eagleton specialises in the criticism and critical theory of the last hundred years or so. But his knowledge includes criticism written not only by British critics but those in Europe, Russia and America, even though there is little to suggest that he has made contact with foreign critics in any foreign language. Nevertheless, Eagleton's reading in theory compares well with that of the arch-historian of critical ideas, René Wellek. But Eagleton himself is not an historian, nor can his treatment be equated to that of the harmless, would-be fair-minded neutrality of the now numerous standard guides to modern literary ideas. Eagleton, to an admirable extent, is personally and passionately engaged as a man on a mission in much that he writes: 'Since there is in my opinion no "neutral", value-free way of presenting it, I have argued throughout a particular *case*, which I hope adds to the book's interest'.[2] Eagletonian opinions are consequently drummed and dinned into the reader. An imagery of conflict flows through his prose. The enemy (and hostile forces are often in view) is time and again given short shrift. The enemy for Eagleton is the (in his view) blinkered and covertly partisan establishment of bourgeois literary studies. Of this Eagleton is himself a product, and given his present Oxford position, ambiguously a part. But it is nevertheless to the credit of Eagleton that the questions he poses, and attempts to answer, are the largest of all, and notably unparochial: what is the particular character of literary language? What is the relation of language to meaning? What is literature? What is criticism? What is the relation of literature to society? How is critical thinking formed by the society in which it is shaped, in the past, or today? And what is the real worth of values by which we aspire to live? None of these questions is new. Eagleton's criticism finds a modern idiom in which to bring them alive.

But though a reader of theory, and an advocate of it, Eagleton himself is only sometimes a theorist. He can therefore appeal to readers whose interest is not theory of literature, theory of criticism (or theory in criticism), but literature itself. Theory is applied. Ideas (however foreign) are tested against the English literary works that his students must read. Although, increasingly throughout his career, the ideas become more important than the works, and necessarily direct attention outside them, Eagleton's writings taken as a whole cannot be reduced to a theory. As a critic, Eagleton insists on commitment. He despises (almost as a moralist) those who refuse to nail their colours honestly to the mast, and show loyalty to them. But in his practice, Eagleton inevitably over the course of time shifts his ground, as all critics must (unless wholly unsusceptible to new experiences, enthusiasms or thoughts, in which case they are disqualified as critics). Consequently, Eagleton can reject former friends, as he does at one point Raymond Williams, but then remake the bond: Eagleton's Obituary review of Raymond Williams is moving and humane.³ As a 'radical', Eagleton has in any case to change with the times, to keep abreast of the new, to find current debates in which to 'intervene', to catch the popular drift. Given Eagleton's interest in theory, his tendency to try to promote literary ideas as part of a formal programme or theoretical mission, much is predictable in any new Eagleton book. There is considerable, perhaps partly unconscious, duplication of thinking across the range of his works. But there are always surprises. For example, nearly all of Eagleton's books have different form, if only in that some are substantial while others are slight, even very slight. But less obvious aspects of Eagleton's variety become apparent when moving from earlier to later examples of his work.

Almost all Eagleton's output is either criticism of criticism (and its manifold political and social, particularly Marxist, implications) or is criticism in the sense of comment upon works of creative writers. His earliest publications exhibit a religious (Roman Catholic) emphasis, one where interest in the Church, and Christian commitment, are seen as part of his general allegiance, jointly, to literature and politics of the Left. In the series of essays published in 1966 as *The New Left Church*, Eagleton states that his aim is 'to persuade Christians that being in the church involves commitment to imaginative culture and the political left'.⁴ More recently, Eagleton's religious commitment seems to have split from his literary studies, and, as time has gone by, his doctrine of commitment becomes increasingly political–artistic, less church-based, in terms. But the militant tone of *The New Left Church* has survived, as have certain strands of Eagleton's (again Roman Catholic) *The Body as Language* (1970),⁵ Eagleton's contribution to the exploration of a once fashionable, now not very fashionable, idea. But, from reinterpreting the concept of the Word as Flesh, it has been an easy transition to the world of semiological concerns, in the particular context of the challenge launched by 'radical' theory to assumptions about the transparency of language. Before about 1970, however, Eagleton's commitment to literature stood within a framework he has since come to reject: that of the humanist. In this he seems to have drawn inspiration from Leavis: 'The "basic living deference", the reverence, is shared equally by the Christian, the artist, and the radical humanist'.[6] At that date, it was possible to be 'radical' and 'humanist' at the same time. Between then and now, Eagleton's sense of these terms has diverged. Eagleton's writing on creative authors began in 1967 with his first book-length study: *Shakespeare and Society*.[7] This is a solid, now quite uncontroversial and, compared with later work, ideologically understated study of eight Shakespeare plays. Eagleton argued, as Samuel Johnson had once argued in the eighteenth century, against the notion that individual identity is everything in Shakespeare. Eagleton claimed that in Shakespeare, as in life, a man exists only in relation to society. The book is 'For Raymond Williams' (Eagleton's Cambridge colleague). It reflects the combination of literary and social preoccupations which is the hallmark of its mentor. The modesty of this enterprise is clear. Eagleton's challenge to received interest in Shakespeare is tentative. He suggests the reciprocal illuminating interplay between reader and text in the following terms:

> The problems which Shakespeare confronts are in some ways very much the problems which concern us, and we cannot examine these problems as they are present in his plays except through the focus of our own experience, as we cannot fully understand our own experience except through an understanding of Shakespeare. What we judge in the plays as relevant, what we actually see, is shaped by what we see in our own culture, in ourselves.[8]

At the time of *Shakespeare and Society*, Eagleton's critical principles are perfectly in tune with values of common humanity, though this is based on 'eternal verities' he is later to scorn. Here, however, we are told that common humanity is realised within us through our contact with literary works. It, in its turn, gives meaning to works.

Eagleton, in 1967, is thus able to appeal to values which, while palatable to him in terms that refer to the emergent discipline of cultural studies, are nevertheless humanist in kind. He appeals to the same values in his next book, *Exiles and Emigrés*, published three years later. This book, Ph.D. thesis-like in scope and design, establishes him as a critic of the twentieth century.

Containing essays on Conrad, Waugh, Orwell, Graham Greene, T. S. Eliot, Auden and Lawrence, its aim is to trace a common thread in twentieth-century authors who write from positions spiritually and, often, geographically, external to the culture they address. A purpose of the book is to attack notions of Englishness in English literary tradition. In his 'greatest work' (*Under Western Eyes*), Conrad 'was able to transcend those English assumptions, achieving a vantage-point beyond them from which they could be probed and illuminated'. Waugh's 'Upper-Class Novel', meanwhile, connives with the very conventions of upper class English life it at the same time attacks. Yet Eagleton, we see, is still attracted to the idea of 'great literature' and 'great art'. The period between the death of Henry James in 1916 and that of Conrad in 1924 was 'the highpoint of literary creativity in the twentieth century'. More general judgements emerge from minute and detailed attention to tone, texture, attitude and stance (implicit and explicit) in particular passages. Passages represent in condensed form general qualities of whole works discussed. Evidence of Eagleton's contact with Leavisite tradition is again apparent: 'This last passage from *Mrs Dalloway*, trivial as it is in its context, expresses an important truth about the world of Woolf's novels in particular and the English upper-class novel in general...'. The same is true of Eagleton's comment on the end of *The Power and the Glory*, similarly 'a characteristic moment in Greene, and one which demands analysis'. Eagleton's way of approaching a work, and questions he asks about it, suggest what he has learnt from Leavis. Thus Waugh's 'cool externality of style,' in *A Handful of Dust*, 'is not, at root, a "placing" externality at all...'.[9] But, as in *Shakespeare and Society*, Eagleton's impulse is to broaden the field of attention from textual to social. In a way that is hardly, in itself, at odds with Leavis, though may actually owe more to the influence of Williams, the author's and reader's sense of society, as a whole, are brought into critical play.

The relation of literature to society is the theme of Eagleton's next full-length book: *Myths of Power: A Marxist Study of the Brontës* (1975). Like *Exiles and Emigrés*, the emphasis, in which Eagleton has perhaps begun to depart from the high valuation of specifically 'English' literature in Leavis's writing, is non-Anglocentric. Here, however, it appears in terms not of subject but critical approach. An explicit ideology of approach is signalled by the title of the book. But within its covers, the basic humanism of Eagleton's attitude is, in large measure, preserved. Claims made explicit in the Introduction suggest concern to identify a 'categorial structure' in the Brontës' fiction. But the Introduction also contains less specifically Marxist statements of Eagleton's critical credo. In 1975, Eagleton seems to have been drawn to a Marxist approach for reasons that are both liberal and humane: because of the freedom and scope that it gave him, and because it offered a needed alternative to the dead end into which literary criticism, as Eagleton saw it, had got itself trapped. This dead end Eagleton associated with both literary scholarship and, above all, Cambridge traditions of 'practical criticism'. To this combination of evils, his 'Marxist' study, and his promotion of 'historical' criticism, supply the required response. The aim:

... is not to add specialist footnotes to literature; like any authentic criticism, its intention is to possess the work more deeply. To attend to the words on the page is excellent advice for a critic: all that needs to be added is that, unless we attend in that act to the history of which the words are the opaque but decipherable signs, we should not pretend that we are actually reading the work.[10]

At this date, 'historical' criticism for Eagleton is just one of several (or perhaps many?) 'authentic' criticisms. But whatever route to critical authenticity is sought by the critic, it will never be enough, Eagleton is saying, *just* to attend to the words on the page. In 1975, Eagleton's ambitions are pluralist in the sense that he is calling for more complex critical apprehension; greater breadth of critical view. Against the orthodoxies of practical criticism, Eagleton is proposing a dual vision whereby the critic, in order to 'read' the work, must rise to the occasion and break with the mental habits, the critical routines, of everyday self. To this extent, Eagleton's position may at this date be described as 'liberal–humanist', in a sense that is perhaps hard to despise as reactionary because it is a position which even Eagleton then saw not as impeding critical innovation, but encouraging it. The fundamental aim of authentic criticism, after all, is 'to possess the work more deeply'. Deciphering of signs (words on the page) is merely a *means* to this end. Criticism can be 'authentic', and it can be inauthentic, like that which aspires only to 'add specialist footnotes to literature'. But the measure of authenticity is criticism's power in helping the reader to possess the work. For Eagleton in 1975, as at various times in the past for Pope, Johnson, Wordsworth, Arnold and Leavis, the true ('authentic') critic is defined as capable of fuller, more comprehensive, vision of the work under critical inspection. In *Myths of Power* Eagleton's critical position was fundamentally at one with the traditions of criticism he was soon to reject. And as the moment of *Myths of Power* recedes, Eagleton's radicalism becomes the opponent of humanist critical ideals.

Parts of the Introduction to *Myths of Power*, it is true, anticipate a revolution in method. But it is not effected in the body of the work. There is, in the course of the book, search for, and discovery of, ambiguities. But this does not, one might have thought, amount in itself to a Marxist approach, since 'ambiguity' has interested non-Marxist critics, for example Empson. The Brontës' novels are discussed in relation to class; the conclusion being that they are 'deeply informed by [the] bourgeois ethic . . .'. But this concern is merely an historical, and not necessarily ideological, fact of the novel as a form, itself a product of its scope and not shared by, say, poems. Perhaps the distinctively Marxist note is then rather to be heard in the constant insistence on oppositional and comparative relations: the impulse to find a coherent scheme. Thus 'In *Jane Eyre* the choice between "Romantic" and "rationalist" is clear-cut'. In *Shirley*, 'Shirley and Moore are complementary rather than contradictory types.' More generally, 'The friction between "realism" and "imagination" . . . manifests itself not only as theme but also as a problem of how to write.'[11] The effect (if not the theory) of Eagleton's 'Marxist' approach in *Myths of Power* is therefore not 'radical' except in the sense of strengthening impressions of the academic formality of his critical work, and in emphasising the schematic nature of his framework of ideas. It is not 'radical' in the sense of having its readers 'possess the work more deeply'.

But in Eagleton's gathering enthusiasm for Marxist political analysis, critical method (rather than the author or work to which any method is applied) becomes the important thing. Method, first a Marxist one but then others, begins to emerge as an interest in its own right. To this point, Eagleton's critical writing is reactionary (in what are now explicitly, but were not then, his own terms) in one key respect: its dominant concern is the creative author. It is author-centred. The approaches tried, though at times in danger of overwhelming works, and thus defeating their own purpose, are subordinate to the end of bringing authors more clearly before us. Cultural theory is merely a means, and Eagleton, in his critical priorities, remains consciously if not enthusiastically in contact with humanist (primarily Leavisian) roots. But later, Eagleton is to go out of his way to put Leavis in his place. This begins to occur in Eagleton's writings when critical theory begins to supersede specifically literary criticism, i.e. the criticism of literature. It signals the moment when Eagleton is to find in issues of criticism outlets for his recurrent attention to literary questions that are, for him, implicitly political questions, and therefore, as he comes to see it, larger than literature. Eagleton's first book *on* (rather than *of*) criticism is *Criticism and Ideology: A Study in Marxist Literary Theory*.[12] Raman Selden, in *A Reader's Guide to Contemporary Literary Theory* (1985), has found here 'a radical revaluation of the development of the English novel'.[13] According to Patrick Parrinder, on the other hand (*The Failure of Theory: Essays in Criticism and Contemporary Fiction* [1987]), Eagleton revives Leavis's 'Great Tradition'.[14] The basis for saying this is the writers he chooses for comment: Arnold, George Eliot, Dickens, Conrad, James, T. S. Eliot, Yeats, Joyce, D. H. Lawrence. As Parrinder suggests, the selection indicates the influence of Leavis. With few additions, this *is* Leavis's *Great Tradition*. The difference is that in Eagleton's study, concern with critical ideology subsumes the authors to which it is illustratively, not substantively, applied: Eagleton's writing has therefore become theory- not author-led. The authors are pushed to the back of the book. This is perhaps because Eagleton recognises that theory is now a more exciting pursuit than the problematic search to possess the work more deeply. As Logan Speirs notes in his review of books by Eagleton in *The Cambridge Quarterly*, 'None of the insights sound as new or as profound as the theorising that precedes them.'[15] Eagleton's discussion of Conrad supports this view. It recalls treatment of Conrad, published sixteen years earlier, in *Exiles and Emigrés*, and now recommended in a footnote. In *Criticism and Ideology*, Eagleton repeats a point about ambiguousness in Conrad's position, and in almost identical terms: *Heart of Darkness* has as its message 'a viewpoint which disturbs imperialist assumptions to the precise degree that it reinforces them'.[16]

Where, Eagleton asks in *Criticism and Ideology*, is English Marxist criticism going? In his attempt to answer this question, this book is to many Eagleton's (and British criticism's) most substantial contribution to Marxist critical thought, as it is his most ambitious work of theory. The book begins with an attack on bourgeois criticism for infuriating pretence of ideological innocence. The chief culprit here is the literary criticism of *Scrutiny*. The problem with this criticism is the criterion of human experience. *Scrutiny* thus contrasts with Marxist criticism which is now incompatible with 'empiricist and intuitionist techniques' but pursues the 'end of criticism' which is to make conscious all that the text cannot know about itself. The 'function of criticism' is that which Marxist criticism is more adequately fitted to perform: 'to furnish the terms in which the text can know itself, rather than the terms in which what the text does not and cannot know can be disclosed'. But although Eagleton is in this way using *Criticism and Ideology* to widen the gap between himself (as Marxist critic) and *Scrutiny*, his practice suggests that his attitude to the 'English' values of *Scrutiny* is not subversive, except in the sense of going back to values of criticism that *Scrutiny* itself was reacting (subversively) against. Surveying the history of criticism, Eagleton therefore begins with Sidney's *Apology for Poetry*, an especially parochial choice for a critic concerned with European dimensions of critical thought. But it anticipates the standard critical history that Eagleton goes on to outline. Eagleton is more subversive (in terms of his own book) when he is echoing the *Scrutiny* positions the *Scrutiny* critics, to their discredit, scrutinised least. In this way, Eagleton's account of the 'neoclassical' phase in the history of criticism is indistinguishable in its conventionality from Leavis's:

> Once more, criticism becomes a crucial ideological instrument – but now in the struggle to stabilise an ideological formation which will seal the contradictory unity of those social classes which compose the hegemonic bloc. In the drive for order, proportion and propriety, the demand for socially cohesive categories of Nature and Reason, the need to reduce and systematise social life to a series of ordered practices, history once again selects criticism as both paradigm and instrument of such a project.[17]

The old romantic stereotype of the 'neoclassical' age has surfaced yet again.

Yet Eagleton, as far as he is concerned, is now diametrically at odds with attitudes and assumptions of *Scrutiny,* and with Leavis, and writes with the air of someone breaking new ground. But Eagleton's charge against Leavis, though explicitly hostile, is not hostile in a new way, but rather recalls George Watson, writing in *The Literary Critics* of 1962: 'It is the central paradox of his achievement that, while it challenges the reader with its apparent severity and fierce discrimination, it refuses to discuss the criteria by which it proceeds.'[18] Eagleton, like Watson, is irritated with Leavis's maddening refusal (as he sees it) to come clean about standards, and to make them as explicit as he thinks he is making his own. At the same time, while Eagleton wants Leavis to make his standards explicit (and thus write a criticism which conforms more closely to his image of his own), he also wants to depose *Scrutiny,* which has gone unchallenged by ideological opponents. Even Raymond Williams, Eagleton regrets, failed to depose *Scrutiny* because he was infected by the notion of experience as literary test. Eagleton sees himself as free from infection, which is confirmed in the following terms, at the end of Chapter 1, where he can now distinguish between the idea of criticism as 'midwife to the text' and what, in his opinion, it really is:

> Criticism is not a passage from text to reader: its task is not to redouble the text's self-understanding, to collude with its object in a conspiracy of eloquence. Its task is to show the text as it cannot

know itself, to manifest those conditions of its making (inscribed in its very letter) about which it is necessarily silent.[19]

This is a novel insight, for Eagleton at least, in so far as Eagleton is now prepared to offer for the first time an explicitly reductive conception of non-Marxist literary criticism: the belief, new for Eagleton when we think of his insistence that the purpose of criticism was to have the reader possess the work more deeply, that criticism, while still justifying its name, may be regarded as the simple smoothing of the passage for the text; redoubling, or repetition, in 'conspiracy of eloquence', of what the text is saying for itself. It is not a novel insight in so far as Eagleton suggests that criticism demands a measure of critical detachment from the work, and that the origin of the work's making is to be found in its detail (its 'very letter'). But Eagleton, at this point in his career, since he claims no longer to believe in eternal values or common human experience, may be consequently less sensitive to the possibility that earlier values might resemble his own. Being Marxist has become, for him, the same thing as being new, which, for him, of course, as fresh convert, it is; even though Eagleton's Marxist position seems in reality to have been evolving over a period of years and is not, as we have seen, a sudden personal awakening.

Eagleton's commitment to Marxism had surfaced in the book on the Brontës. In a less focused way, it was also there in Eagleton's early concern with cultural questions and with politics of the Left (Eagleton was a founder-editor of *Slant*, the forum for leftist Catholic thought). Following publication of *Criticism and Ideology*, Eagleton sought a more popular form in which to convey his interest in Marxist critical thought. *Marxism and Literary Criticism* (1976), a short book intended for beginners in the ideological critical field, is nevertheless a clear and closely discriminating volume. Here, Eagleton opens himself fully and directly to theory in a sense that includes, but is not limited to, Marxist theory. But at the same time Eagleton's ability to perform particular analyses (to do them in practice) seems to have gained in sensitivity and force. Perhaps this is because Eagleton is now writing on authors who, like him, are theorists, inspiring in him deeper enthusiasm. There is freshness about

Eagleton's discussion of, say, Marx's draft manuscripts of 1857 (known as the *Grundrisse*), not found in his Marxist approach to canonical 'creative' authors of the late nineteenth century that appear in his Marxist study of the Brontës, and in *Criticism and Ideology*. And it is when writing on Marx and Marxists that Eagleton is able to be more sharply evaluative than he allows in his own, applied, Marxist critiques. Distinctions are drawn: 'I find the comments of both Althusser and Macherey at crucial points ambiguous and obscure'.[20]

One of the Marxist critics nevertheless celebrated in this beginners' guide is Walter Benjamin, friend of Bertholt Brecht. Benjamin is the subject of Eagleton's next, far weightier and more narrowly specific study, *Walter Benjamin or Towards a Revolutionary Criticism* (1981),[21] and to date Eagleton's first and only book-length study of a single Marxist critic. The first part of the book is on Benjamin himself. The second is more broadly concerned with revolutionary criticism, a thematic disunity which no doubt reflects the fact that sections had been previously published in article form. But it is also, according to Eagleton, 'in the manner of Benjamin himself'. Writing on Benjamin, Eagleton thus finds a distance from his personal, merely individual and perhaps therefore from his point of view worryingly bourgeois concerns as Marxist critic and is using him as mouthpiece, or *persona*. But it is in this book that we also see signs of Eagleton's suddenly expanding consciousness of his own growing critical importance and influence that being a Marxist has helped him achieve. In the Preface, he reflects for the benefit of increasing numbers of readers following his career on his personal development and change of perspective, since the time of *Criticism and Ideology*. As well as 'the pressure of global capitalist crisis' and the effects of the 'influence of new themes and forces within socialism', he confesses that there have been 'certain deep-seated changes in my own personal and political life since the writing of *Criticism and Ideology*'. In his own mind, Eagleton has moved from being merely a writer *on* the relations between the individual and society (as in *Shakespeare and Society*) to being a living example *of* them. Eagleton's consciousness of his own significant historical role appears in the dynastic catalogue of 'names of the major Marxist aethesticians of the century to date' on page 96: 'Lukács, Goldmann, Sartre, Caudwell, Adorno, Marcuse, Della Volpe, Macherey, Jameson, Eagleton'.

Yet Eagleton is also responding to non-Marxist features of 'revolutionary literary criticism' in his book on Benjamin, even though, in 1981, these new, in some ways complementary, in some ways rival, wings of the 'radical' critical movement were not as congenial to him as they have since become. Radical feminism (to 1981), though recognised by Eagleton as in many senses an ally of Marxist criticism, is strongly chastised. In a series of agonised, self-flagellating 'reservations', it is stigmatised as follows: 'Anti-theoretical, rampantly idealist and frequently sectarian, such "radicalism" represents the presence within the women's movement of a familiar brand of petty-bourgeois ideology.' Fellow Marxists are warned of likely 'tragic' consequences of its success. The advent of Deconstruction, the 'death drive at the level of theory',[22] is more extensively considered, as linked to and yet fundamentally at odds with the Marxist programme. In its non-commitment, it is in many ways only an 'inflection' of the liberal humanism from which Eagleton now sees himself as completely divorced.

But Eagleton overcomes these reservations in his next book, *The Rape of Clarissa* (1982). Although the ostensible subject of this book is the work of the novelist Richardson, it differs from Eagleton's earlier, author-specific, studies on nineteenth and twentieth-century literary works in an important respect. Where *Criticism and Ideology* is the vehicle for Eagleton's Marxist theory, *The Rape of Clarissa* becomes the vehicle for the theoretical positions which were once seen as at odds with Marxism: feminism and deconstruction. In the Benjamin study, Eagleton had noted in passing that '... nothing could be easier to hear than the ideological and psychoanalytic discourses that truly "write" Pamela and Clarissa, discourses that resound scandalously through the cohering letter of the subject'.[23] Eagleton takes up these themes in the Richardson study, analysing *Pamela, Clarissa,* and in a Postscript *Sir Charles Grandison.* In so doing he suggests the increasing appeal that non-Marxist movements in radical critical theory have begun to have for him, perhaps partly under the acknowledged influence of such Oxford feminist critics as Toril Moi. As Eagleton (within limits of this 'radical' school) accommodates himself to these other 'radical' approaches, Marxism 'pure' is proportionately demoted. Marxism, or 'historical materialism', Eagleton says simply, is now merely his book's 'third method'. The other two (now quite comfortable bed-fellows rather than rival radicalisms) are 'various poststructuralist theories of textuality' and 'a feminist and psychoanalytical perspective'.[24] By 1982, Eagleton's Marxism has merged with a family of third or fourth generation Marxian notions and is no longer at loggerheads with them. In Richardson's *Clarissa*, Eagleton has found a focus for his expanded empire of radical ideas. He is therefore now able to take up, via *The Rape of Clarissa*, the patriarchal oppression of Woman, arguing that Woman is incarnate in Clarissa, victim of forces (embodied in the seductive aggression of Lovelace) that history is later to overthrow. As feminism is blended with Marxism, modern feminist preoccupations are given voice (albeit by a male critic) in study of the historical and artistic developments of the Novel. Class is still a significant issue; but Eagleton is not concerned with relations between the middle class and the workers, as at least to some extent he may have been in his Marxist study of the Brontës. What interests him now is the changing relation of the aristocracy to the middle class as it is signified by the re-negotiated formal and sexual relations between women and men. Since the writer of *Clarissa* was an author-cum-printer, at least one aspect of the old–new Marxist conception of literary creation can however be retained. *Clarissa*, in an unusually literal sense, is the fruit of a 'system of production'. But Eagleton is also opening the door to semiological concerns for which his choice of text is tactically convenient. In the epistolary novel, such as *Clarissa*, the text (a novel) and the subject (a series of letters) really are one. By the same theory Richardson, as author, is important only in providing Eagleton with a text with which to display his grasp of the latest (to Eagleton) body of critical ideas.

In *Literary Theory: An Introduction,* the best-selling students' guide to critical ideas published in the following year, Eagleton is however unimpeded by need to relate comments to any particular author. Though the work gives theoretical support to the relationship between text and critic appearing in applied form in the Richardson study, for the time being Eagleton has abandoned the need to apply his ideas. Instead, Eagleton's survey of theory becomes itself an opportunity to advance theory. But although Eagleton is all the time drawing on Marxist or structuralist or feminist theory, all of which imply the possibility of common ground (the common human nature which Eagleton had at one time valued), his own theory wishes to deny it. The reason literary works seem to retain their value across centuries, says Eagleton, is that 'we always interpret [them] to some extent in the light of our own concerns'. Ostensibly, Eagleton is here recalling the appeal to common human nature made earlier in his career. Actually, he is rejecting this position (they do not retain their value though they seem to) by extending the case to the point where each generation's, even each individual's, interpretation produces a different work. Therefore whatever people may think they are appreciating, the critic can always know better:

> 'Our' Homer is not identical with the Homer of the Middle Ages, nor 'our' Shakespeare with that of his contemporaries; it is rather that different historical periods have constructed a 'different' Homer and Shakespeare for their own purposes .... All literary works, in other words, are 'rewritten', if only unconsciously, by the societies which read them; indeed there is no reading of a work which is not also a 're-writing'.[25]

In appearing to clarify the thought, Eagleton transforms it. From 'to some extent', we have moved in a few sentences to something much more hard and fast. Though use of inverted commas around 'our', 'different', 'rewritten' and 'rewriting' perhaps suggests that Eagleton is hedging his bets, Eagleton adapts the (now to him) old system-of-production theory of literary and critical history to give a whole new freedom of movement to the individual critic. Since our Homer and Shakespeare are not identical to the Homers and Shakespeares of times past, and since their works (like 'All literary works'), are in any case rewritten by each age, Eagleton's own critical procedure may be vastly simpler. The only critical assumptions one now ever need bother with are one's own.

From the individualism (but not in one sense the Marxism) of this position, Eagleton can attack the negative collectivism he diagnoses in 'The Rise of English Studies', a conspiracy of twentieth-century bourgeois political, social and educational forces responsible for the stability he abhors in the English literary canon. These forces have produced the spurious unity of the subject 'English'. The persons who have channelled them have not done so because, unlike him, they are untheoretical (as Eagleton had once claimed of Leavis), but for the opposite reason: because the rise of English studies has accommodated a variety of apparently hostile but really mutually sustaining literary theories, theories of criticism or approaches to literature. These theories, Eagleton's *Literary Theory* (in a way as apparently accommodating as those Eagleton wishes to attack) then goes on to survey: 'Phenomenology, Hermeneutics, Reception Theory', 'Structuralism and Semiotics', 'Poststructuralism' and 'Psychoanalysis'. But in the conclusion Eagleton changes his tack. Having spent so much time in his book on theories, the whole notion of 'literary theory' is questioned on the grounds that literature itself, as discrete category of phenomena, does not, or should not, exist. And since literary theory depends on literature, and literature is a construct of bourgeois (and therefore, for a critic with residual Marxist proclivities, uncongenial) political assumptions, literary theory (by which Eagleton also means literary criticism) should give way to the study of 'discourse', or rhetoric. The fruits of this would be a new educational programme. More time would be spent studying Hollywood films, the press and working-class writing. Literature, as the term is presently understood, would take part in, but not dominate, this programme.

But, in Eagleton's next critical book, it becomes clear that Eagleton himself, whatever his own theory, is not the one to be actually tackling a widened artistic field. Instead, Eagleton's *The Function of Criticism* (1984) looks inwards to his favourite genre:

criticism of critics. As in *Literary Theory*, Eagleton is advancing a personal theory. But where, in *Literary Theory*, Eagleton is drawing up the terms of reference for others, in *The Function of Criticism* he may be seen as opening a way for himself. How has modern criticism, he asks, become what it is? As an answer Eagleton outlines the story of literary criticism from the eighteenth century to the present with particular respect, at different points in history, to relations between criticism and society. Eagleton's point is that the function of critics has changed with society. In Addison's day, the critic was the voice of a public. He shared in ideals of classical bourgeois culture. Now, through socially and politically polarising influences of the nineteenth century, the literary critic has assumed a professional, specialist and socially alienated role. But while *The Function of Criticism* maps this progress, it also records Eagleton's frustration with the political and social impotence of modern criticism, including perhaps his own. Since political and social commitments have not been enough to change society, Eagleton's advice to the modern critic is that his role is, after all, traditional. It is in essence Addison's. But this is not quite the *volte face* it seems. Eagleton is not now seeking a return to eighteenth-century critical ideas but rather the opposite: the modern critic, like the critic in the eighteenth century, must avail himself of the intellectual life of his times; become more, not less, a creature of his age as Eagleton has himself tried to do. Eagleton's theory of criticism's function is thus adapted to conform with his own broadened conception of legitimate study outlined in *Literary Theory*: ' "English Literature" is now an inherited label for a field within which many diverse preoccupations congregate: semiotics, psychoanalysis, film studies, cultural theory, the representation of gender, popular writing, and of course the conventionally valued writings of the past.'[26]

But does Eagleton ever live up to this critical ideal in his practice? To decide this, we can turn to one of the most recent examples of Eagleton's applied theoretical work. In *William Shakespeare* (1986),[27] Eagleton returns to methods of *The Rape of Clarissa* and thus contributes to the last of the categories designated in *The Function of Criticism* as legitimate areas for the modern critic's concern: 'the conventionally valued writings of the past'. But in so far as he is concerned with the 'conventionally valued', Eagleton seems here to have stayed safely within the academy's walls, where Shakespeare is for many critics other than Eagleton the keystone in a liberal–humanist arch they all want to demolish. *William Shakespeare* is thus intentionally radical: a far cry from the staid, pre-Marxist 1967 study, *Shakespeare and Society*. In the earlier volume Eagleton had written as a young critic, in hope of approval from elders and betters. In *William Shakespeare*, Eagleton's comparative boldness (as it appears) is that of an established critic, General Editor of the 'Re-Reading Literature' series. Even so, Eagleton is not trying to write Shakespeare off; or even to diminish his importance in the literary canon. Instead, he seems rather inspired, albeit rather late in the day, by the searches that fellow radical theorists have conducted for an *'Alternative* Shakespeare'. Therefore compared with *Shakespeare and Society* Eagleton can seem to have more to say, and take more exuberant pleasure in saying it. Readers will be either irretrievably hostile and therefore not matter, or already in the club and not need persuading.

Even so, there are clearly similarities between earlier and later books. Of the eight plays (plus *Timon of Athens*) considered in *Shakespeare and Society*, seven are recalled in *William Shakespeare*. Several passages are reminiscent of the earlier study. Chapter 1 of *Shakespeare and Society* had been devoted to analysis of *Troilus and Cressida*. Here, Eagleton had focused on the circular structure of debates between Troilus and Hector in Act II, on Helen's value. Hector believes in 'permanent values accessible to reason'. Troilus, meanwhile, believes that value 'is a human creation, humanly conferred': '... things have value in so far as an intensity of human activity gives them it, and value is thus something which grows within the process of activity .... The conflict is a direct one, between essentialist and existentialist vision.' Hector 'sees value as an amalgam of the intrinsic worth of a thing, and the actual worth it derives from its context ...'.[28] Twenty years later in *William Shakespeare*, Eagleton discusses the same passage from *Troilus and Cressida* in similar terms: 'Hector wants a fusion of intrinsic and assigned values ... Troilus, by contrast, holds to an existentialist rather than essentialist theory of value.'[29] The basic point is the same: meaning is relative. But while in *Shakespeare and Society* the determinant was cultural, in *William Shakespeare* the orientation is linguistic. The difference reflects Eagleton's widening contact, in intervening years, with post-Saussurean critical thought.

But *William Shakespeare* is also a narrower, more personal (less Marxist?) study than *Shakespeare and Society*. Eagleton rejects the appeal to common humanity – a point of reference (the 'radical' substance) of the earlier book: 'On the whole I have written about the plays which interest me, with the aim of developing a particular case about Shakespearean drama ...'. Replacing common human values in *William Shakespeare* are the ideas of various specialised radical cults. Shakespeare is important to the extent that he anticipated such ideas; he exists as far as he can be reconstructed through them, in which view Eagleton is practising the theory of *Literary Theory*. He can therefore frame the (chronologically nonsensical) statement that Shakespeare: '... was almost certainly familiar with the writings of Hegel, Marx, Nietzsche, Freud, Wittgenstein and Derrida'. This is because while writing on Shakespeare, Eagleton's stance is defined entirely in terms of a personal assortment of modern critical, political, sexual and linguistic dicta. Three plays are discussed in each of the chapters of the book. With each chapter, Eagleton starts from an abstraction designed to reflect a current theoretical domain: Language, Desire, Law, 'Nothing', Value, Nature. The new readings of Shakespeare take place in relation to these concepts, even if they seem to depend on a body of rather old readings of Shakespeare, such as the application of an 'Elizabethan World Picture' conception of Shakespeare in the claim that: '[Shakespeare's] belief in social stability is jeopardized by the very language in which it is articulated'. That Shakespeare believed in social stability can be simply assumed. Eagleton can knowingly attribute to Shakespeare views he is sure that Shakespeare held, though he may not in turn seem to have much respect for Shakespeare's ability to rise to the sophistication of his (Eagleton's) beliefs: '... marriage is the organic society in miniature, a solution to sexual and political dilemmas so ludicrously implausible that even Shakespeare himself seems to have had difficulty in believing it'.[30]

But, knowing Shakespeare's beliefs, Eagleton, by virtue of a privileged contact (chronologically denied to Shakespeare) with post-Marxist, post-Freudian, post-Saussurean and feminist ideas, can point out the dilemma that any belief entails. Shakespeare's dilemmas thus defined serve to anticipate modern radical struggle in all its forms. Thus in the section devoted to 'Desire', we learn that Shakespeare's witty excess at points in his comedies reveals workings, through language, of anarchic sexuality. Concern with marriage runs counter to the anarchy of sex. In political terms, Shakespeare, despite shortcomings, is for Eagleton a pre-Marxist warrior in a post-Marxist war:

> Social and sexual identities have the mystifying mutability of a paltering language or counterfeit currency; anything can be exchanged with anything else. This is particularly worrying for Shakespeare, since it seems like a grotesque caricature of his traditionalist belief that all identity is reciprocally constructed, constituted by social bonds and fidelities.[31]

Whether in fact Shakespeare did hold 'traditionalist' beliefs is not at issue. The matter, as far as Eagleton is concerned, has been settled satisfactorily elsewhere.

Eagleton's 're-reading' of Shakespeare thus rests on academic notions of Shakespeare's plays that ought to have been hostile to him (from all he seems to have been saying about the rise of English Studies and the role of *Scrutiny*), but the validity of which he does not question. But his study of Shakespeare does not lack the lustre of a modern critique. The modern social, sexual and political implications of Shakespearean drama, he says, can be found for example in *Macbeth*. The witches in *Macbeth* '... by releasing ambitious thoughts in Macbeth, expose a reverence for hierarchical social order for what it is, as the pious self-deception of a society based on routine oppression and incessant warfare'. In Eagleton's *Macbeth*, the witches are therefore 'the heroines of the piece', a fact not recognised by Shakespeare (nor, for that matter by 'almost all literary critics'). This judgement is based on a variety of Freudian, linguistic and feminist values and ideas: the witches inhabit 'their own sisterly community'; they are 'devotees of female cult, radical separatists who scorn male power and lay bare the hollow sound and fury at its heart'; their 'teasing wordplay infiltrates and undermines Macbeth from within'; they 'figure as the "unconscious" of the drama'. These Freudian, linguistic and feminist values and ideas replace ordinary human ones used by past critics to judge the plays. Eagleton announces his book in the Preface to *William Shakespeare* as an 'exercise in political semiotics'. Macbeth, accordingly, 'ends up chasing an identity which continually eludes him; he becomes a floating signifier in ceaseless, doomed pursuit of an anchoring signified.' Eagleton illustrates this remark with a famous speech by Macbeth on life:

> Life's but a walking shadow, a poor player
> That struts and frets his hour upon the stage ...

In the actual speech, Macbeth had compared 'life' to the figure of an actor. But Eagleton does not make life (the subject of Macbeth's speech) but Macbeth himself (who is supposed to be speaking the lines) the actor: 'He is reduced to a ham actor, unable to identify with his role.'[32] Eagleton interprets Shakespeare's 'poor player' as 'ham actor'. ('Poor', for Eagleton, means 'bad', just as, in *The Body as Language,* Eagleton had written that Macbeth 'comes to see himself, finally, as a bad actor, full of sound and fury but signifying nothing'.)[33] Eagleton substitutes a Stoppardian preoccupation with relations between actor and role. He thus excludes the universal human application of Macbeth's speech, prohibiting possibility of sympathetic fellowship with the actor's plight. It is one of many moments in *William Shakespeare* where Eagleton's attitudes are precisely and deliberately the reverse of the common and human. In *Measure for Measure* Isabella, by risking her brother's life to preserve virginity, is protecting society from all such blackmail attempts. (It is beside the point that there is little in Isabella's words to suggest social conscience of this kind.) In *The Merchant of Venice,* it is to Shylock and not, as is traditionally the case, to Antonio or Portia that we are to look for the ethical 'baseline' of the play. In standing up for law as abstraction, by insisting on his pound of flesh, Shylock overrides a bourgeois obsession with the rights of individual humanity on which Eagleton's own criticism seems all the time to insist. Antonio, in this scheme, is a 'racist', while Shylock's stance is subversive of 'class law'. Portia's famous speech in defence of mercy is, by this standard, 'dubious': 'Would it have been admirably merciful, or an obscene insult to the dead, to have allowed a later anti-semite, Adolf Eichmann, to go free?'[34]

William Shakespeare thus says more about the strategies and conventions that are possible in modern criticism than it does about Shakespeare; and it is surely intended to do so. Though on the one hand the 'text' is the thing, and not Shakespeare, reader-responses to Shakespeare's text (his words, phrases, images, speeches and poetic effects, etc.) are on the other hand not invited or encouraged. They are permitted only so far as they are bounded by the intellectual walls of Eagleton's current collection of 'radical' ideas. From these, dissent is forbidden and escape impossible. Eagleton's critical patter is constant and diverting, his technique being to place one challengeable assertion next to another, and then another, creating an unbroken string. Since one does not know where to start first, one generally does not bother. Apparent through all is the extraordinary agility, verbal novelty and intellectual derring-do of the cult-critic Eagleton himself. The impression his criticism creates depends on our being intrigued, shocked or amused, not by Shakespeare, but by him: Eagleton's criticism replaces an interest in the Shakespearean text, which is used as a foil. In his 'radical' strokes, Eagleton is often self-consciously iconoclastic, and reminiscent of a lecturer who has mastered the means to capture an audience's attention by fair means or foul. Chapter 4 begins with the following sentences in this vein: 'There is some evidence that the word "nothing" in Elizabethan English could mean the female genitals. From a phallocentric viewpoint a woman appears to have nothing between her legs, which is as alarming for men as it is reassuring.' A common device (and rhetorical habit of the French structuralist critic Roland Barthes) is to counter, with its opposite, a contention that no one in the first place (including the critic) has ever suggested is true. Thus we learn in the chapter on 'Nothing' that: 'The unpalatable implication of all this is that jealousy is not a form of sexual desire: sexual desire is a form of jealousy.' On the following page, likewise, we have: '*Othello* is not a play about sexual deviancy, but about the deviancy of sex.'[35]

But pointedness of this kind is not the staple of Eagleton's prose. In small doses his style is more compelling, because clearer, than most structuralese: hence Eagleton's popularity as critic. But long stretches of text can be tiring. This is because of the absence of modulation in Eagleton's critical prose; the lack of that quality which would normally mark and control writings by a critic sensitive both to the varying emotional contours of his literary text, and the interest likely to be taken by readers in comments upon it. Eagleton's prose, by contrast, has the texture of something that is able endlessly to regenerate itself, for its own ends, according to laws of its own, independent of reader and text. Therefore it may, when experienced in large swathes, seem churned out. With Eagleton turning the handle, the text-as-product rolls without let or hindrance off the end of the critical–theoretical assembly line. The effect is to reduce the variety of emphasis that we normally, if unconsciously, rely on to enable us to know when the important point in a critical discussion is being made. Eagleton is somehow always elsewhere; an absentee from his text, he is never quite available for challenge in the sentence one happens at any time to be reading. But in this way, Eagleton's critical manner achieves the relativity desired by his critical theory. No one statement quite stands on its own, or answers for itself. Since all is relative, he (the critic) cannot be pinned down. We are left with his critical text. The text may not 'know' Shakespeare either. But long after Eagleton has ceased to profess with any enthusiasm the virtues of a Marxist critique it realises, in practice, his Marxist critical dream: it 'knows' itself.

Even in Shakespeare – the test of an English literary critic – there seems little to bring Eagleton up short. He is never struck dumb, as Samuel Johnson was at the death of Cordelia. The most painful scenes in Shakespeare are not problematic because they hurt. They are painful because they embody conceptual contradictions of binary opposition. On this topic, Eagleton is particularly eloquent. The liberal–humanist ideology of a Johnson is fearlessly exposed by the following remarks from his account of *King Lear*. In the chapter on 'Value', the death of Cordelia is 'covered':

> Cordelia blends largesse and limitation on her first appearance in the play, when she reminds Lear that her love, though freely given, must be properly divided between himself and her future husband; and the same balance is present in her combination of physical rootedness and freedom of spirit. In this sense, she symbolically resolves many of the play's formal antinomies.
> The only problem, however, is that she dies.

Edgar's closing words in the play denote 'that organic unity of body and language, that shaping of signs by the senses, of which Cordelia is representative; but the play has also demonstrated that to speak what one feels is no easy business'.[36] In dying, Cordelia fails to resolve many of the play's formal antinomies. But poetical justice is after all done: she is punished for speaking her mind. In dying, she proves that speaking one's mind is 'no easy business'. The sardonic comedy of this understatement is presumably meant.

The main difference, then, between *William Shakespeare* and the writings of the range of European theorists Eagleton has come to admire is its linking of theory to practice. It urges the domestic student audience, for which it is primarily intended, to apply modern critical theories to English texts. By the precedent it sets, the study claims that theory is not enough on its own. In so doing *William Shakespeare* exemplifies as well as any of Eagleton's books the relations between his 'radical' aims and the effects of his practice; but not, contradictorily and characteristically enough, in the sense of actually questioning and itself replacing worn out, because critically disengaged, ways of thinking and writing about Shakespeare's plays. It points instead to the apparently unfortunate dependence (as far as Eagleton's practice and theory are concerned) of radical 'theory' on radical 'style'. The former is negatively signified by the latter, as any sign, in Eagleton's own recent terms, is inclined to reveal the unspoken in the text, that which is there though the text may not know it. Eagleton's style and the energy behind it, the unshakeable *will* he displays, are radically conscious enough, too clearly for their own ends. But they do not make up for the unconscious absence of radical 'practice', i.e. the lack of any deep split with post-*Scrutiny* treatments of Shakespeare where Eagleton is especially, and adversely, sensitive to them: on 'Eng. Lit.' courses in British secondary and higher education (where particular ways of thinking and talking about Shakespeare have effectively preserved the reactionary ideology in literature as in politics that Eagleton despises). Eagleton knows that, while Shakespeare cannot be abolished, he needs to be rescued from reactionary criticism. To this end, and beyond all Eagleton's books to date, *William Shakespeare* is a cornucopia of terms designed to confirm its 'radical' credentials. 'Deconstruction', 'sign', 'signifier', 'transgression', etc. draw attention and raise hopes of rescue on every page. But the 'revolutionary' language overlays an approach as sadly conservative in a literary as perhaps also political sense as the context and occasion of Eagleton's criticism would tend to suggest: it is academic, and traditional. Like Shakespearean critics of the nineteenth century, and their academic imitators in the twentieth, Eagleton is preoccupied by Shakespearean characters. Though he is not much interested in the psychology of characters or their human individuality, the plays nevertheless exist for him in character terms. His re-readings of Shakespeare, his politicisation of the issues of the plays, are character-dependent. We hear little reminiscent of an even older emphasis in Shakespearean criticism, where character in Shakespeare was second to 'the progress of his fable and the tenor of his dialogue'. And there is certainly determined rejection of the same writer's insistence that the value of Shakespeare lay in his 'human sentiments in human language'.[37] We do hear loudly, however, albeit with a new accent, the voice of an academic Oxford and Cambridge of the forties and fifties. Eagleton without knowing it echoes the academy he is supposed to be revolting against. His criticism is therefore the ideological opposite of what he intends.

Are we then still justified in thinking of Eagleton, as he thinks of himself, as a 'radical' critic? In critical practice he is not radical, even within his own definition of the term. Eagleton believes in the death of the author. He attacks the canon. And, to an increasing extent as his career proceeds, he is scathingly dismissive of the *Scrutiny* conception of the shape and progress of English literary achievement:

> The main thoroughfares on this map ran through Chaucer, Shakespeare, Jonson, the Jacobeans and Metaphysicals, Bunyan, Pope, Samuel Johnson, Blake, Wordsworth, Keats, Austen, George Eliot, Hopkins, Henry James, Joseph Conrad, T. S. Eliot and D. H. Lawrence. This *was* 'English literature': Spencer, Dryden, Restoration drama, Defoe, Fielding, Richardson, Sterne, Shelley, Byron, Tennyson, Browning, most of the Victorian novelists, Joyce, Woolf and most writers after D. H. Lawrence constituted a network of 'B' roads interspersed with a good few cul-de-sacs. Dickens was first out and then in; 'English' included two and a half women, counting Emily Brontë as a marginal case; almost all of its authors were conservatives.

Eagleton dislikes the *Scrutiny* map of literature in English, but it is the one he uses himself. On the one hand, he uses it to suggest the limits of our currently received idea of literature. Shouldn't it, logically, contain *Superman* comics and Mills and Boon novels? On the other hand, there is little to suggest that any serious revision of the scheme quoted here is either possible or desirable. In practice, the difference between Eagleton's and the *Scrutiny* scheme is not that it is wider, to allow more in, but that it is narrower. It represents an intensification and institutionalisation of post-*Scrutiny* taste. Even Eagleton's particular judgements have a Leavisian ring. Illustrating the Russian Formalist critics' attitude to language, Eagleton draws on a Leavis-like reading of the poetry of Hopkins:

> By having to grapple with language in a more strenuous, self-conscious way than usual, the world which that language contains in vividly renewed. The poetry of Gerard Manley Hopkins might provide a particularly graphic example of this. Literary discourse estranges or alienates ordinary speech, but in doing so, paradoxically, brings us into a fuller, more intimate possession of experience.[38]

But by comparison with the essays in *Scrutiny*, Eagleton pays very little attention indeed to poetry. Fiction and drama, but mostly fiction, claim his attention to the virtual exclusion of all poets except Yeats, Eliot and Auden. There is little in Eagleton's criticism to suggest, for example, why Chaucer is still worth reading today, or why he should be abandoned; what ideological conditions have removed Spenser to the B roads of English literature; what alternative history of the seventeenth century, with what poets, needs to be constructed to escape from the admittedly persistent modern fixation with Donne and the Leavisian 'Line of Wit'; why Dryden or Pope, but particularly Dryden, enjoy such a low estimate among modern readers compared with Wordsworth and Keats. On all these questions, a critic sensitive to the ideological implications of modern literary enquiry might have much illuminating to say. Eagleton does not. He rejects the *Scrutiny* line on the shape and history of literature in English. He can do little as a critic of poetry to revise it.

Nor, perhaps, has Eagleton done a great deal to revitalise ideas of the novel. *Exiles and Emigrés* contains essays on Conrad, Waugh, Orwell, Greene and Lawrence. *Criticism and Ideology* offers brief analyses of George Eliot, Dickens, Conrad (again), Henry James, James Joyce, and Lawrence (again). As previously noted, such lists may suggest the impact on Eagleton of Leavis's *Great Tradition*, which Eagleton, in his conscious mind, wishes to damn. But they also mark the chronological outer limits of the Eagletonian literary unconscious. There are exceptions in his critical writing to this privileging of a Leavisite analysis of fictional history, such as *The Rape of Clarissa*. But this is a special case because it enables Eagleton to articulate a collection of feminist and structuralist ideas. Generally speaking, Eagleton's radical theory is sustained by, and applied to, an historically received, pre-selected and centrally canonical catalogue of literary 'greats'. On the novel, Eagleton follows in the footsteps of an earlier generation of literary critics, and his own work on this genre largely consolidates the position of nineteenth and early twentieth century authors. Some of these, like the Brontës, were done to death years ago by a doubly fatal dose of proliferating academic research and popular over-promotion. Perhaps it is enough, however, that Eagleton's theory is new, if only to the British student and scholarly audience he is keen to initiate. If it is, it is also nevertheless the case that Eagleton himself prizes the theory less for its novelty than for what it has in common with that of other once new but now old, and mostly dead, theorists. Not surprisingly, therefore, the effect of applying it, whether to prose fiction, Shakespeare, or English poetry, is not to revise or revitalise taste, but to ossify it. If Eagleton's own style subverts the critical standards of the generation of his father and grandfather, his tastes and ideas make them stronger than ever.

A sign is the backwardness of Eagleton's eighteenth century. Like other critics before him, he acknowledges works and authors that seem, to otherwise hostile modern eyes, agreeably to prefigure elements of post-modernist consciousness or stylistic innovation. So Swift receives favourable mention. Sterne does too: *Tristram Shandy* is 'the greatest "anti-novel" of all time'.[39] Richardson, as we have seen, provides opportunity for discourse on a variety of post-structuralist and feminist ideas. But Eagleton's response to the eighteenth-century novel occurs within the established (though now exhausted) historical caricature of the 'rise of the novel'. Therefore exposure to eighteenth-century works cannot seriously threaten modern consciousness, which has to be read back to them intact, as in Eagleton's treatment of Richardson in *The Rape of Clarissa*. The radical de-centring of modern consciousness to come from contact with currently alien enthusiasms expressed by those living then, and not now, is not found; though nor is it sought. Instead, Eagleton presents the literary landmarks of the eighteenth century in a manner which confirms the unexciting, homogeneous, conventional image that characterised Romantic reaction against the so-called neo-classical age. Beyond that, it is largely if not wholly a vision of the period created by Victorian and Edwardian taste. Hence we find Eagleton attending to the minor eighteenth-century critic, Addison (on whom his contemporary, Pope, poured regulated scorn in his portrait of 'Atticus'). In his critical–historical study, *The Function of Criticism: From the Spectator to Post-Structuralism*, Eagleton's account suggests not so much first-hand contact with the values of the eighteenth century, such as Pope's, but a debt to Leslie Stephen's gentlemanly conception of a genteel age. This is the more surprising because, in his time as a Marxist critic, Eagleton, as in his study of the Brontës, 'radicalised' criticism (at least in his own terms) by analysing the links between literature and the society contemporary with it. But where the eighteenth century is concerned, Eagleton's Marxist sympathies are negatively operative: he quotes the long superseded authority of Beljame on the eighteenth century's social conditions (perhaps because it tends to sustain his own, dated, portrait). As may be suggested by the following passage from *Literary Theory* (where doubtless the simplification for student consumption is partly to blame), Eagleton's eighteenth century can bring out an unusually crude (as much standard-stale academic as radical Marxist) sense of historical and social conditions of literary production:

> In the eighteenth century . . . literature did more than 'embody' certain social values: it was a vital instrument for their deeper entrenchment and wider dissemination. Eighteenth-century England had emerged, battered but intact, from a bloody civil war in the previous century which had set the social classes at each other's throats; and in the drive to reconsolidate a shaken social order, the neo-classical notions of Reason, Nature, order and propriety, epitomized in art, were key concepts. With the need to incorporate the increasingly powerful but spiritually rather raw middle classes into unity with the ruling aristocracy, to diffuse polite social manners, habits of 'correct' taste and common cultural standards, literature gained a new importance. It included a whole set of ideological institutions: periodicals, coffee houses, social and aesthetic treatises, sermons, classical translations, guidebooks to manners and morals. Literature was not a matter of 'felt experience', 'personal response' or 'imaginative uniqueness': such terms, indissociable for us today from the whole idea of the 'literary', would not have counted for much with Henry Fielding.[40]

Victorian ideas and scholarship buttress the apologetic enthusiasms located at the fashionable end of specialist twentieth-century academic enquiry.

For the work of a 'radical', Eagleton's criticism therefore expresses an exceptionally unquestioning reverence for the traditions of twentieth-century academic taste, though his writing is liberally sprinkled with remarks indicating desirability of mixing canonical and non-canonical works: ('... sign systems ... all the way from *Moby Dick* to the Muppet show, from Dryden and Jean-Luc Godard to the portrayal of women in advertisements ...'; '... literary theory can handle Bob Dylan just as well as John Milton').[41] In his practice, Eagleton in fact spends little or no time at all on the Muppet show, or Bob Dylan or advertisements. Contemporary cultural studies are urged, but not personally pursued. Doing them is other people's business. Eagleton himself sticks safely to the world of approved canonical authors. Perhaps this is the reason he is strangely silent on the living writers in poetry, drama, fiction and prose. Unless of course they happen to be theorists. Eagleton's real enthusiasm is reserved for the men of ideas themselves. When he is discussing thinkers and critics, Marx, Macherey, Williams or Leavis, his criticism comes fully alive.

This is as true in the critically negative as the positive sense. When writing on critics, especially those who do not qualify for approval as theorists, or suggest that criticism requires qualities beyond the ability to do with literature what Eagleton personally wishes critics would do, Eagleton, often, is satirical and caustic. The most enjoyable passages in his writings are therefore those where he puts others down. Despite his liking for theory which denies the validity of evaluative judgement, Eagleton's practice is rich in evaluative criticism. It is only *not* 'criticism' in as far as Eagleton's judgements of other critics may seem partisan, occasionally tendentious and sometimes unfair, as polemical writing, if not criticism, must often be to achieve its ends. It is nevertheless criticism in the sense of reflecting the relief of a man heaving the weight of an oppressive and absurd literary–academic education from his shoulders. The jibing and taunting is done with a sense of disproportion between pretentious official claims for the importance of literary works, and the actual (often dismal) experience of people both inside and outside the system of British education who confront them. It is a deliberately deflating approach, forcing the mind to a dead level of reality which, though not the whole truth, is a reality nevertheless. It is a position that cannot be argued against, any more than the insistence of a blind man that something does not exist because he cannot see it.

But in vanquishing one set of cherished illusions, Eagleton exposes others. He is often crushingly flip at others' expense. Playing for laughs, he operates effectively as every lecture-going student's longed-for debunker of the hallowed idols of the world of books, even if the great literature debunked is already halfway debased by Eagleton's own unconscious but nevertheless tactically effective assent to the expired conventions of its academic appropriation. Presented thus, it is no wonder the students are impatient. The jokes are easy to make. But Eagleton can swing from this to the opposite extreme; to the murkily theoretic, the esoteric and the supersubtle. In destroying one élitism he replaces it with another. And when he is not being dismissively funny and is talking seriously about what matters to him, he can degenerate into sentimental journalese and melodramatic idealism. He then patronises his readers. One instance of this appears in *Literary Theory*, where Eagleton is describing the tumultuous social conditions in France that prepared the ground for Roland Barthes's crucially important critical book of 1973: *The Pleasure of the Text*. The passage has all the marks of an 'A' level history essay gone out of control:

> *The Pleasure of the Text* was published five years after a social eruption which rocked France's political fathers to their roots. In 1968 the student movement had swept across Europe, striking against the authoritarianism of the educational institutions and in France briefly threatening the capitalist state itself. For a dramatic moment, that state teetered on the brink of ruin: its police and army fought in the streets with students who were struggling to forge solidarity with the working class. Unable to provide a coherent political leadership, plunged into a confused melée of socialism, anarchism and infantile behind-baring, the student movement was rolled back and dissipated; betrayed by their supine Stalinist leaders, the working-class movement was unable to assume power. Charles de Gaulle returned from a hasty exile, and the French state regrouped its forces in the name of patriotism, law and order.
>
> Post-structuralism was a product of that blend of euphoria and disillusionment, liberation and dissipation, carnival and catastrophe, which was 1968.[42]

Neither the dash, nor romantic nostalgia, of this passage is wholly untypical of its author.

Notes

1. Quoted from Robert Louis Stevenson's fable *The Three Reformers*. See W. W. Robson, *The Definition of Literature: and other essays* (CUP: Cambridge, 1982), p. 92.
2. Preface to *Literary Theory: An Introduction* (Blackwell: Oxford, 1983; reprinted 1983 [three times], 1985), p. vii. For an attack on liberal humanism, see 'The Bankruptcy of Liberal Human Values in Literary Studies', reprinted as 'The Subject of Literature', *The English Magazine*, **15** (Autumn, 1985), 2.
3. *The Independent*, 28 January 1988: 'Williams shaped generations of students not only by his powerful intellect, but by the deep humanity he almost tangibly radiated. He had an innate dignity and authority, combined with a quick sympathy for the common and popular. He was the kindest, most generous of men . . .' For another opinion of Raymond Williams, see *New Left Review*, **95** (January–February, 1976).
4. *The New Left Church* (Sheed and Ward: London, 1966), p. vii.
5. *The Body as Language: Outline of a 'New Left' Theology* (Sheed and Ward: London, 1970).
6. *The New Left Church*, p. ix.
7. *Shakespeare and Society: Critical Studies in Shakespearean Drama* (Chatto and Windus: London, 1967).
8. *Shakespeare and Society*, p. 1.
9. *Exiles and Emigrés: Studies in Modern Literature* (Chatto and Windus: London, 1970), pp. 32, 14, 36, 108, 49.
10. *Myths of Power: A Marxist Study of the Brontës* (Macmillan: London, 1975), pp. 13–14.
11. *ibid.*, pp. 26, 83, 83–4, 86.
12. *Criticism and Ideology* (Verso/NLB: London, 1976; 1978).
13. *A Reader's Guide to Contemporary Literary Theory* (Harvester Wheatsheaf: Hemel Hempstead, 1985), p. 42.
14. *The Failure of Theory: Essays in Criticism and Contemporary Fiction* (Harvester Wheatsheaf: Hemel Hempstead, 1987), as reviewed by Kenneth Parker, *THES*, 3 July 1987.
15. *The Cambridge Quarterly*, **XV**, i (1986).
16. *Criticism and Ideology*, p. 135.
17. *ibid.*, pp. 17, 18–19.
18. George Watson, *The Literary Critics: A Study of English Descriptive Criticism* (1962; Penguin Books: London, 1968), pp. 213–14.

19. *Criticism and Ideology*, p. 43.
20. *Marxism and Literary Criticism* (Methuen: London, 1976; reprinted four times to 1985), p. 19. For Eagleton's involvement in *Slant* see Terry Eagleton and Brian Wicker (eds) *From Culture to Revolution: The Slant Symposium 1967* (Sheed and Ward: London, 1968).
21. *Walter Benjamin or Towards a Revolutionary Criticism* (Verso/NLB: London, 1981).
22. *Walter Benjamin*, pp. 99, 136.
23. *ibid.*, p. 16.
24. *The Rape of Clarissa* (Blackwell: Oxford, 1982; reprinted 1985), p. viii.
25. *Literary Theory*, p. 12.
26. *The Function of Criticism* (Verso/NLB: London, 1984). Reviewed (with first three books in 'Re-Reading Literature' series) by Peter Conrad, the *Observer*, 31 March 1985, p. 27.
27. *William Shakespeare* (Blackwell: Oxford, 1986).
28. *Shakespeare and Society*, p. 25.
29. *William Shakespeare*, p. 59.
30. *ibid.*, pp. ix, 1, 21.
31. *ibid.*, pp. 22–3.
32. *ibid.*, pp. ix, 2, 3.
33. *The Body as Language*, p. 11.
34. *William Shakespeare*, p. 47.
35. *ibid.*, pp. 64, 68, 69.
36. *ibid.*, p. 83.
37. Samuel Johnson, 'Preface' to his edition of *The Plays of William Shakespeare* (1765), *Yale Edition of the Works of Samuel Johnson*, VII, pp. 63, 65.
38. *Literary Theory*, pp. 32–3, 4.
39. *Walter Benjamin*, p. 16.
40. *Literary Theory*, pp. 17–18.
41. *ibid.*, pp. 207, 205.
42. *Literary Theory*, pp. 141–2.

2
Radical Theorists II: Catherine Belsey

Catherine Belsey, second only to Eagleton among modern British 'radical critics', has fewer 'revolutionary' flights. But her criticism raises similar questions concerning the relation of expressed 'radical' intentions to achieved critical effects. In common with Eagleton, she is in regular employment as a University academic. Her publishing life, though comparatively short, has been long enough for her to emerge as a significant voice of her times, with a large following in Higher Education. Two major features of her work have contributed to this: her brisk intelligence and her unswerving sense of personal direction. Belsey's productions are densely argued, and her aim throughout them has been to establish an advanced 'critical practice': a 'project' in critical thought. This project is not simply personal: it is a communal aim. Belsey belongs to a radical caucus. She stands shoulder to shoulder in ideological solidarity with modern critics of the Left. And just as it has become the established convention among modern critics (whether or not they are 'radicals') to link Leftist politics to commitment to Theory, Belsey, like Eagleton, sets out to wake up modern readers of criticism and literature, and especially readers of English literature, to recent 'advances' promoted in British criticism by an amalgam of critical philosophy, psychology and contributions to political thought. The object of the exercise is to produce 'revolution'; not, in the first instance, on the streets or in government, but more fundamentally (Belsey would argue), in our root sense of the relations between language and things. Academic writing on matters of language and literature may serve as the means. But the ultimate goal, nevertheless, is to change the world; and to cooperate, in so doing, with grand processes of change which go beyond the political in the limited party or social sense and embrace, by politicising it, reality itself. To this purpose, Belsey focuses repeatedly on existing socially and politically constructed assumptions, as she sees them, that we bring to examination of literary texts. She reminds us, sometimes scoldingly, that we read with one ideology, bound by culture and time. Too often, we are happy to remain unconscious of its limits. For Belsey herself, at the same time, there appear to be no mysteries, no mystifications. She, in common with her fellow theorists, sees things as they are, confidently exempt from the otherwise universal conditions under which the rest of us labour. Belsey thus resembles Eagleton in exemplifying a current characteristic of the modern academic critic: a sense (which is shared with the medieval church) of special privilege in respect to the diagnosis of contemporary intellectual and spiritual evil.

The main difference between Belsey and Eagleton is that Belsey, while promoting theory, does so by *explicitly* arguing for (and not just embodying) the importance of critical practice. Critical practice, as suggested by the title of her best known work, published in 1980, is at the centre of her 'project' and explicitly discussed: Belsey's other major critical studies are *The Subject of Tragedy: Identity and Difference in Renaissance Drama* (1985) and *John Milton: Language, Gender, Power* (1988).[1] Belsey, in contrast to Eagleton, rarely in any of these studies rises to the comprehensive account of any whole play, novel or poem (preferring to operate by snippets and short passages). But all are alike, and resemble Eagleton's work, in their intention to bring a different kind of critical attention, with different assumptions, to the analysis and eventual subversion of an established literary canon. Belsey joins with Eagleton in aiming to undermine literature as perpetuator of what she sees, and he has come to see, as 'liberal–humanist' attitudes and tastes. These, in their turn, they regard as having had a reactionary influence in politics and society. But although Belsey concentrates on practice, practically as well as in theory, her critical practice, in practice, is always a consequence of theory (never the source). Therefore the practice of all of her books is always subordinate to the needs of a common theoretical mission. So it is in *Critical Practice* itself, which invokes extracts and texts, that we find the leading statement of Belsey's theoretical concerns. These concerns are then reproduced, often in similar words, in the subsequent books where, again, the practice is not just discussed but done. But although in later books principles of *Critical Practice* are brought to examination of a more narrowly defined 'field' of literary scholarship, the range of English writing that Belsey's books collectively embrace is wide. Her practice may, or may not, as we shall see, have achieved much. But her ambitions in one meaning of the term are as 'liberal' (in a sense Belsey shares in common with the 'liberal humanism' she dislikes) as they are 'radical'. They are those of a general critic, interested in the nature, social and cultural relations, origin and effect of literature as a whole, as total phenomenon, unconfined by limits of any historical period or 'field'.

Less 'liberal' perhaps (in her own 'radical' theoretical terms) is the abstraction necessary to this generality of approach. This can be seen in Belsey's contribution to proceedings of the Cardiff Critical Theory Seminar of 1979. Papers presented to this Seminar were edited by Belsey under the title *Workshop on Lacan*.[2] Belsey herself contributed a paper on 'Lacan's Copernican Revolution'. Modern theorists, she argues, are in process of effecting revolution on a scale comparable to that of Copernicus's dismissal of the idea of a universe with the earth at its centre. Here, in condensed form, we find ideas which are to inform so much of her critical writing in the 1980s. All the key names are present: Althusser, Marx, Freud, Lacan, Barthes, Macherey, Derrida and, of central importance, Saussure. What, in the middle ages, Copernicus did to de-centre the earth, Freud, in the twentieth century, did to de-centre the mind. Criticism now faces an analogous challenge. Belsey's definition, in her paper to the group, of criticism's task is that it is: 'to establish the unspoken in the text, the absent centre around which its consciousness is constituted and which it can neither conceal nor display, to de-centre the work in order to provide a real knowledge of it'.[3] That is to say that the relationship of a critic to a text is, or should be, that of a psychoanalyst to a patient. A familiar collection of radical tenets is outlined in this paper. Various items in the liturgy of radical credo are preached. None of them is new to the reader of Eagleton's work: the 'death' of the Author, the idea that 'the meaning of a text is to be *produced* by the reader, not *consumed*, ready-prepared by the author', that words *create* things, etc. Later, Belsey is to state these 'radical' claims in relation to particular authors and works. But Belsey, even here, remains a highly unradical academic in one respect: the fact that so much of her criticism is rooted in specialist research. Yet this seems not to frustrate 'radical' ambitions. Quite the opposite, it seems, is the case. The one thing brings out the other.

Compared with Eagleton, Belsey's reading in literature (as distinct from the reading in theorists and literary critics in which Eagleton excels) is that of the specialist. She is therefore adept at 'background studies'. This can be seen in 'The Case of Hamlet's Conscience', a substantial article, also published in 1979, in *Studies in Philology*.[4] The article is interesting in introducing us to Belsey's concern with (1) language and (2) Renaissance drama and its context. But it also throws light on the origin of her own (and other 'radical' theorists') 'radical' method. In effect, Belsey's article is like the *Workshop on Lacan:* anti-liberal–humanist. But it differs in so far as it does not seek to attack 'liberal humanism' by explicit intent but by adopting its methods at their specialist, historicist extreme, thus creating the effective (illiberal) equivalent of Eagleton's anti-historicist treatment of Shakespeare. Belsey takes issue with traditional ('Romantic') readings of Shakespeare on the grounds that they are unhistorical. 'Conscience' has been mistakenly interpreted as 'consciousness' in the line: 'Thus conscience does make cowards of us all' (*Hamlet*, III, i, 83). Belsey argues for 'an altogether more vigorous Hamlet, struggling to determine the "nobler" course, but caught up in the moral ambiguity that what seems a great enterprise is forbidden by conscience'. Hamlet should be seen as victim of moral rather than psychological dilemma. Evidence for this reading is brought to the fore in a manner entirely in accord with academic scholarship's established procedures: by considering *Hamlet* in closer relation to the role of Conscience in morality tradition. This tradition supplies 'conceptual patterns which are not so readily apparent in the twentieth century'. Belsey therefore offers a contextual study: more intimate contact with systems of ideas that inform the contemporary scene. To establish a sense of this scene, several obscure documents are brought down from the shelves. William Perkins's 'widely influential' *A Case of Conscience* (1592), *A Discourse of Conscience* (1596) and *The Whole Treatise of the Cases of Conscience* (1606) are invoked. So are Wager's *Enough is as Good as a Feast* (c. 1559–70) and *The Castle of Perseverance*, 'the first complete extant morality play'. Some of these works, such as Nathaniel Woodes's *The Conflict of Conscience*, offer 'parallels' with *Hamlet*. The figure of Wrath in *The Castle of Perseverance*, is 'relevant to the audience's response to Hamlet'. In a footnote, George Wither's 'Of Revenge' is described as an 'analogue'.[5] By associating *Hamlet* with contemporary and earlier art and thought, Belsey creates an ethical 'setting' for Shakespeare's play. The aim is to dispel anachronistic, 'Romantic', and therefore psychological assumptions. Belsey's object is to replace these assumptions with a framework of ideas closer to those of Shakespeare's time. In terms of method, nothing could be safer; or less 'radical'.

But Belsey's historical scholarship is the corollary (even the vehicle) of her 'radical' campaign as a 'new' and, by intent, quite unconventional modern critic: the proponent of Freud, Marx and Lacan. The careful respectability of her article contains the seeds of an attitude that will soon place her securely in the ranks of 'radical' critics. In drawing attention to the context of plays, 'The Case of Hamlet's Conscience' anticipates the 'de-centred subject' that is to become a Belseyan trademark. Though little within the article diverges from the oldest of academic routines, Belsey, by virtue of her method, sees *Hamlet*, as Eagleton in his consciously Marxist phase sees all literature, as culturally produced: a product of its encircling contemporary culture, which in turn 'explains' the old work, and provides the terms for our modern relationship to it. Nothing so ideologically specific is actually said in the article, which seems continuous in spirit and approach with other unexceptionable offerings in the learned and respectable pages of *Studies in Philology*. But like other traditional criticisms, the article stresses the context of the play. And this (not Shakespeare, its author) is to be seen as defining its moral and literary world, and therefore meaning: the subject is de-centred. Thus 'The Case of Hamlet's Conscience' prepares the ground for the explicit radicalism of Belsey's publication of the following year: the widely known, and openly revolutionary *Critical Practice*. In Belsey's work as a whole, new procedures and old orthodoxies share important fundamentals in common. While, at times, these may be regarded as two sides of the same coin, in *Critical Practice* internal contradictions are involved. These emerge when the practice of this work is compared with its aims.

Belsey's *Critical Practice*, like Eagleton's *Criticism and Ideology*, is a critical manifesto, conscious of its 'radical' intentions, and conceived with an eye to the critical future it sets out to mould. To this end, Belsey assaults modern critical assumptions, themselves shown to depend on past critical assumptions, which hamper revolution. But since her assault has historical sources (as all appeals to revolution must), it therefore looks backwards as well as ahead. Its effect is therefore in a way unintended by Belsey, that of a critically and ideologically reactionary text which reinstates a number of the very doctrines (with their associated tastes) it is meant to demolish. This, the primary contradiction of *Critical Practice*, stems from Belsey's debt to the ideals of Romantic criticism, the original, though largely unacknowledged source of her attempted twentieth-century revolution. Belsey, like the Romantics, rejects 'common sense', associated for her, as for them, with the norms and ideals of a conservatively neoclassic body of rationalist critical thought and linking the present restrictively to the values of the immediately previous age. To Belsey, in the twentieth century, as to the Romantics in the nineteenth, 'common sense' is hostile to the progress of criticism, or, in Belsey's terms, to progressive criticism. Attempts have been made to oust it. But these have not been powerful enough. Therefore the time has come to recognise it for the ideological construct that it is, and acknowledge its dominant but imprisoning influence on critical thought. The basic delusion of common sense, according to Belsey, is the pretence of non-commitment. And criticism, for Belsey, as it comes to be for Eagleton, is necessarily committed. This is so, apparently, whether the critic admits it or not. It is not enough not to want to be committed. Criticism, like everything else, is political, like it or lump it. And if criticism is political, the criticism which rests on, or celebrates, 'common sense', is by that same token conservative (with a small 'c' and perhaps sometimes with a capital one). The direction of Belsey's critical argument may therefore be described as that of a 'New Romantic'. An old age is out. Catherine Belsey is prophet of the new.

But here Belsey reflects a second contradiction of the 'radical theory' which her criticism exploits. For in order to attack common sense, she has to employ it. In order to persuade, others must be carried along. The 'sense' she is talking must be experienced as common, available for all to understand. It must first convince before it can convert. (Otherwise, there is no point in writing a book, and Belsey's insights, intended like many of Eagleton's to influence a student audience, would have to remain the private property of a private club: that of the Cardiff Critical Theory Seminar or some other.) Her crusade against 'common sense' forms part of a wider campaign: against 'humanism', 'realism' and 'subjectivism'. In so doing, it is fiercely 'reasoned', in one sense of the word. And it is wholly consistent with the approach of the learned contributor to *Studies in Philology:* arguments rest on examples. On the evidence of Belsey's own practice (and in a book whose very title highlights questions of practice) it is clear that the values of evidence are given fervent respect. The problem is that the point of the argument is to cast 'common sense' in a hostile role: the value that has to be displaced. This is because like her Romantic forbears in the nineteenth century, Belsey sees 'common sense' only as a negative criterion. It is synonymous with the unproblematic, and therefore at odds with the kind of literature she happens to prefer. An appeal to 'common sense' is too simply, and too often, the easy way out. It is based on 'assumptions . . . which appear obvious and natural'. According to Belsey, a feature of 'common sense' is that it 'is not called on to demonstrate that it is internally consistent'. For Belsey, in her theory if not her own practice, standards have to be explicit. But the real worry about common sense may not be that it fails 'to demonstrate that it is internally consistent', but that, once made explicit, it is the wrong standard. Belsey links these two (different) charges. In the following sentence it is claimed that: '. . . an account of the world which finally proves to be incoherent or non-explanatory is an unsatisfactory foundation for the practice either of reading or of criticism'.[6] The 'sense' of the attack on 'common sense' depends on our accepting that there is no difference between these two things. At this point, the form and matter of *Critical Practice* are wholly in tune (though not in a way that builds confidence in the 'sense' of the book).

Precise language would not be important were explicit attention not drawn to the central importance of language in creation of meaning. We must therefore examine the relationship between what Belsey is saying, and how she says it. 'Common sense', she argues, is not only 'obvious', it is untheoretical. Theory, a positive value, is synonymous with intellectual disinterest. It counteracts the emotional, unconsciously receptive, response. It stands for complexity, not simplicity. At the same time, it seems that while Belsey is arguing in a general way for a more theoretical approach to, and conception of, critical study, she is herself primarily interested in advancing claims, not of theory in general, but of one particular theory: the 'post Saussurean'. In promoting Saussurean analysis, the disinterest of theory has to be put to one side. It is replaced by commitment to *a* theory. Thus Belsey's own practice does not really sustain greater intellectual, more 'systematic' grasp, or resist the confusedly 'affective' bourgeois critical tradition. It is 'radical' in a different way: in restoring to modern critical discourse the tones of the pedagogic and the liturgic. This can be seen when, in summarising 'common sense', Belsey is led to summary of her second *bête noire:* 'humanism'. In order to facilitate the attack, which would otherwise be harder (and problematic in a way Belsey at other times seems to require), attention is drawn away from what might or might not be signified by the term 'humanism' to the signifier itself. This is allowed only token value, reduced to italics and brackets and syntactically divorced from ideas it is intended to represent and must therefore parody. 'Humanism', according to Belsey, is an expression of 'common sense', and: '... common sense urges that "man" is the origin and source of meaning, of action, and of history (*huma*n*ism*)'.[7] 'Read, mark, learn and inwardly digest,' this seems to be saying. The device relies upon play upon words: 'man'='hu*man*ism'. 'Humanism' is offered as convenient label, a deliberately distorting verbal caricature that may be readily noted, recalled and recited. Here, the rejection of 'common sense' is reflected in the logic used to attack it. Meaning is not to be sought in the author. Therefore, it must be found in the language. Not being one, it must be the other. It is the approach of the either/or ultimatum. If one thing is not true then its opposite must be.

Belsey's polarities, in that they unconsciously reproduce the polarities of Romantic criticism, shape her in the mould her 'radical' ambitions are trying to have criticism break. But consciously, she uses a similar logic to displace the nineteenth-century values she explicitly does not favour, such as 'realism'. Past attempts to leave behind assumptions of 'realism', she says, have not been decisive enough. The theories of various quasi-radical critics, such as Frye, Fish, Jauss and Iser are surveyed and found wanting. They do not constitute a sufficient departure from 'the propositions of common sense'. Belsey, by virtue of her theory, is committed to total departure. Confronted with the following statement in writings by Swift or of Pope, the effect would probably strike most readers as ironic: as satire on nonsense. But in Belsey the statement is not intended to be funny at all:

> The failure of each of these theoretical assaults on expressive realism to break with the commonsense view of language has meant that while each in turn has had a fashionable following, and while New Criticism even came to prevail as an orthodoxy, particularly in the United States, common sense has continued to flourish and expressive realism, with only minor concessions to its opponents, has survived largely unscathed.

It is to ensure common sense does not continue to flourish, and that realism does not survive any longer unscathed, that Belsey appeals to insights modern criticism has derived from the French linguist, Ferdinand de Saussure. The key tenet (and basis of Belsey's revolt against the nineteenth century) is that literature does not reflect reality. It is not a mirror of life. Instead, it is like advertisements: it is a signifying system, albeit a complex one. According to Saussure, whose thinking Belsey adapts and applies, all meaning is relative; words express 'difference', not things themselves:

> Only a small social group can generate signs. Noises which have no meaning may be purely individual, but meaning, intelligibility, cannot by definition be produced in isolation. The sign is in an important sense arbitrary – the sound *dog* has no more necessary or natural connection with the concept *dog* than has *chien* or *Hund*.[8]

But Belsey goes no further back than Saussure. Now, historical considerations, which are the thrust of Belsey's contextual argument in her article on *Hamlet,* do not have to apply. The reflections of, say, Samuel Johnson on the frequently apparent, but usually arbitrary (socially constructed) relationship of the sound of words to their sense cannot be recalled. The reasons are perhaps obvious enough.[9]

Belsey's debt to Saussure forms the basis of her attack on the nineteenth century. Thus we learn that just as society constructs language, so ideology, inscribed within discourse, constructs the 'subject'. This link is explained with the aid of Althusser and Benveniste. According to the latter, whom Belsey quotes: ' "Language is possible only because each speaker sets himself up as a *subject* by referring to himself as *I* in his discourse." ' The thought is enforced by the following 'argument': ' "If one really thinks about it [sic], one will see that there is no other objective testimony to the identity of the subject except that which he himself thus gives about himself." ' Therefore even the idea of 'Literature', according to Belsey, reinforces liberal–humanist norms. The exception is when Belsey herself is examining literature (and thereby implicitly acknowledging the idea of it). In this case, the process simply confirms as valid the theory that makes construction of the subject *the* important target for 'radical' critics. In Belsey's own practice, criticism is selectively applied: some literary areas are exempt; some are not. Sometimes, identification of the subject serves merely to demonstrate the scale of the humanist threat it is an aim of *Critical Practice* to expose. Belsey lights on moments in which subjectivity is itself the subject (in the everyday sense of topic) of discourse. She discusses Richard III's speech 'What do I fear? Myself?' (V, iii, 182), where Richard, on the eve of Bosworth, is playing with the image of his own identity. Here we are given 'a crisis of subjectivity'. The idea of the subject, as topic, is reinforced, too, by poetry of the nineteenth century: 'It is readily apparent that Romantic and post-Romantic poetry, from Wordsworth through the Victorian period at least to Eliot and Yeats, takes subjectivity as its central theme.'[10] 'Radical' excitements of this insight are not very clear. We learn that Wordsworth's *Prelude* is a poem about himself; and that Tennyson's *In Memoriam* is like that too. We do not learn how subjectivity is a 'central theme' of less literally subjective works: *Michael,* say, or *The Palace of Art.* Belsey does not condemn poetry of the nineteenth century for fostering the 'subject'. It is there to confirm the validity of the idea: the *objet trouvé* of modern critical thought.

But it is a different matter with the nineteenth-century novel. Now, with 'classic realism' in view, the 'subject's' appearance is strongly condemned. In what sense, then, may this be considered to belong to a 'radical' judgement? In some ways, it is radical *only* in the sense that it is a product of seeking in the literature of the past evidence of political issues consistent with modern 'radical' theory, as Eagleton does in *William Shakespeare,* and as Belsey does herself when she looks at the Renaissance. The deficiencies of classic realism, and the nineteenth-century fiction which sustains it, are brought out by contrast with Renaissance drama. Here, in what Belsey calls the 'interrogative text', contradiction (not unity, which she associates with the nineteenth-century novel) is the principle of the work. Thus in *Macbeth* 'the discontinuity of the ego and the explicit division of the subject have become a structural principle of the play'. In Marlowe's *Tamburlaine,* we find a 'recognition of political contradiction'. In Shakespeare's *Julius Caesar*, meanwhile, 'political contradiction is rendered emblematic in Brutus's speech immediately after the assassination of Caesar.' *Coriolanus* 'dramatizes the contradictory truth that heroic individualism is both necessary to and destructive of a militaristic society'.[11] But Belsey is radical in a different sense when she is turning to Renaissance drama to repel the aesthetic ideals she sees as underlying the nineteenth-century novel. In repelling the novel, she is also questioning the demand for consistency in character, whether in the novel itself (which she sees as the source of the demand), or in the Renaissance plays to which she sees the demand as having been improperly (and unhistorically) applied. While therefore Eagleton's 'radical' treatment of Shakespeare is character-dependent, and thus in an important sense not radical, Belsey's attitude to Renaissance drama, including Shakespeare, is radical by virtue of challenging the concept of character integrity which has dominated criticism of the plays, including, in Eagleton's case, 'radical' criticism. It is not radical in being the only criticism of Renaissance drama ('radical' theoretical or otherwise) to do this.

In judgement on the nineteenth-century novel itself, Belsey's objections are again not in themselves new. But her position apparently justifies the term 'radical' in a way that Eagleton's treatment of the same literary field does not. This is because Eagleton's conscious commitment to Marxist beliefs, at one time in his career, directed his attention to relations between the nineteenth-century novel and its social context. Consequently Eagleton is committed ideologically to a favourable judgement of the realist novel. He can stress with approval, as in his *Marxist Study of the Brontës*, the immediate, daily, reality against which the novel, as art, requires to be measured. Belsey differs in that she does not favour attention to the social background of the novel any more than she hangs on to the idea of character that Eagleton preserves in his criticism of Shakespeare. Belsey uses 'reality' to stigmatise the unfortunate influence (as she sees it) of the form. For her, the problem is not that criticism has ignored the social context and political implications of the novel. It is that these features of the nineteenth-century novel have encouraged an illusory, too literally imitative, notion of relations between literature and life. The notion has sustained a bourgeois myth, which, like Eagleton, she sees as hostile to radical change. Above all, for Belsey the specialist Renaissance scholar, it has effaced the message of Renaissance drama. To effect change, criticism must emerge from obsession with the nineteenth century's main creative mode because this is irredeemably linked to emergence of a realist ideal which Renaissance drama, her researches reveal, leaves open to question. Belsey contributes to, and does not actually break with, the twentieth-century post-*Scrutiny* fashion for Renaissance drama studies. But she does have a claim, at least in appearance, to be radically displacing the nineteenth-century novel.

Except that, when this argument informs Belsey's critical practice, it takes more 'conservative' form: Belsey still thinks of the nineteenth-century novel as a unified literary enterprise. By examining extracts from classic realist texts the intention is to identify 'privileged discourse' through which the author exerts authority (the pun is intended to solidify the link). But this is at odds with a critique of 'realism'. Belsey wants art to present itself as art; as the non-realist, 'artificial' thing that it is. But she appeals to the notion of 'privileged discourse' 'which places as subordinate all the discourses that are literally or figuratively between inverted commas'. This suggests some impatience when the hand of the artist is apparent; i.e. when artificiality (and thus non-realism) is manifest in the work. On both counts, however, the classic realist texts incur negative valuations. But since literary evaluations are part of an ideologically hostile critical mode, they are blamed, hedgingly, not for their intrinsic error, but for influence, as a form, on later work: Belsey therefore cites but does not *directly* criticise George Eliot's *Mill on the Floss*. Although she sees the work as part of a movement representing an historically conservative force, the fault is that of the form, not the work's. This is because for Belsey 'classic realism' is not just a label, neutrally summarising historically and critically related texts. She conceives of it as active doctrine, aggressively at odds with radical theory of today. For her, the abstraction functions as agent. 'Classic realism', in the abstract, then, 'proposes a model' in which: '... author and reader are subjects who are the source of shared meanings, the origin of which is mysteriously extra-discursive. It thus does the work of ideology in suppressing the relationship between language and subjectivity.' But it is hard to escape the impression that unfortunate consequences (as Belsey regards them) of 'classic realism' *are* the fault of particular authors. The 'problem' in the passage quoted from George Eliot's *Mill on the Floss* is precisely that of the *author's* control and the reader's knowledge. Such knowledge exceeds that of characters in any situation portrayed, creating a conspiracy between author and reader. Belsey's real objection is to the unwarranted simplification of the text that this seems to entail. Worst of all, it squeezes out language: 'The context... points more or less irresistibly to a single interpretation which appears as the product of an intersubjective communication between the author and the reader in which the role of language has become invisible.'[12] George Eliot has produced the 'single interpretation' (where in a different, Belsey's preferred, form of art – such as that of Renaissance drama – many were possible).

But Belsey's principle has to be extended to Belsey herself. She too offers a 'single interpretation'. Her appeal to non-subjectivity is itself a subjective move. It is interesting therefore that her key quotation from George Eliot should be taken from one of George Eliot's most autobiographical (and therefore, arguably, most 'subjective') of novels, *The Mill on the Floss*, attacked by non-radical critics on similar grounds. *Critical Practice* does not acknowledge this valuation, but nor does it wish to displace it. Nor, any more than Eagleton's criticism, does it in the event subvert the idea of a 'great tradition'. Classic realist novelists have their role in this tradition confirmed: George Eliot, Dickens, Charlotte Brontë and Henry James are all invoked. Because Belsey's aim is to effect radical dismissal of classic realist art, the same figures, *en bloc*, must remain essentially linked. Belsey's argument only works if the balance is not upset; if literary history of the period covered by these writers, and as outlined by Leavis, is actually endorsed. *Critical Practice* thus makes a fundamental concession to the critical convention it seeks to escape. And we must therefore conclude that its own 'critical practice' qualifies (even subverts) its radical intent, even when Belsey is writing about those moments in literary history which stand in contrast to classic realist achievement in her terms. These, according to Belsey, coincide with appearance of the 'interrogative' text (the preferred alternative, in Benvenistian–Belseyan terms, to the 'declarative' text of classic realist fiction): 'The epoch of classic realism coincides roughly with the epoch of industrial capitalism. But at times of crisis in the social formation, when the mode of production is radically threatened, for instance, or in transition, confidence in the ideology of subjectivity is eroded.' But the taste which supports this theory is not new. Belsey chooses examples from earlier literary periods to suggest 'times of crisis in the social formation'.[13] But she takes them from authors highlighted (on similar if less consciously ideological grounds) by such unradical critics as the post-*Scrutiny* contributors to the *Pelican Guide to English Literature:* Donne, Wordsworth and, of course, the Renaissance dramatists themselves. The elements of this taste are not undermined. They are effectively reintroduced.

Therefore *Critical Practice* resembles the criticism of Eagleton in central respects. The style and manner of the work convey its 'radical' aims; but the taste and method on which this 'radicalism' rests (once demystified by means of the critic's own conscious standards) are unusually orthodox. Although on the one hand, a 'radical' philosophy is applied to works from the past (as in one strand of Eagleton's criticism), on the other, the works are judged in terms of their age (a stance in which Belsey and Eagleton are also at one). On the surface, the approach is anti-evaluative. But in fact, whether particular works are or are not favoured depends on (1) when they were written and (2) whether they satisfy personal (subjective) *genre* criteria that Belsey lays down, for example those of the 'interrogative text'. Thus *Critical Practice* (in practice), and despite 'radical' aims, is deeply indebted to the values of a literary–academic critical establishment with which it feels itself consciously at odds but which it cannot reject. New distinctions are invented or developed (the realist text, the interrogative text). But only some texts are 'interrogative'. And these are only good because they lend themselves to 'new' critical practice: the political–theoretical one the book's 'project', as distinct from its actual, observed, practice, wants to advance.

But for all her stress on the virtues of the 'interrogative text', Belsey does not see art as intrinsically 'interrogative', an enduring radicaliser (when and only when it is art) of the consciousness of humanity. The 'common sense' on which she relies herself to express her ideas is intra- not inter-social. It is determined by norms established in a specific society at a particular time: the Renaissance, the age of classic realism, the moment of the *Workshop on Lacan*. 'Common sense', as far as it aspires to become inter-social, or therefore 'natural', is bad: unearned and available without the effort that characterises modern radical theoretical 'struggle'. While this involves a personal cost, 'common sense' reflects back on the reader his own complacently held assumptions, and leaves them unchallenged. It must therefore be rejected. Radical theory interrogates; 'common sense' reassures, dissolving contradictions. An idea of what Belsey is tilting against can be gathered when she defines the duties of her new kind of critic. Drawing on Barthes and Macherey, she rises to a statement describing the crucial turning point in modern literary criticism:

> The object of the critic, then, is to seek not the unity of the work, but the multiplicity and diversity of its possible meanings, its incompleteness, the omissions which it displays but cannot describe, and above all its contradictions. In its absences, and in the collisions between its divergent meanings, the text implicitly criticizes its own ideology; it contains within itself the critique of its own values, in the sense that it is available for a new process of production of meaning by the reader, and in this process it can provide a real knowledge of the limits of ideological representation.

In Anglo-American criticism, in contrast to Macherey's, too much time has been spent making 'sense' of texts; accommodating them to values of dominant (liberal–humanist) ideology rather than allowing contradictions to come through. But Belsey's vision of Anglo-American criticism does not merely echo, it re-erects, consciously in order to knock down, unconsciously in the tastes and methods it reflects, traditional expressions of the type, for example *The Elizabethan World Picture*. It may be with such studies consciously in mind that she writes of Anglo-American critics' 'quest . . . for the unity of the work, its coherence, a way of repairing any deficiencies in consistency by reference to the author's philosophy or the contemporary world picture'.[14] But deliberately, unwittingly, but either way 'unhistorically', the dissensions internal to Anglo-American criticism are not brought out. And it is tactically necessary they should not be, since an image of the mediocrity of bourgeois liberal–humanist Anglo-American criticism is required as a foil to the 'radical' claims of Belsey herself. Belsey's 'radicalism' thus rests on this mediocrity and effectively extends it. *Previous* criticisms of post-*Scrutiny* taste, in Britain or the United States, have to be ignored. For the same reason, as we have seen, Belsey must leave out of account the trans-historical 'sense' which is permanently interrogative, shocking for every generation to confront, even though Belsey herself is widely in debt to critics from the past. Her 'sense', in practice, *is* 'common' in the sense of which she disapproves. It is simply that while some critics and thinkers with whom she shares ideas (Johnson, the Romantic critics, Leavis) are present though undeclared in *Critical Practice*, others (Brecht, Althusser, Lacan, etc.) are also present but persistently and openly acknowledged.

What Belsey says of the text in general terms, that it 'implicitly criticizes its own ideology', is true of her own text. *Critical Practice*, in practice, offers in some ways the reverse of what its 'radical' theory appears to imply and what she, apparently, thinks it has achieved. Belsey asserts that today's revolution in critical theory is 'radically undermining traditional ways of perceiving both the world and the text'. It is nothing less than 'Copernican'. And this 'de-centring' of literary assumptions is intended to highlight alternative texts. These texts accompany readings which 'would ultimately have the consequence of redrawing the map of "Eng. Lit." '. When however examples of texts are produced the claim is illustrated in relation to extended discussion of the stories of Sherlock Holmes(!). With Belsey's 'radicalism', as with Eagleton's, there goes an accompanying reluctance to move far from the established canon, however loudly it appears to be shouted down. There is no break with the mythologies of bourgeois taste. The myth, if there is one, is that bourgeois taste is somehow denied. With Belsey, symptomatically, where there is a conscious shift (unconsciously and effectively there is none), it is from the historically and academically established, such as George Eliot's novels, to the respectable popularity of Conan Doyle. Of course, interest in the Sherlock Holmes stories is presented in terms wholly congenial to preoccupations of modern self-consciously de-mythologising modes of critical enquiry: 'The project of the Sherlock Holmes stories is to dispel magic and mystery, to make everything explicit, accountable, subject to scientific analysis.' But the real literary heroes of *Critical Practice* are not creative writers in the ordinary sense. They are the theorists whose names are dropped time and again in the course of discussion: Althusser, Barthes, Marx, Macherey and Lacan. All 'creative' authors, George Eliot, Henry James, Shakespeare or even Conan Doyle, have only the reality of their text. But with theorists it is different. There, the author retains authority, his status as an Arnoldian *point de repère*. He (and it is usually a 'he' – by virtue of which Belsey is at odds with certain strands of radical feminist criticism) is the source of the 'truth' and 'sense' beside which the common sense of other authors (those not approved) is denied. Summarising, this time with unqualified approval, the views of Lacan, Belsey writes: 'The Death of the Author, the Absolute Subject of literature, means the liberation of the text from the authority of a presence behind it which gives it meaning.'[15] Whether, then, you are an author whose death is proclaimed depends a great deal on who you are. In its own practice, *Critical Practice* is an evaluative criticism. Selections are made. In another respect it seems uncritical: all the magic circle, Freud, Marx, Macherey, Althusser, etc. are taken over wholesale and freely applied.

But, modestly, Belsey does not lay claim to impeccable logic. Her case, she concedes, has 'dangers'. In warning of these, however, her tone is not so much self-critical, designed to uncover the flaws she suspects in her logic and to do something about them. It is confidential. It is a question of finding a way forward nevertheless. She therefore addresses the reader in the hushed voice of a fellow strategist speaking to those whose loyalty to the cause can be taken for granted. In the conspiracy between author and reader (such as Belsey condemns when she finds it implicitly present in realist writing) it is a matter of plotting the details of the campaign. Thus, with some of Lacan's formulations, 'there is a danger [i.e. a danger for us as fellow radical theorists] . . . of inverting the Cartesian problematic rather than doing away with it.' By this point in the book, Belsey hopes to be preaching to the converted, assuming her readers were not converted from the start. For the previously and persistently unconverted, there seems more to provoke than to persuade, though this, it might be conceded, is the spirit of contradiction that Belsey values in literature itself, and (by intention at least) in criticism of literature. Even so, *Critical Practice* becomes less confidently provocative as the conclusion draws near. As details of the new critical practice are produced, a note of caution is heard. With the new idea, we learn that 'the work of criticism is to release possible meanings'. Milder than earlier comments, the definition of criticism is now exceptionally uncontroversial, precisely designed not to point up the differences between liberal humanism and radical theory. Perhaps, in the closing pages, Belsey realises that there is, after all, no more to argue; that belief is all, and that affirmation (based on faith) should take over. Even then, there is a certain desperation in such statements as: 'Traditional boundaries, constructed in language and in ideology, no longer hold . . .'[16] The dramatising points to some doubt.

In her response to such doubt, Belsey reverts to the academic–industrial. Since some concepts are admitted to be 'vulnerable', 'this means only that there is more work to be done.' Any logical objections we might have are merely a 'source and evidence of [the] vitality' of the new procedures. *Critical Practice* ends with a hopeful glance at the appetising prospect of future labours. The questions which remain: ' . . . invite us to go on to solve the problems which new forms of understanding must inevitably generate, to produce a critical practice which is fully pertinent to those forms of understanding, without evading the difficulties necessarily involved in the development of a new mode of production.'[17]

If then the Belseyan 'theory of practice' of *Critical Practice* seems undermined by its own practice, that is only because it is merely the start, not the end, of Belsey's critical project, a necessarily incomplete part of the total picture to be built up one work at a time. Its general argument is replicated in her essay on Shakespearean comedy, 'Disrupting sexual difference', printed in *Alternative Shakespeares* (1985).[18] And in the same year, it appears in *The Subject of Tragedy: Identity and Difference in Renaissance Drama*, where practice is put into practice in extended form. Like *Critical Practice*, however, the argument of *The Subject of Tragedy*, while it respects the documentary evidence necessary to any effort of critical revision, aims to bring new light to bear: an applied grasp of the forms of understanding found in what Belsey regards as the new 'radical' theory of the twentieth century.[19] At the same time, given perhaps that Belsey is now directing herself at teachers of students as well as students themselves, it offers a somewhat more complex vision than *Critical Practice*. We read the past, Belsey claims in the Introduction to her book, while confined by the present. Eagleton would say that for this reason each age has a different Shakespeare, or different Homer, which the modern critic may, in his own exclusive terms, re-construct (which Eagleton himself does in his *William Shakespeare*). But Belsey is interested to discover more precisely the import both of the past's 'difference' from ourselves, and the 'identity' of present and past. We know only the present, of course, and to think that, even in imagination, we can return to the past to recreate fully the context of any past work is, she says, an illusion. In her own field (the Renaissance), Belsey finds both difference and identity: identity because the present (i.e. the modern age) began in this period; and difference because we also feel the period's distance from us; its pastness as part of the past. *The Subject of Tragedy* can thus reassert Belsey's radical concerns alongside her scholarly interest. It does not matter that many works invoked in the book suggest the familiar territory of studies in Renaissance drama: *Arden of Faversham, Julius Caesar*, etc. As in *Critical Practice*, the theory which Renaissance drama study serves to sustain (by identity) and to back (by difference) is for Belsey radical enough.

But where this occurs depends, in practice, upon the logical needs of the moment; the strictly local tactical requirements of the book as a whole. The central tactic is the device of the title, *The Subject of Tragedy*. Here, divisions between conventional and revolutionary dissolve within Belsey's key term: 'the subject'. This functions as a pun without humour: its political sense (meaning 'subject' as 'citizen' of a monarchical, pre-revolutionary, state) flows freely into its use to suggest point of view, stance or attitude of a literary work, as embodied in the person, author or central character responsible for each. Thus, by accepting the terms in which Belsey conceives her study, we are helpless against mergings of the political and the literary (and politicisation of literary) the book aims to promote. In the Preface, Belsey writes of her first purpose being 'to contribute to the construction of a history of the subject in the sixteenth and seventeenth centuries'. But a sense of the extension of the term 'subject' is already presumed. Therefore the argument, without having begun, is already over. We are told how the 'subject' is to be seen at the centre of a newly organised vision of human activity: 'The subject is to be found at the heart of our political institutions, the economic system and the family, voting, exercising rights, working, consuming, falling in love, marrying and becoming a parent.'[20] It is merely to *explain* the oneness of these things that the history of the 'subject' (that part of it which is traceable in Renaissance drama) is then written. But this history of the 'subject' (as difference) is intended as a lesson to the present: a prophetic identity. The present, we should see, is sustained by assumptions which came into being or were dramatically strengthened at the time of the Renaissance. Contemplating radical change in the past suggests possibility of radical change in the future. Therefore the 'subject' can be displaced; 'liberal–humanism' can be extinguished; human nature is not, at bottom, the same. Everything changes. In making this claim Belsey speaks as a period specialist, scrupulously enumerating peculiarities, special features and the modern relevance of her favourite historical field. But, at the same time, she is a radical critic, rejecting unchanging nature as 'conservative' notion. The old scholarship is extended to the status of a modern, explicit, political–intellectual dynamic: a radical credo. Without having itself to change, the scholarly orthodoxy of the past becomes the road to the future.

But Belsey's analysis is still *literary* criticism. It thus implicitly sustains literature as a revolutionary medium. For Belsey, literary knowledge is a prerequisite knowledge coming *in advance of* political or social change: 'To propose an alternative to the humanist version of literary history is to offer a contribution to that rearrangement of our knowledge which signals the end of the reign of man.' The first half of the book is on 'Man', the second on 'Woman'. But it is the literary treatment of these issues that Belsey is interested in. Woman remains Man's 'other'. But concern is more literary than feminist. It is scholarly–historical (not sexual–political) justice that first needs to be done. For Belsey, the root problem is that Renaissance drama is still not understood. Thus liberal–humanist readings find 'Unity' in 'interrogative' texts. But scholarship reveals that in the Renaissance there were two modes, emblem and illusion, which often collide. *The Revenger's Tragedy* (1607) is cited as one example: 'On one plane Vindice is . . . a wronged man . . .; on another he is vengeance, as his name implies.' But many plays do not conform to liberal–humanist readings, though some conspire to strengthen the liberal–humanist self, stressing the realm of the inner mind, its power and durability. This 'interiority' is to be found in *The Second Maiden's Tragedy* (1611), where 'the mind is a place of retreat, defined by its difference from the exterior world.'[21] Even then, liberal–humanist criticism has not recognised that self-assertion in Renaissance tragedy is at one with Evil. Where liberal–humanism fails, Belsey's scholarship steps in: it shows that Renaissance drama does not always sanction the private world of the inner mind. This is because, as Belsey's research has uncovered, the within and without were not clearly defined in Renaissance drama, even where the free-standing individual self is dramatically prominent, as in soliloquies.

Hamlet has no interiority. Hence the endless search by critics to find it.

Thus *The Subject of Tragedy,* though it reflects post-*Scrutiny* academic concern with Renaissance drama, implicitly and explicitly reiterates Belsey's critique of nineteenth-century realist critical norms. In this it appears to offer a refreshing departure from the kind of criticism (against which *Scrutiny* had already reacted) that insists on character study, where focus is on who is saying a particular thing, not what is said. 'What', not 'who', is the starting point of Belsey's latest study, on Milton. 'This book is not about John Milton,' she insists on page 5 of *John Milton: Language, Gender, Power* (1988). In common with her previous publications (as this attempt to disconcert the reader suggests, and as does her placing of 'Milton' in inverted commas), it is a book offered, along with the others, with self-consciously radical intent, the latest stage in the progress of her 'radical' project. According to Eagleton, the General Editor, *John Milton* is: '. . . a subtle double reading of Milton's work, attending at once to its most negative ideological features and to those troubled "textual" moments when his poems significantly equivocate, running against the grain of their official convictions'. As this suggests, the outlook of this latest book is consistent with that of the others. Just as Belsey appears to dislike the simplification and unity (as she sees it) of George Eliot's 'classic realist' literary art, so she is drawn, correspondingly, to the complexity of Milton's. Milton's texts represent an offshoot of her interest in Renaissance drama: 'My project is . . . to locate in Milton's texts, sometimes in defiance of the author's apparent convictions, the turbulence within the writing which demonstrates the conflicts that occurred in the process of establishing some of the meanings we now take for granted.' Going to Milton, as to Renaissance drama, is to address a modern problem of being: 'Is it possible in the twentieth century, as both the cultural relativity of humanism and the metaphysics of logocentrism become apparent . . . that we might share the work of producing meanings . . . by which to live?' Milton, like Renaissance drama, offers 'identity', access to meanings the modern world needs. Thus for example, the angels in *Paradise Lost* provide the reader with 'momentary vision of a world beyond essences' of which the result is 'imaginable as sexual plurality for each individual, and the consequent release of sexual being from power'. Milton accordingly has a place in the current debates of sexual politics. His poetry has a bearing on the present. He is like the Shakespeare of the comedies, who, Belsey had written in her essay printed in *Alternative Shakespeares,* has plays which enable us to 'glimpse a possible meaning, an image of a mode of being, which is not asexual, nor bisexual, but which disrupts the system of differences on which sexual stereotyping depends'.[22]

But *John Milton* aims only to interpret Milton. Belsey's interpretation is intended to contrast with, and supersede, two other sorts of interpretation: the biographical, and that carried out on the basis of what many have supposed to have been Milton's intentions as writer. As Belsey's own critical writings themselves show, the intentions and meanings of a work may be two different things. But, while she questions the kind of interpretation desirable in existing criticism of Milton, she does not question the assumption that criticism *is* interpretation. For her that is all that it is: 'The interpretation I want to offer does not seek out an apparition; instead it attends to an appearance, the signifying surface of the text, not an essence concealed by the words, but the textuality of the words themselves.' From this it follows that the issues raised by, and reflected in, Milton's poems should be (manifestly) permanent issues: palpably enduring matters of debate. Were they not, there would be no point in seeking them out in Milton's poems. The link is captured in tones of occasionally impatient directness. The opening sentence of Chapter 3 of *John Milton* is '*Comus* is about rape.' But, if Belsey's tone is 'radical', it is also true that the attention she gives to each of the poems of Milton (to illustrate the theory) is neither unusual nor unconventional in any substantial degree. *Paradise Lost,* naturally enough, features centrally in the study. It has on the one hand the historical interest that Belsey requires of literature, as it 'records the emergence of humanism'. But like other Milton poems, it is also one of the 'turning points' which 'address in the process questions concerning the location of authority'. But in *John Milton* only certain issues, ones with current, theory-sanctioned appeal, appear to have their permanence acknowledged. These are signified by chapter headings, reminiscent of the section headings in Eagleton's *William Shakespeare*: Poetry, Gender, Sovereignty, Narrative. The first is most important, as it concerns 'the textuality of meaning itself', a feature demonstrated in analysis of Milton's 'On the Morning of Christ's Nativity': 'The project of such poetry is to inscribe the Word in the word...' Neither in intention, then, nor in effect, can *John Milton* be said to have broken new ground: the 'radical' analysis merely allows Belseyan tenets of 1980 to be recalled, unmodified, in 1988. The application is new; but the theory, if only by virtue of the ongoing project to which it belongs, is old, an orthodoxy in its own right. And Belsey is now in danger of labouring her point: 'The project of the classic realist narrative is to repress its own textuality, constructing the illusion of a knowledge which is inter-subjectively shared by narrator and reader, and which transcends the text itself.'[23]

But what does Belsey's criticism, taken as a whole, say about her practice as a critic? Negatively, it tells us that for work by an expressed 'radical' critic, with ambitions that go far beyond literature to politics and society, her criticism, in revolutionary effect, displays features of a narrowly historical, contextual and specialist approach. These then seem to become, by virtue of their use by a self-declared 'radical critic', revolutionary. Thus, Belsey's practice resembles Eagleton's in exposing the unconscious conservatism behind the 'radical theory'. Belsey's methods and personal canon of literature make this clear. Her 'map' of 'Eng. Lit.' in fact matches closely the map of mid-twentieth-century academic taste she is ostensibly reacting against, but can't, because her criticism depends crucially upon it for its ends.

Of the earliest English literature, Chaucer is mentioned only in passing and, even in treatment of the Renaissance (Belsey's specialist area) we do not learn where Spenser say, or Sidney, fit into, or inspire, the character of the age. The scene is dominated by Renaissance drama. The Renaissance drama that bulks largest in Belsey's writing is Shakespeare's. But she also invokes non-Shakespeare plays, or works that are not plays at all. This blurs (as the criticism of Eagleton, who is not a Renaissance scholar, does not) the very differences between Shakespeare and his contemporaries that give modern relevance (an identity-in-difference other than that Belsey identifies) to Renaissance studies. But then it is Belsey's aim to fragment the subjectivities of her chosen authors, so long as they are not theorists, to make thematic considerations square with her own, self-specified, 'radical' aims. Even the extended examinations of single Shakespearean plays are short, and conducted with regard to single aspects of each play: revenge, 'split subject' and so forth. Shakespeare *in toto* as author is not faced: but nor, for that matter, either as authors, or through whole plays, are Shakespeare's dramatic contemporaries and immediate successors. The *positive* merit of Belsey's practice as critic is that she draws into the forum of modern critical speculation works that might be thought the business of Renaissance studies at its most narrowly historical. In Belsey's hands, Renaissance studies may, for a time, seem not to be so.

But Belsey's seventeenth century non-dramatic poets are those prominent in *The Pelican Guide:* Milton, Donne and Marvell. These lend themselves to a theory of critical practice (either by virtue of their form or *genre* or because they are readily treated by the procedures of Practical Criticism). But the critical practice has undergone a conversion to revolutionary terms. Thus, Marvell's 'A Dialogue between Soul and Body', by virtue of its dialogue form, keeps open matters which classic realism, within the polarities of Belsey's criticism, would have poetry close. Likewise, Donne's 'Death be not Proud' 'dramatises the speaker's fear of death in its imagery and syntax even while asserting death's powerlessness'. Belsey's 'revolution' therefore not only upholds the position in the canon of both poets, but does so on what may once not have been, but now are, very conventional grounds: complexity, contradiction and ambiguity. Not that Belsey wants to concede that her grounds are conventional. She is always at odds, in her own mind, with the judgement of (non-radical) mankind, even in the very moment of having her readers attend more closely to it where it supports contradiction. Thus she can write of the contrary positions of Marvell's 'Horatian Ode': '... to smooth over the contradictions in the "Horatian Ode" by attributing to Marvell a non-contradictory ideology of Loyalism is to refuse to enter into the debates about revolution, authority and tyranny initiated in the texts.'[24]

Beyond the limits of her most recent study, Milton is a presence in Belsey's criticism only in passing, and then as prose writer (of Puritan tracts) rather than poet. Dryden exists as playwright, and even in that role the most extended treatment of him is comparison between Shakespeare's and Dryden's versions of the story of Anthony and Cleopatra. This is not a novel approach. Pope appears hardly at all, perhaps because for Belsey, as for the early nineteenth-century and Victorian critics (and for Leavis), his poetry is associated with a system based on discredited liberal–humanist values of reason and order. The potential for 'contradiction', of tensions offered but unresolved, in Pope's (as in Marvell's) verse, is not explored, and therefore is not discovered. Swift, on the other hand, is approved. Invoking Eagleton's judgement of *Gulliver's Travels,* Swift offers an example of 'the absence of a clear authorial and thus authoritative point of view'. But the possibility of enjoying this same 'absence', one signally afforded by the great Augustan translators of classical and medieval poetry, is not pursued. Perhaps because his writings impress characteristics of an 'authoritative point of view', Samuel Johnson is also all but ignored, though in a short review, '*Re-Reading English* and the Uncommitted Reader' (1984),[25] Belsey refers to him as 'arch-empiricist and exponent of bluff common sense'. She may also be tilting at Johnsonian notions (of general nature) when she rejects in the Introduction to *The Subject of Tragedy* the view that 'change is always only superficial, that human nature, what it is to be a person, a man or a woman, a wife or a husband, is palpably unchanging.'[26] As 'New Romantic', Belsey believes that radical change, if not in the facts of life, then in its meanings, can occur. 'People have always, we may reasonably assume, made love, and always died,' she writes in the opening of her article 'Love and

Death in "To his Coy Mistress" ': 'But the meanings of love and death are discursively and historically specific.'[27]

The nineteenth century, as far as it is a source of 'liberal–humanist ideas', is therefore also anathematised by Belsey. But it also offers numerous exemplifications of 'radical' features of texts. Belsey, as noted, sees it as apparent that 'Romantic and post-Romantic poetry, from Wordsworth through the Victorian period at least to Eliot and Yeats, takes subjectivity as its central theme' – a judgement based on the number of works in this period whose subject (meaning in this case 'topic') is the person of the author. The following well-known passage from Wordsworth's *Prelude* (1805) is quoted to instance the 'interrogative text', notable for 'a distinction between a past "I" and a present "I"':

> I would stand
> Beneath some rock, listening to sounds that are
> The ghostly language of the ancient earth,
> Or make their dim abode in distant winds.
> Thence did I drink the visionary power.
> I deem not profitless those fleeting moods
> Of shadowy exultation: not for this,
> That they are kindred in our purer mind
> And intellectual life; but that the soul,
> Remembering how she felt, but what she felt
> Remembering not, retains an obscure sense
> Of possible sublimity . . .

In introducing this quotation, a commonsensical reading of the passage is decisively set aside. More grandly:

> Here the project of the text is to ensure a convergence between the subject of the *énoncé* and the subject of the enunciation to create a unified identity which is intelligible as the product of past experience: what the poet *was*, we are to understand, is the source of what he *is*. Thus the narrative passages employ the past tense and there is a clear transition from narrative to meditation in the present tense.

Other Romantic poets are mentioned: for example, contributors to the *genre* of the 'Romantic ode'. But detailed comments, such as they are, suggest a fairly uncontroversial reading; one in accord with commonly expressed academic views. Thus, in

Keats's 'Ode to a Nightingale': '... the escape from mortality is to a world of mutability. The nightingale's "happy" song becomes a "requiem" and finally a "plaintive anthem", and the transcendent vision succeeds only in recalling the world of loss which was its antithesis.'

Victorian poetry finds its place in Belsey's criticism in examination of Matthew Arnold's 'The Scholar Gypsy', where, in the central section, 'The dissatisfaction of the text with the logic of its own argument ... is everywhere apparent'.[28] But the point made here, in Belsey's first book-length study, is also made in her last, where these are her reasons for writing on Milton. The example is different: the idea is the same. Belsey advocates change, but remains constant herself.

Belsey, then, like Eagleton, exhibits the non-fallibilist confidence of modern critical–academic writing. If this is not infallibly consistent in the relation of theory and practice, then it expresses an admirable determination to bring theory into the cross-current of a relationship with authors and texts. The theory itself may be anti-humanist; but its interest is necessarily human. It expresses the social commitment, zest and intellectual topicality of what it means to be a modern critic; and asserts that it is too easy to do modern literary studies in a state of naïve unconsciousness of the cultural forces that have shaped the world, academic institutions, the subjects we pursue and our mental constitutions. There is an outspoken sharpness, rancorous edge, persistent abrasiveness and occasional moody anger in the work of both critics which join with the natural repugnance aroused in us all by the whole unwittingly snobbish ethos of bourgeois bookishness; the irresponsible and introspective concern with the 'higher things' of life that literary study so often seems to foster and invite. Eagleton and Belsey stamp their feet in joint protest at the insidious gentility of literature and criticism, and direct our minds to the permanent forces that can both create and topple the apparently secure but in reality fragile compositions of contemporary society that allow literary study to take place at all. Both challenge the pretentions of literary study, but simultaneously express them. If, therefore, they have helped bring literary criticism to the forefront of intellectual fashion, they have also inherited the values of the British critical establishment they abhor. The difference is that in their works, the genial decencies of an earlier age have given place to the polemicism, sectarian entrenchment and scientistical show that make the critic, in the absence of the (now) dubious virtues of grace and ease, a genuine spokesperson for contemporary society. In their hands, criticism no longer aspires to noble aloofness from the failings and faults of ordinary, inward-looking, humanity. It writes them large, and is proud to do so.

Notes

1. *Critical Practice* (Methuen 'New Accents': London, 1980); *The Subject of Tragedy: Identity and Difference in Renaissance Drama* (Methuen: London, 1985); *John Milton: Language, Gender, Power* (Blackwell's 'Re-Reading Literature': Oxford, 1988).
2. Ed., 'Workshop on Lacan', *Lettera* **18,** 1979, 204–42.
3. *ibid.*, p. 216.
4. 'The Case of Hamlet's Conscience', *Studies in Philology*, **76,** 127–48. Other specialist contributions to Renaissance drama studies include 'Shakespeare's "vaulting ambition" ', *English Language Notes*, **10** (1973), 198–201, and 'The Stage Plan of *The Castle of Perseverance*', *Theatre Notebook* **28** (1974), 124–32.
5. *ibid.*, pp. 129, 131, 133, 137, 138.
6. *Critical Practice*, pp. 3–4.
7. *ibid.*, p. 7.
8. *ibid.*, pp. 37, 41.
9. See Johnson, *The Rambler*, No. 92: 'It is . . . in many cases, apparent that this quality [of beauty] is merely relative and comparative; that we pronounce things beautiful, because they have something which we agree, for whatever reason, to call beauty . . . . It is, however, the task of criticism to establish principles . . . . There is nothing in the art of versifying so much exposed to the power of the imagination as the accommodation of the sound to the sense.' (*The Yale Edition of the Works of Samuel Johnson*, IV, pp. 121–2).
10. *Critical Practice*, pp. 59, 88, 67–8.
11. *ibid.*, pp. 89, 95, 96.
12. *ibid.*, pp. 70, 72.
13. *ibid.*, pp. 85–6.
14. *ibid.*, p. 109.
15. *ibid.*, pp. 130, 109, 111, 134.
16. *ibid.*, pp. 145, 144, 145.

17. *ibid.*, p. 145.
18. 'Disrupting sexual difference: meaning and gender in the comedies', in John Drakakis (ed.), *Alternative Shakespeares* (Methuen: London, 1985).
19. An earlier example of Belsey's ability to relate her Renaissance scholarship to modern theoretical and social concerns (revised for inclusion in *The Subject of Tragedy*) is 'Alice Arden's Crime', *Renaissance Drama*, **13** (1982).
20. *The Subject of Tragedy*, p. ix. For Belsey's discussion of the 'subject' in Renaissance literature, see also 'Tragedy, justice and the subject', *1642: Literature and Power in the Seventeenth Century* (ed. Francis Barker *et al.*), (University of Essex: Colchester, 1981), pp. 166–86.
21. *The Subject of Tragedy*, pp. 33, 31, 35.
22. *John Milton*, pp. viii, 14, 45, 67; *Alternative Shakespeares*, p. 190.
23. *John Milton*, pp. 6, 36, 16, 18, 20, 101.
24. *Critical Practice*, pp. 98, 95.
25. Rejoinder to Peter Barry's review of Peter Widdowson's *Re-Reading English* (1982), *English in Education*, **18**, 2 (Summer 1984), 85.
26. *The Subject of Tragedy*, p. 2.
27. 'Love and Death in "To His Coy Mistress"', in *Poststructuralist Readings of English Poetry* (eds. Richard Machin and Christopher Norris), (CUP: Cambridge, 1987), p. 105.
28. *Critical Practice*, pp. 67–8, 87, 122, 120.

3
Media Dons I: John Carey

If critical stability is something the 'radical theorists' aim to subvert, the 'media dons' belong to a majority party whose perceived aim, as far as the 'radicals' are concerned, is to defend it. We have seen that the 'radical theorists' have practised a criticism outwardly at odds, but inwardly at one, with the critical establishment they seek to dismantle. But the existence of 'media dons' points to a critical establishment also definable as at odds with itself. In the figures of the most famous literary professors of recent years, we find literary critics – whom the 'radicals' would regard as establishment critics – securing academic distinction and position by locating a more general audience for their views through the press. In their use of the press, their reviewing or occasional radio broadcasts, *they*, and not the 'radicals', have conducted critical discussion in a language and form that has opened it up to an audience outside academic life; even though their success in effecting critical revolution may seem no greater than the 'radicals'' own. Carey, the subject of this chapter, summarises this stance. On the one side he shares the specialist interests of the literary professor and textual scholar. On the other he is susceptible to the pressures of the public, and commercial, domain. The 'radical theorists' want to widen the range of texts admissible within the 'literature' criticism is equipped to discuss. The media dons, for their part, want to widen the forum for discussion. One turns to politics; the other to journalism. But their secondary effect is by different outward means the same: to challenge (from a position that is simultaneously centrally part of the modern academy) the modern academic monopoly on literary critical values and in so doing to ensure it. With the 'media dons', as with the 'radical theorists', potentially unshackling instincts again act to reinforce the literary values of a shared *status quo* jointly preserved.

Carey differs from the 'radical theorists' in not always being *explicitly* hostile to the critical establishment whose values that he, like the 'radicals', in many respects shares. He is an eminent scholar with a senior position in the university system: that of Merton Professor of English Literature at Oxford. At the same time, Carey's critical writing stands as an implicit (and occasionally explicit) criticism of this university world by virtue of the fact that Carey enjoys a 'popular' outlet for his criticism as regular (and some think brilliant) reviewer for *The Sunday Times*. That Carey is in neither role of the theorists' camp does not, in itself, make him 'right-wing', or mean he is always trying to rebut the 'radical' attacks on the literary canon of critics like Eagleton or Belsey. (He mostly ignores them.) We therefore do not gain from Carey an image of modern criticism 'in crisis'. But Carey is at the centre of the critical life of his times in a different respect. His writings reach those outside the exclusive world of fellow senior academics; outside the limited, and in Britain select, population of college and university students at which 'radical theory' is now aimed, and even beyond mere *readers* of criticism (if Carey's occasional radio appearances are taken into account). But Carey is no 'media personality' (a critic–entertainer like Clive James). His authority – both the source of his media success and sustained by it – continues to come from the fact that he is an Oxford don, but one able to bridge the gap between academic and popular sides of a cultural divide. Carey has a foot in two camps. One is academic life; the other is journalism. Where Eagleton and Belsey aspire to transform the moral and political climate of future society, Carey is compelled to interest the reader of the moment. Positively, this means that Carey is one of modern criticism's liveliest academic critics. Negatively, Carey's 'brilliance', however much a challenge it appears to the image of the grey academic, may at times seem a matter of academic manners smartened by mere journalistic gloss, superficially impressive, but critically inert. Carey may then offer no more than a further version of the facile substitution of values of one clique by those of another. At worst, the values of don and journalist subtractively combine.

Positively, Carey brings literary scholarship alive to a wide audience, even when he is not actually writing reviews for the press. His academic criticism, to this end, is astutely marketable, from his little book on Milton designed for sixth-formers and students to his major works on Dickens, Thackeray and Donne.[1] Despite the popularity with the student audience of some of Eagleton's 'radical' studies, from Carey's critical output, it is clear that the market for 'liberal–humanist' literary criticism, both inside and outside that of the student reader, is far from exhausted. All of Carey's studies are author-centred (as for that matter are many of Eagleton's). But Carey differs from Eagleton in adopting more often than not the type of biographical approach – the interest in a given author's 'vision' – that 'radical' theorists must always dismiss, since their authors are 'dead'. In the material they assemble, Carey's books are the products of lengthy research. They do not, however, read as research studies, written for an audience of scholars. All, though they include an audience of academic readers, are also calculated to appeal to readers whose literary (or simple human) interests are unacademic. That this may have required a deliberate effort on Carey's part, a transition between critical cultures, may be judged by glancing at Carey's early scholarly work; that which formed part of his 'serious' academic publishing career inaugurated in the sixties. In 1968, as co-editor with Alastair Fowler, he published an edition of *The Poems of John Milton* in the series of 'Longmans' Annotated English Poets',[2] where Carey's job was to edit the 'Minor Poems' plus 'Samson Agonistes'. This he did by printing the poems in formal academic dress. The controversies surrounding individual words, lines or passages in the poems are traced to multitudinous articles and 'contributions to knowledge', and the concern with sources is as minute as the extraordinary (almost obsessive) attention to the readings, theories and suggestions of fellow (or rival) scholars. However, not even Carey seems to think that all the inclusions have something worthwhile to say. While a proportion of the notes are there because they are there, others are expanded to a point out of all proportion to the scale of the issue in view. In the end it is the editor's knowledge, rather than the poet's, the edition exposes.

There is no doubt, nevertheless (or, more cynically, for this very reason), that Carey has enjoyed a 'successful' career as a specialist scholar. And the Milton edition must be seen as contributing to this. But Carey achieves a more publicly accessible role for his criticism (and a wider reputation as a scholar) in his three major books. The cautious specialism of the Milton edition contrasts with the boldness of his *The Violent Effigy: A Study of Dickens' Imagination* (1973). Carey's approach in this book is refreshingly direct. Now, the questions of literary context that necessarily dominate his edition of Milton are pushed to the side. Carey's method appears consistent with the implicit (and explicit) conviction about literary art voiced in the book itself: that it matters because, as Leavis might have said, it speaks for itself. In making this claim, Carey has to deny a strength of Dickens's fiction attributed frequently to him: that Dickens is important as a social commentator on the evils of Victorian society. This he does, while at the same time challenging the 'radical' idea which rests on this conventional picture of Dickens's achievement: that a work of art – as Eagleton's study of the Brontës suggests – is directly (or indirectly) a 'product' of society's forces, economic or historical. According to Carey, we feel the power of Dickens's imagination, the richness of his comedy, for their own sake, or we miss the point of his works. Carey is not interested in Dickens as moralist. He does not want to extract 'truths' from the novels. He claims that the meaning of the work lies in its inherent energy, its power to compel the reader to attend. Its rightness is its force. Dickens is subversive not because of the political philosophy or ideology focused by his work, but because he is funny. Dickens's comedy, like all great comic work, exists to destabilise the *status quo*. In its wit, compactness, energy of delivery and awareness of the needs of the general reader, *The Violent Effigy* is a 'formal', 'academic' critical work informed by qualities of literary journalism at its best. But Carey's book also reveals the subtractive *relationship* between journalist and scholar at their joint worst. The witty detachment of the one (a product of the cult of the columnist who is monarch of all he surveys), and the professionally requisite chilly disinterest, externality and remoteness of the other appear to unite. In so doing they place the critic firmly outside the text, insulating him personally from its effects. These effects then merely reflect back attention on the critic, making us conscious of his presence as mediator between ourselves and the work. The consequence is conservatively unchallenging, and effectively obstructs the Dickensian subversiveness it offers to portray, to the extent that it resembles Eagleton's 'radical' theoretical account of Shakespeare's plays: the presenter supplants the presented.

The self-projection nevertheless occurs at some of the most lively moments in Carey's book. As twentieth-century academic studies of Dickens's writings go, Carey's *The Violent Effigy* is one of the most eloquent celebrations; packed with detailed reference to the works, unpolluted by jargon and free from burdens of the theory that only the specialist (or modern student) has time for. Carey bombards the reader with example after example from the novels. He moves mesmerically from novel to novel, and from character to character, evoking, with great energy, the richly populated world of Dickensian fiction. At the same time, his book overflows with self-conscious 'technique', a show of wit which means that it is Carey's account of a scene, not Dickens's, that we usually come to admire. Often, therefore, while he is ostensibly concerned with a feature of Dickens's style or subject, Carey seems also to be making a point on his own behalf, and drawing attention, not to his response to the text, but to the effectiveness of the image of himself responding: as where Carey is explaining Dickens's obsession with images of violence and zestful brutality, where he is showing, or perhaps showing off, how unsqueamish he can be. The details of Dickens's accounts of executions, violent assaults, threats of cannibalism, riot and destruction, are lovingly reproduced and dwelt on. Carey approves with wholehearted relish the amoral vigour of for example Quilp:

John Carey

When amused, Quilp screams and rolls on the floor. He delights in tormenting animals as well as people. Finding a dog chained up he taunts it with hideous faces, and dances round it snapping his fingers, driving it wild with rage. He keeps a huge wooden figurehead of an admiral, sawn off at the waist, in his room, and diverts himself by driving red-hot pokers through it. He is, in short, a masterpiece of creative energy in comparison with whom Little Nell and her grandfather and all their part of the novel are so much waste paper.[3]

But Carey is striking a pose in this account of Quilp. He sets out to shock. The commentary depends very much for effect on Carey reacting in a studiedly uncensorious way to the violent scene he describes, and while shocking us, appearing himself unshockable. Carey, at this point in his book, comes before us in the role of the critic with a jut-jaw. In a way which has *something* in common with 'radical theorists' ' impatience with the vagaries of the affective reader response, he seems deliberately to trample on the idea of the critic as moist-eyed or effete; as in some special way a creature of tender emotions, or fragile sensibilities. But while the 'radicals' attribute their reading of a text to a theory, in a critical act in which, by their own account, individual participation is minimal, in Carey critical personality is asserted: Carey differs clearly from the 'radicals' in seeing the critic as a man of the world, a sharp-witted, unsentimental iconoclast, robust and confident in his common sense. Carey-as-critic is a figure of independent power.

Within this personality, Carey can appreciate the positive value of ordinary things that other more explicitly politically committed critics have been unable, or not wanted, to see: Dickens's obsession, for instance, not only with violence ('contradiction'), but also with order, especially the order of domestic life. The 'bourgeois' delight to be taken in Dickens's domestic interiors (such as Lieutenant Tarter's room) is minutely explained. For Carey, as could never be the case for Eagleton or Belsey, the independent Englishness evoked by these interiors may be freely enjoyed: Wemmick's 'castle', is much admired. And Carey can also enjoy Dickens's critique of bourgeois values, just as he is impatient with what are in his opinion the pretentious, non-essential features of Dickens's art: 'We could scrap all the solemn parts of his novels without impairing his status as a writer. But we could not remove Mrs. Gamp or Pecksniff or Bounderby without maiming him irreparably.' Comedy makes morality fly out of the window and is often black. Sometimes, Dickens's comedy is 'jocose'. Sometimes, it is 'facetious'. Sometimes, Dickens provokes laughter when in all decency we should be appalled, as in the 'comic' account of the degradations of the climbing boys in *Oliver Twist*. On other occasions it is a question of *grave hauteur*. Sometimes, Dickens's skill 'degenerates into sarcasm'. It is not always an attractive humour: sometimes we find a 'disdainful and supercilious note'.[4] Carey, in his awareness of the different voices of Dickensian comedy, and of its levels of success, is brusque and no-nonsense in his critical approach. Premature 'interpretation' of the novels is thus kept at bay. What they 'mean', in the 'radical theoretical' sense of the term, remains secondary to that which they cause us to see or to hear. Carey, in following Dickens, has his own way of delving beneath the layers of the bourgeois myth, even if he thereby confirms the critic as the bourgeois individualist the 'radicals' reject.

In so doing, however, the other, less attractive, even slightly 'sick' side of this attitude (as of Carey's journalistic temper) is exposed in cold sensationalism. The truth, when revealed, has to be one of horror and of shock, if only to make the impact Carey requires on what he judges to be the (compared with him) insensitive mass-market reader. Therefore a short step from black comedy is the macabre. Dickens, as Carey sardonically avers 'never missed a human carcass if he could help it'. And Carey, no more than Dickens, whose attitude is the source of his own, shrinks from such moments. Instead, he delights in Dickens's preoccupation with the paraphernalia of death. Devoting a whole chapter to 'Corpses and Effigies' he shows that he is not a critic to pale at the strong stuff Dickens deals out. The strange beauty of Dickens's descriptions of dead or living-dead humanity, automatons, grotesques, people-puppets and those who exist only in terms of their gestures, parts of the body, or their clothes, exerts a compelling fascination for Carey. Where some may see in these evidence of Dickens's poisoned imagination,

Carey finds imaginative vitality. The description of Mrs. Skewton in *Dombey and Son* going to bed and having her maid take off her false hair, eyebrows and the rest prompts praise of the 'brilliance of the writing'. The scene shows Dickens's imagination 'involved as the able-bodied heroes and heroines can never involve it'. According to Carey, descriptions of characters shaking hands show us, 'in miniature, why Dickens is a creative genius. He is intransigent. He won't accept that what's normally thought to be seen is what he sees.' Where Belsey rejects the realism she finds implicit in the classic realism of the nineteenth-century novel, Carey, by contrast, consistently requires it. Thus, he distinguishes between Dickens's sense of the symbolic import of any thing, such as the sea, and his sense of it as a reality, informed by experience. When Dickens waxes symbolic, Carey shows that his prose falls apart. Dickens's yearning for the significant, not justified by a sense of the real, prompts scorn. His 'symbolic writing is best . . . when it sticks closest to physical objects and doesn't break out into abstract – and especially religious – annotation'. Dickens's best 'symbols' are not really symbolic *of* anything: they simply exist – powerfully: 'He fills his novels with objects that vividly loom – locks, graveyards, cages – intensely themselves, not signs for something else.' But Carey resembles Belsey in one respect. In making his negative criticisms, as for example of the way Dickens is carried away in his portrayal of children's deaths, his impulse, like hers, is to contrast Victorian taste unfavourably with the other half of his own taste. For him, as for her, that is the Renaissance: Little Nell's being told she will become an angel after death, 'would have seemed preposterous to Milton or Donne' (the subjects of two other of Carey's books):

> For the seventeenth century the angels were all created long before the first man, and immensely excelled man in power and intellect. They were not remotely like a dead child. In *Paradise Lost* they wear armour and hurl mountains about. The deterioration of the angel is a further sign of Victorian religion ebbing into sentiment.[5]

Carey shows the connection between this and Dickens's obnoxious portrayal of women, acceptable only as submissive little girls.

Grown up they exist as a threat, surrounded by needles, pins and sharp scissors.

In *The Violent Effigy*, then, the text, though it appears to 'speak for itself', actually does not because it is mediated by a critic whose personality it in effect foregrounds and exalts, enabling him to condescend to the wider readership the book is designed to address. While Carey is stressing the text's independent life, it 'lives' (and is subversively comic) only in so far as it throws light on the liveliness of the critic's engagement with it, and whose standards it is seen at all points to inform, never to challenge or usurp. In reading Dickens, Carey has discovered nothing about himself of which he was not already aware. He reads Dickens but finds Carey, as do his readers. It is perhaps therefore ironic, though tactically essential to the preservation of Carey's scholarly credentials, that Carey should explicitly insist on the purity and authority of the naked text, this time in scholar's guise, when three years later he reflected on its power to stand on its own in his inaugural address to the University of Oxford on becoming a Professor of English.[6] This address, a critical theoretical 'policy statement' on Carey's part, reflects his growing confidence in his position in the critical establishment, and rests on the claim that as far as they challenge the supremacy of the author by their habit of re-wording his text, modern critics (though not presumably Carey himself) should be seen as critically presumptuous. In promoting a due scholarly respect for the text, Carey is therefore able to demote other scholars (and thus reinforce his own position, on what are scholarship's own terms). By returning to Coleridge, Carey's argument is that 'To reword is to destroy'. This is because, contrary to the assumptions of, say, Dryden in the seventeenth century, form and content, though we have two words for them, are indivisible. Arguing that 'literary critics spend much of their time destroying the meaning of literature', Carey takes four examples to sustain this charge; all by twentieth century critics. The first is from William Empson's *Seven Types of Ambiguity*, 'probably the most important seminal work in English criticism this century, and one that is almost entirely composed of rewordings and re-rewordings of pieces of literature'. With reference to this, and to other examples from criticism (of Spenser) by C. S. Lewis and (of Milton) by Christopher Ricks, Carey shows that what a critic says that an author is saying is often, manifestly, different from what is in front of our eyes. The critic's version will frequently distort the text. Thus Ricks had, in passing, called Samson's pulling down of the temple's pillars 'genocide'. Carey comments:

> The word 'genocide' is here superimposed upon, or rather substituted for, the two hundred lines of dramatic verse which Milton has used to organize and control our response to the catastrophe. 'Genocide' brings vividly to mind the racial atrocities of the twentieth century, and invites us to equate these with what Milton is writing about.[7]

Carey claims that not only does the word 'genocide' mislead the reader ('Should we wish to substitute a technical term for Samson's deed — which we don't — it would have to be tyrannicide, not genocide'), the process of rewording a great poet is inherently reductive. It is as criminal, apparently, as defacing a picture in the National Gallery. Unless the criticism is instantly forgotten, the 'text' (i.e. that which constitutes what we might agree to call the meaning of the work as well as its form) is no less 'damaged'.

In warning criticism to recall the limits of its province, and attacking criticism for getting in literature's way (by for example offering substitute literature such as students' guides to the real thing), Carey reminds his audience that works of literature must speak (like Dickens's novels) for themselves or not at all, so justifying his critical practice in the past. But he also prepares the ground for, and similarly justifies, a new development in his personal practice, albeit one that seems the precise opposite of the first: the critic, we are now told, should build up a context 'linguistic, social, biographical — within which any given piece of literature originally existed'.[8] Literature is now not after all to be judged in terms of the present (because 'we are restricted to those values and responses which our period has itself fashioned'). By this means, in the address to the University of Oxford, Carey finds a position through which he can link his past and future specialist preoccupations to emergent, and otherwise incompatible, public and commercial aims. Carey thus opens the way for an historical and biographical approach to criticism (that of the 'Life and Works') which is as popular in its appeal as it is consistent with his new, elevated, Oxford role.

That this new formula has not produced in all cases a critically entirely inert amalgam is shown by Carey's next major book: *Thackeray: Prodigal Genius* (1977). While Carey's *Thackeray* resembles his *Dickens* in that it is concerned with the author's imaginative vitality, his creative energy, it is also a more 'scholarly' work, if not in the manner of preserving the purity of the text in sense (1) of Carey's Inaugural Address, then in the opposite respect of sense (2): that attention is given to the social and biographical context of the novels and the writings as a whole. This change of approach has the additional convenience of enabling Carey to indulge his taste for literary gossip that is as donnish as it is journalistic. So, correspondingly, does the subject itself: Thackeray himself was a literary journalist addicted to the same sorts of things. It is therefore this side of Thackeray's work that Carey sets out to explore. The outcome is a book which, while undoubtedly a work of scholarship, is not designed for scholars alone, but aimed at the broad readership that literary–biographical writing has always enjoyed. To this end, the opening chapter is on Thackeray's colourful life, and here, needless to say, Thackeray's sexual adventures and peculiarities (his cultivation of a public schoolboy relish for physical punishment, which, as a schoolboy, he had hated) are given great play. He is brought on stage as one of the great 'characters' of English literature (like Boswell's Johnson). In these respects Carey's *Thackeray* is journalistic in a sense that detracts from its critical force: in that the treatment provides Carey with a good opportunity to be knowing; to peer behind the scenes of the great novelist's work to the private 'reality', the intimate 'human interest' story that journalists love (or make up when they cannot find it). On the other hand, by relating his criticism to what might be called a sense of life (in the 'realist' terms the 'radical' theorists have sought to deny validity), Carey brings within the scope of his otherwise academic criteria values that potentially challenge the academic appropriation of literary studies.

Once examined, however, they actually confirm that appropriation. Carey, by exploiting a popular romantic image of the writing life, maps the 'life' (of one sort) of the ups and downs of Thackeray's career, giving the story immense biographical appeal. Biography functions as scholarly background, buoying up the thesis of the book: which is that Thackeray's best writing is autobiographical in kind and to be found in and before *Vanity Fair,* after which it becomes decorous and sentimental. Therefore in one way (i.e. within the limited terms of 'Thackeray studies'), the book breaks new ground: it aims to show us the neglected 'spurts', or miscellaneous bits and pieces of Thackeray's output, such as the fruits of his 'brilliant gift for the impromptu'. At times, however, the wit we are meant to be admiring is not always as good as Carey appears to believe: Thackeray's reaction to the picture of a woman with big breasts (' 'Tis true 'tis titty, titty 'tis, 'tis true,') so amused him with its impromptu 'brilliance' that he made a point of praising it again in a review.[9] Nevertheless, Carey's interest in 'life' in Thackeray's writings makes his criticism in *Thackeray* into his liveliest study. We are shown how Thackeray's eye as a practising painter influenced his eye for detail and colour, light and shade in the literary art on which his reputation rests. The same eye is responsible for visual presentation of the best literary pieces. It sees things sharply in the earlier work, but constructs them more mechanically and contrivedly in the later. Carey's test of Thackeray's 'life' rests on his liking for the 'concrete particulars' in Thackeray's writing. But though Carey, in Arnoldian terms, praises Thackeray's evocation of the thing itself: 'The thingness of things, their intractable otherness, intrigued Thackeray . . . . In his own writing things regain their status as things,'[10] Carey's gloss on the idea of the thing itself is sometimes no more than materialist, as becomes clearer in the chapter entitled 'Commodities'. By 'things', Carey is including reference to Thackeray's unabashed attachment to the material world in its most trivial manifestations: the buttons, jewels, hats, gloves, the appurtenances of a comfortable and glamorous life are lovingly dwelt on. The 'life' Carey enjoys most in Thackeray is therefore often no more than the Good Life, by which he is entranced. His pleasure is apparent here and in the chapter on 'Food and Drink', where Carey goes to some lengths to anatomise Thackeray's fascination with food. On the one hand, this taste is linked closely to Carey's down-to-earth attitude to art: it is a thought which appeals to the critic as plain man, contemptuous of over-sophisticated notions of the function of art. Art (as literature) = food (for the spirit). On the other hand, it appeals to the critic as don, and to the hedonism of the world to which Carey belongs. It is a world which, for Carey, Thackeray's novels pleasingly reflect.

The congeniality of this attitude to journalistic values appears when Carey discusses Thackeray writing on the theatre. Here, Carey sees Thackeray challenging and then finally giving way to the restricting codes of Victorian sexual morality. Thackeray's love for the theatre, we are told, is that it is overtly a sham; a self-conscious pretence: 'Theatre provided Thackeray ... with an alternative world, which suited his restless purposes admirably, because it could so quickly be turned inside out. The bright side enchanted him, and transcended his reason and scepticism. But the shabby side, the patent sham, remained available for reason and scepticism to play upon.' At his best, according to Carey, Thackeray is able to see through the hollow values of his society. Sharing the *mores* of the Victorian world, he can yet move beyond them. While Carey, as scholar, is fascinated by the tension between Victorian primness and Victorian prurience that Thackeray embodies, occasionally, life behind the scenes inspires something akin to the droolings of the popular press. Here, Carey seems thrilled not so much by the text itself, as by the idea the text prompts in his private imagination:

> For Thackeray ... behind-the-scenes life meant dirt and violence and beauty. It was fantastic and alluring, the meeting place of dream and of the waking world, where strangely-garbed and painted figures swarmed and revelled. It was low and mysterious, located beyond the area-railings of middle-class decency, down unwholesome mews and alleyways and up dilapidated flights of stairs. Coarseness, ignorance and duplicity pervaded it, as Pen's Miss Fotheringay amply manifests...[11]

At its worst, there are many signs, such as this, of journalistic voices overpowering those of criticism in Carey's *Thackeray*. At its best, however, these values constructively combine with Carey's scholarship to reassert important critical values (themselves a consequence of Carey's taste for Thackerayan particularity). This is the case, in the book as a whole, when Carey, in a way which draws on his own journalistic–satirical powers, ensures that our sense of the strength of Thackeray's best work is sharpened by confrontation with *him* at his worst: Carey sees Thackeray at his worst (after *Vanity Fair*), collapsing into a morass of snobbish vacuity and empty idealisation, precisely resultant from his own 'populist' wish to flatter the prejudices and fatuities of his contemporary audience. Thus, Carey claims, Thackeray is too close to his characters, too lost in admiration for them as embodiments of popular ideals: thus Clive in *The Newcomes* is 'meant to illustrate . . . the entirely delightful results of the unequal distribution of wealth', when the reverse, in fact, is the case. In his praise, based as it is on a sense of the failings of Thackeray, Carey is more 'radical' than any of the 'radical' theorists' analyses of the nineteenth-century novel, even if his praise serves in the end rather to confirm, not overturn, the strength of this aspect of twentieth-century taste. Carey admires Thackeray for the same reason that Leavis had admired Tolstoy (*Vanity Fair* compares with *War and Peace*). In his praise of *Vanity Fair*, Carey stresses the internal self-criticising juxtaposition of the characters of the novel; the cross-currents of the reader's judgement and those of the author, which is only to re-echo what Leavis himself once defined as the morality of a dramatic literature able to justify itself as art: '. . . the life-principle of drama as we have it in the poetic–creative use of language – the use by which the stuff of experience is presented to speak and act for itself'.[12] In *Thackeray*, therefore, Carey escapes via journalism the scholar's inhibitions with regard to evaluative criticism, even though in so doing he is unable to offer a fundamental revaluation of any element of twentieth-century taste. He therefore merely expands, and does not subvert, the Great Tradition. But his work nevertheless has an important modifying role. It displays, within albeit limited terms, a consciousness of the re-evaluative role of literary criticism that consciously 'radical' criticism does not.

This could not be said of Carey's next work, *John Donne: Life, Mind and Art* (1981), which although it is the most ambitious of his three major books, with the air of a definitive study, and richly textured with Carey's critical wit, apt quotation and densely woven prose, is by comparison critically flat. Here, Carey is no longer able to rest his case on a sense of a strong antipathy of good to bad. While, in *Thackeray*, Carey had aimed to revive and bring within the terms of critical discussion an author unfairly neglected, in *John Donne* he seems rather to be further institutionalising an author whose works are already widely admired. A parallel apparatus of biographical and historical scholarship is applied to Donne's poems. But it is applied without critical point, even though Carey seeks to widen the field of concern for Donne's poetry beyond the limits of his *Songs and Sonnets*, which we are shown interlock in their imaginative preoccupations with Donne's other works: Carey reveals how they recall at multiple points the Donne of the 'Satires', the 'Problems', the 'Paradoxes' and the 'Sermons'. In this way, Carey outlines the case for the oneness of Donne's mind and art that justifies the title. But the critical outcome (as distinct from its embodiment of a successful modern academic marketing formula) is little more than a somewhat late tribute to Donne, whose claim to distinction is now quite unchallenged, since the critical contest for Donne's place in the canon was fought long ago, when Grierson, Eliot and Leavis all lent their authority to the effort to have him read and admired. Critically, then, Carey's book simply confirms, if confirmation were needed, the success of this campaign. Critical objections to Donne are brushed swiftly aside, and Carey seems almost to assume that Donne's status as poet had never sparked much critical dispute, or ever could. Alternative accounts are simply out of the question. Carey is merely confirming decisions of an earlier generation of critics. The critical genesis of the central claim is admitted in the Introduction:

All this is perhaps no more than a rephrasing of what T. S. Eliot meant when he said that Donne picked out ideas because he was 'interested in the feeling they give' – only I would argue that what Eliot observes is not an individual aberration on Donne's part but, however we may disguise it from ourselves, the universal practice.[13]

John Donne is a work of confirmatory criticism; a sanctification of what has long been a leading orthodoxy of twentieth-century literary taste. Thanks to this book it is likely to remain so.

The novelty of the study comes rather from the sensationalism we have noticed in Carey's other two books, of which, in *John Donne*, one example is the description of the terrible tortures inflicted on Catholics in Donne's age. By this means, Carey 'spices' his account, unsparing of the gory details of human suffering that accompanied religious repression in sixteenth-century England. Little is left to the reader's imagination: 'Other bystanders held his arms and legs while an executioner cut off his genitals and took out his bowels,' etc., etc. But while shockingness of this kind is an effective attention-getting tactic, it helps also to disguise the staleness of some of the literary critical insights. In a commentary on a passage from Donne's 'Satire III', we are offered a cliché of conventional homage to John Donne: Donne's poetry is powerful, we learn, because it resembles speech: 'No one before Donne had written English verse in which the pressures of passionate speech could be retained with such unhindered power.'[14] At the same time that Carey is inviting the reader to observe the crises at the core of many poems, whether of love or religion, as a consequence of Donne's inner turmoil – the product of his apostasy (or change of religion), no valuation of any poem discussed in these terms is allowed to affect Donne's standing as poet: it matters only how the poems come about. Thus in a fashion that is typical of the combination of ingenuity and knowingness in Carey, Donne is perceived to transfer his sense of disloyalty to the women in his poems, making them inconstant and not him. But just as the critic's power over his author and his text is preserved (Donne is revealed indulging in a 'manoeuvre'; as having a 'paranoia about betrayal'), the effect is to protect, not undermine, Donne. On one occasion, Donne's 'Holy Sonnet' beginning 'What if this present were the world's last night' is criticised, and Carey describes it as a poem in which 'Donne's logic is patently worthless.' But seeing what lies behind an unsatisfactory (and in some ways offensive) poem, we are to read it (and enjoy it?) in terms of the poet's personal plight. Donne's status as religious poet remains unimpaired by negative criticism of his poem. In this way detractors, caricatured as critics 'who fancy that religion is a sedate affair', are disarmed, and serious questioning of Donne's value as a poet in the 'Holy Sonnets' dissolves in matters of biographical speculation. On the 'Holy Sonnets' in general, Carey forces, or wills, a favourable judgement: their illogic, it turns out, is their strength: 'If, as Louis Martz suggests, these sonnets began as calmly plotted devotional exercises, intended to extirpate fear and despair, we can only say that they failed as exercises, and so succeed as poems.' We later learn of Donne's 'Holy Sonnet' 'Death be not proud': 'It is part of the strength of this poem that its argument is so weak.' The poetic strength revealed is in fact the condition of the poet: Donne's 'inner disarray'.[15]

The consequence is that Carey, without needing to offer anything in the way of a new or original overall valuation of Donne's poetry, can nevertheless adopt a would-be iconoclastic position as critic by virtue of praising qualities in the poetry which, when he has identified them and pointed them up, he knows the rest of us may or must disapprove, and which often tell us more about the critic than they do about Donne. Thus Donne's selfishness, egotism and coldness are justified as a 'precondition of his complexity', even though in his account of the metaphysical poets in his 'Life of Cowley' of 1779, Samuel Johnson had written that 'their courtship was void of fondness, and their lamentation of sorrow,'[16] and intended it as a criticism. For Carey, such features of Donne's poetry contribute to the 'self-consciousness' of Donne. The awkward expression of some poems is a sign of Donne's 'power'. His lack of elegance 'only convinces us more forcibly of the resolution behind the whole encumbered enterprize'. Such stylistic features are shown as related to the 'will to power': the one which made him Dean of St Paul's. In the chapter entitled 'Bodies', dedicated to an eager (and sometimes colourfully sickening) account of Donne's exuberant poetic realisation of his anatomical interests, Carey sports a coolly delighted appraisal of Donne's poem 'The Comparison'. The pose, with its slightly unpleasant relish, is that of the hardened and unshockable connoisseur. The disgusting and revolting images in the poem, like some of the scenes of violence in Dickens's novels, are proffered with a stubborn and studied refusal to be revolted. In this way Carey distances himself from the vulgar cringing reader who has no stomach for lines that a real critic (used to this kind of thing) can lap up with pleasure:

> As Donne handles it . . . the poem is not simply a list of insults, but a rich, ingenious and medically informed physical experience – especially the disgusting parts, such as the description of the other woman's sweat:
>
>> Ranke sweaty froth thy Mistresse brow defiles,
>> Like spermatique issue of ripe menstruous boiles.
>
> Here we can see Donne pursuing his interest in the body's excremental secretions, and speculatively blending four of them – sweat, pus, sperm and menses – in order to gain something more satisfying than mere sweat.[17]

The hysteria of the lines, implicit in their descriptive and imaginative qualities, is simply not acknowledged. In *John Donne*, the journalist supplies the stylistic *élan* and eye for sensation; the academic tailors them both to the needs of the critical *status quo*.

The extent to which Carey's writings as a whole reinforce this *status quo*, and thus extinguish the challenge to the norms of academic taste his role as modern media don would seem to promote, can best be gathered by looking more closely at the journalism itself: those areas of Carey's work where he is liberated from the constraints and expectations of academic forms that make his critical monographs on Dickens, Thackeray and Donne, while all, in their ways, 'journalistic', still successful as serious and sustained academic studies. Carey's *Original Copy: Selected Reviews and Journalism 1969–1986*[18] was itself reviewed, savagely, in the first number of the satirical magazine, *The Digger*.[19] The reviewer, placing its author among the 'Gilt-edged glitterati', as the 'new Godfather of the Oxford–London literary mafia', here pours withering scorn on 'the smarmy chorus of puffs with which it is being sacramentalised', and the asperity of the review suggests what violently polarised feelings Carey's writings can seem to arouse, and not necessarily from 'radical' quarters. Carey, in his role as Merton Professor of English Literature at the University of Oxford, is accused of running a literary protection racket, where special favour is shown to well-placed friends, such as Craig Raine, the poet and Faber editor, whom he grotesquely overrates. And he is accused of preserving, while seeming to attack, the 'academic establishment', as, it is charged, he does in the piece entitled 'Down with Dons', an ostensible swipe at the Oxford scene, and its once notorious ornament, Sir Maurice Bowra. Carey, the review makes devastatingly clear, is the would-be replacement star, on old pals' terms with the massive media personality of Clive James, who receives exorbitant praise in the collection. As lead reviewer of *The Sunday Times*, Carey is portrayed as the critic-cum-journalist *par excellence*, one foot in his Oxford college and the other in Fleet Street.

Savage though this seems, it is true that the critically (and for that matter humanly) negative implications of Carey's stance are there to be felt in some of the essays. In 'Viewpoint from the *TLS*' (1980), in the conclusion to a discussion of the passing of evaluation in literary criticism, appears evidence of Carey's critical convictions at that date. But it is a different story from the one he had told to the University of Oxford in his inaugural lecture as Merton Professor. Now, journalistic criteria transcend scholarly criteria to the point that criticism is effectively abolished. Carey admits that value judgements exist, but he says these are only of use 'when we have acknowledged that they are subjective'. Therefore, they are interesting for what they tell us, not about literature, but the people who criticise it: 'That usefulness lies not in anything they can tell us about works of literature (for they can tell us nothing), but in what they can tell us about the people making the judgements, including ourselves.' Carey is here now quite explicit about the critic's subordination of literature to himself. His explanation is that: '. . . we might come to a clearer knowledge of ourselves, and of the psychological factors which underlie our preferences in art and literature.... True, such a programme would subordinate study of literature to study of people. But then, it is for the sake of people that literature exists.'[20]

The populism of this final remark hides the exclusivism of its real meaning: for Carey, the function of criticism is that it reveals the critic. Writing criticism is therefore a kind of self-investigation prompted by the literary work. The critic can tell us nothing about the work, only about himself (as Carey's criticism, itself, often does). What matters in criticism are the 'people', not the ones inside the books but outside them: one's critical disputants, allies and antagonists. The world of the critic is thereby an enclosed one, looking inwards at itself. Its chief employment is narcissistic observance of itself. This harsh conception of the critical attitude offers a key to Carey's practice as a critic. Here, more than ever in his writings, Carey's acidity comes out. He shows a professionally polished, journalistic command of the sneer, the smirk and the dismissive aside, bolstering the admiration we feel for his 'wit', confirming his own (and now our) superiority to the book, the person, the idea, that happen to come into his range of fire. Of its kind, the most successful writing in *Original Copy* is therefore to be found in the journalism 'pure' rather than the strictly literary reviews. The more that literature is kept out of sight, the more the wit sparkles; so much the more attractive (and genuinely amusing) the tight-lipped terseness of Carey's style is likely to seem. Part One of the book on 'Self', and Part Two 'The English Scene', give the journalist the scope that he needs. Here, from the vantage point of the general reviewer, he can range freely over a hotch-potch of subjects, from his own pleasure in the consolations of vegetable gardening, through the absurdity of aristocratic English life, the Beatles, the 'naturalness' of family love, the awful language of political manifestos, to the comedy and horror of the strange feats of the *Guinness Book of Records.* Throughout, the triviality of the subject, whatever it is, aggrandises the writer. Carey is adept at mocking the afflicted, and the subjects chosen serve to display his skill. The reviewer's framework, with its clear sense of beginning, middle and end, lets him do this with concentrated effect, in small doses. The rapier not the hatchet is used, but negative criticism is Carey's *forte*. He operates at peak efficiency in debunking mode.

By far the largest section of the book is entitled 'Books and Bookmen'. Here, as in two out of three of Carey's extended academic studies, the tactic is to go beyond the writer to the Man. The section is a reprint of a series of reviews of biographical and critical works. But, unlike the 'academic' criticism, Carey's treatment of the Man is on many occasions extremely personal. The physicality, mental peculiarity or sexual oddity of the author discussed is not uncommonly pushed in our face, to waken us up. Not that the critical view advanced is necessarily of any very radical kind. The first in the series, 'Pope's fallibility', is packed with Romantic clichés on Pope: 'His mania for elegance in diction and versification ... provided ... refuge from his ungainly self,' and is among the most impertinent. Thus Pope, the eighteenth-century poet, was a 'dwarf and hunchback' who 'had to be laced every morning into stiff canvas bodices to keep him upright'. These were replaced, Carey informs us (lest the point is missed), 'as his spine gradually collapsed, by a sort of iron cage which locked round him like the chains of a hanged felon, or so it seemed to a friend who saw the shrivelled corpse lifted out after death'. Later, we find that the 'standard view' of Thomas Carlyle is that he was 'so poisonous it's a wonder his mind didn't infect his bloodstream'. The journalist William Howard Russell 'was thirteen stone of unresolved contradictions ...'. Stevenson 'grew up all coughs and bones ... and spent his short life trekking the globe to find a climate in which his lungs would work properly'. G. K. Chesterton 'had a body like a slag heap, but a mind like the dawn sky'. The stress by turns on the fragile, sickly or gross corporeality of writers, besides the indulgence of mild sensation, or pleasure in cheeky gossip, is part of the 'plain man's view' strategy of Carey's critical journalism that is also, to some extent, an element in his academic books. The aim, parallel in some ways to that of the 'radical' critics, is to demystify the cultured world of letters, to deny it the reverence it has for too long enjoyed. But in place of this reverence, Carey substitutes a knowing Sunday-supplement style vision of frail, eccentric and sometimes repulsive humanity lurking behind every mask of fame. With an itching to deride, he portrays writers as characters, or more often caricatures, in a cartoon world. The gaze of Carey's demystifying eye is turned at one point on the demystifiers themselves:

> Structuralism is not a subject that grips the ordinary reader much. Its articles of faith are likely to strike him as a mixture of the self-evident and the impossible. Thus the proposition, solemnly repeated by structuralists, that language is a system of signs (or 'signifiers') seems to him too obvious for remark. Who ever imagined otherwise? On the other hand, the ideas floated by the wilder type of structuralist – that literary texts ought to mean anything we require them to, or that authors do not create their works but are created by them – pretty clearly call for a spell of sedation and devoted nursing.[21]

This crushing verdict opens Carey's (in the end favourable) review of David Lodge's *Working with Structuralism*. The subject enables him to display, once more, that he is tough on pretension, in touch with the 'ordinary reader', not easily gulled by the fads of the hour. Hence the appeals to a brisk no-nonsense approach: 'At this stage you begin to feel that if these are the fruits of working with structuralism it might be an idea to try working without it.' But even the most down-to-earth of critics can turn starry-eyed. Carey, like Thackeray before him, is eventually seduced by the glamour of the literary world whose foibles he scorns. And towards the end of the collection, where living or only recently dead authors are more frequently in view, we find him, though willing to wound, yet afraid or disinclined to strike. This is so in the reviews of books by Betjeman, Dirk Bogarde, Clive James, Larkin, Heaney and Craig Raine. Now there is much less talk, as there had been before with Pope or Carlyle, of oddity, whether physical or mental. A warmer glow suffuses the writing. 'No poet is in fact more precise' than Betjeman. Clive James's 'exuberance with words seems as natural as suntan'. Larkin is 'a modern stoic, today's Seneca', Heaney, 'More than any other poet since Wordsworth . . . can make us understand that the outside world is not outside but what we are made of.' Raine, 'Like Whitman or Christopher Smart . . . applauds the universe' in his 'dazzling new collection' of verse. Even Raine's 'Arsehole' dazzles: 'it is a graceful – almost flowery – attempt to create beauty where ugliness is normally seen'.[22]

But if Carey's criticism, like Eagleton's at times, moves towards journalese (and in Carey's case quite literally *is* journalism), it is partly for that reason not uncompelling or lifeless. Carey's prose, as one might expect of the practised reviewer, is unusually dense and hard-packed, dotted with figures of speech, many of which convey the zest of his critical manner, the pungent quality associated frequently with a quietly furious impatience with all that is vacuously well-meaning, sentimentally unthinking and unrigorously liberal in human beings (as Carey himself tries never to be). Thus in Dickens, an animal or child allows the adult to 'ooze his surplus benignity over the creature, and dominate it, without bothering about its real nature'. Sometimes, a complacent conservatism is Carey's target, as when he writes of the leading characters in the later Thackeray novels that they 'acquire noble hearts, which pump high-grade syrup around their frames'.[23] It is a prose honed by a sense of repulsion from the commonplace idiocies, pretensions and delusions which invade human nature and make it ridiculous. At his best, Carey's criticism conveys the very best of English literary journalism's unsentimental sharpness and edge. Journalists' instincts keep Carey alive to criticism's wider responsibilities, beyond the confines of the scholarly world. Carey's tone, when he mentions other members of that world, is commonly brusque, patronising and dismissive: 'Modern academic expositors . . . have puzzled their heads to discover what he was "really" writing about in the *Anniversaries.*'[24] Carey's criticism is refreshingly free from displays of the would-be cosmopolitan *savoir-faire* that mark the false intellectualism of various modern critical 'movements'. He does not pepper his text with names of uncertainly digested foreign critics or fashionable theorists, and makes no effort to seem easily *au fait* with their work, or to evangelise their views.

This strengthens the sense in which Carey's criticism is anti-elitist. Carey's historical scholarship is not the grand impressionistic sweep of historical and social affairs that sometimes passes for a contextual sense: and nor does Carey accept, with say Eagleton, that the only hold we have over a text from the past is our modern, reconstructed, grasp of its meaning, or suggest that meaning is constantly produced and reproduced, as everything outside the work changes, by a process of cultural determination. Carey is alive to the view that often, literature is the least reliable source of historical fact, and that the contextualised object and its context are very often at odds. While, therefore, it is often useful to know something about a writer's life, 'In order to have a sympathetic feeling for Donne's mentality we must learn something about his life and the society he found himself in,'[25] the context is not merely a framework, whether an old-world commentator's substitute for reading the text, or a new-world ideological scheme to which literature has to adapt. Carey's interest in context, as he increasingly sees the possibilities in turning to a form of critical writing which draws on the 'background' to works, is precise and particular. Thus a page and a half of the Thackeray volume can be devoted to the history of London's water supply during the first half of the nineteenth century, the aim being to disprove a passing remark in *Pendennis:* that 'The poorest mechanic in Spitalfields has a cistern and an unbounded supply of water at his command'.[26] In Carey's hands, things are brought down to earth. They are seen, or made to seem seen, with an ordinary eye. Hence Carey's pointed, often boldly voiced, commonsensical tone. This is sometimes sarcastic, sometimes hard-nosed and sometimes playful. It rests on contempt for the notion of literary experience, or literary pleasure, as an etherial matter divorced from common concerns and unapproachable by ordinary folk. The fact and scale of Carey's attention to Thackeray and Dickens suggest a strong sense of the role of literature as popular art, demystified and uncloistered. Carey's criticism is dedicated to effacing the idea that literature is in any way a special preserve. Man and Writer are made to converge. Genius is as much of the Man as of the Works: an essential component of his vision and consciousness of life. On these occasions, while Carey's belief in the manifest existence of genius suggests debt to a much older school of Oxford criticism, the journalist functions as a critique of the Oxford academic and Merton Professor.

At his worst, Carey is too often out to be in the literary–journalistic swim with his fellow metropolitan wits, at which points his judgements tend towards those of an in-group critic, a member of a clique. This is signalled, in Carey's otherwise serious academic studies, by a style which seems self-conscious and showy, smart in the bad sense, a mere mannerism: Donne's *The Courtier's Library* is a 'bitter little satire, spraying its fire about like a rusty Sten gun'. Now and again, when trying too hard, the colours of Carey's style are apt to clash: 'We feel that charitable humbug has been ripped away, leaving clean air for the truth to be told in.' Often, a swift switch of register is intended both to arrest and to amuse the reader, as here: 'Donne is a celestial sphere floating up the "empty and etheriall way" between a girl's legs.'[27] Writing on Donne, as on Thackeray, provides the occasion for Carey to discuss sex, about which he has a great deal to say. He is never donnishly prim (a charge which could easily be levelled at the older generation of academic critics from which he wishes to distinguish himself), and his freedom from inhibition seems at times almost flaunted, lest the reader should miss it. But it is the preoccupation with sex of the fifties and sixties rather than the seventies and eighties. Discussion of sexual politics is minimal. In the final chapter of *The Violent Effigy*, 'Dickens and Sex', Carey rejects the pervasive Victorian patriarchy of Dickens's fictional treatment of women. But although the treatment is repellent, in Carey's view, objection to Dickens's conception of women and their role in the novels is not a 'gender issue'. Instead, a straightforward human and moral standard is invoked. The problem is seen as the product of Dickens's distorting imaginative vision. Carey is likewise repelled by the stereotypical women that appear in the pages of the later Thackeray novels: in moving from *Pendennis* to *Henry Esmond*, 'Rachel takes over from Helen as angel; Beatrix from Blanche as spoiled minx.' But the problem is one for Thackeray's age, not ours, even though the essential point is made with undeniable punch: 'Beatrix', we realise, 'is the product of an age that demanded its females retarded'. In *John Donne,* Donne is defended for espousing concepts of sexual ownership moderns would reject: 'We are careful to talk, nowadays, as if we believed that the male ought to respect the female's individuality. Donne is above such hypocrisies, and states, with measured resonance, his lethal hunger.'[28] Can Carey really think it just a question of being 'careful'? But, while such knowingness is significant of the penalties attaching to the studied anti-élitism of Carey's critical stance, the élitism that Carey does *not* attack is that of literary greatness. The great works of literature, in Carey's view, remain special things. In his stress on the author's power of literary imagination, the self-justifying imaginative vitality of literary works, the internal architecture, structure and system of tensions which unify, say, Donne's mind, such that the reader perceives it as one, Carey's approach affirms the integrity, if also the strangeness, of artistic personality. It remains an approach (one of the most confident in modern English criticism) dominated by what Belsey would call 'the subject': the author, seen both from within and from without remains stubbornly undecentred.

But so, in Carey's criticism, are the terms of twentieth-century academic taste. Carey may be more explicit about the authors he values than the 'radical' critics, but the significant literary history that his criticism reflects, as it is broadly the same as theirs, is equally conservative. The 'radical theorists' may think they are subverting the established attitudes of their time, but not be. Carey knows that he is not, but that there is no need to try, since the novelty, the new experience, is supplied not by the author but the critic himself. It is his brilliance that counts, and Carey is more 'brilliant' than most. So it follows that there is little incentive for the critic to struggle with a text that is likely to present too great a challenge to the dazzling articulateness on which the reputation for brilliance is based, one for which he has no familiar terms (and where his criticism would have even less of a market); or, therefore, one that lies outside the orthodoxy of Renaissance studies and nineteenth-century fiction.

By contrast with these well-trodden ways, the critic is even more likely to shine; to show command of the material that for many of his fellows and the populace at large, has effectively become 'English Literature'. It therefore follows that Carey, no more than the 'radicals', should not have much time for those periods of English literature that are out of fashion. In the book on Thackeray, Carey had attacked Thackeray's crude caricature of the eighteenth century and its writers, where 'Gentlemanliness, not genius, is at a premium'.[29] But though he was revolted by the shallowness and sentimentality of the eighteenth century according to Thackeray, the period receives little positive recommendation in his own critical work. (Indeed, some things in Carey's criticism, his comments on Alexander Pope for example, seem to suggest a view of the eighteenth century quite in accord with Thackeray's own.) The literature Carey discusses (in order, for the most part, to praise) is that of whose merits students and professional teachers of English are already convinced, but where the general reader, outside the academy, may conceivably yet not be. In which case it is Carey's business to ensure that the academic values of the day are spread, by having them filter downwards. Carey, therefore, no more than the 'radicals', is able to remove the blinkers imposed by a critical tradition which has made certain authors, like Dryden, or whole periods, like the eighteenth century, blindspots for readers. Perhaps attention of that kind would seem too esoteric, or too pretentious a task (too much at odds with the public responsibilities and market orientation of the journalist *or* with the natural conservatism of the literary scholar, even though one might expect the latter to feel it important to keep the unfashionable alive). Whatever the reason, Carey's criticism is confined to familiar fields. Carey knows that the constituency for his criticism, as it is shaped by the existing tastes of the readers of the poets and novelists he treats, is safe. The currently established areas receive professorial endorsement. The not-so-fashionable stay as they are, as yet unsalvaged by Carey's authority. The 'radical theorists' may therefore have every reason to insist that a response to the values of the modern critical establishment must be radical. They do not acknowledge the extent to which those values sustain, and are sustained by, their own.

Notes

1. See *Milton* (Evans Bros, 'Literature in Perspective': London, 1969), *The Violent Effigy: A Study of Dickens' Imagination* (Faber: London, 1973; reprinted 1979); *Thackeray: Prodigal Genius* (Faber: London, 1977); *John Donne: Life, Mind and Art* (Faber: London, 1981; reprinted 1982, 1983).
2. *The Poems of John Milton* (Longmans' Annotated English Poets: London, 1968). Later evidence of Carey's commitment to seventeenth-century scholarship (aside from his book on Donne) includes his edition of *English Renaissance Studies, Presented to Dame Helen Gardner in honour of her seventieth birthday* (Clarendon Press: Oxford, 1980).
3. *The Violent Effigy*, p. 25.
4. *ibid.*, pp. 64, 73, 74.
5. *ibid.*, pp. 81, 91, 98, 113, 130, 140.
6. *Wording and Re-Wording: Paraphrase in Literary Criticism: An Inaugural Lecture delivered before the University of Oxford on 4 June 1976 by John Carey* (Clarendon Press: Oxford, 1977).
7. *ibid.*, pp. 5, 9.
8. *ibid.*, p. 19.
9. *Thackeray: Prodigal Genius*, p. 34. See review of *Thackeray: Interviews and Recollections* (ed. Philip Collins), *Sunday Times* (1983).
10. *Thackeray: Prodigal Genius*, p. 58.
11. *ibid.*, pp. 124, 109.
12. *ibid.*, pp. 160, 161, 162; F. R. Leavis, 'Johnson and Augustanism', in *The Common Pursuit* (Penguin: London, 1952), p. 110.
13. *John Donne*, p. 14. Other work by Carey on 'metaphysical poetry' includes his edition, *Andrew Marvell: A Critical Anthology* (Penguin Critical Anthologies: Harmondsworth, 1969).
14. *ibid.*, pp. 18, 27.
15. *ibid.*, pp. 38, 40, 47, 46, 54, 199.
16. 'Life of Cowley', *Lives of the Poets* (ed. George Birkbeck Hill), I, p. 20.
17. *John Donne*, pp. 118, 122, 141.
18. *Original Copy: Selected Reviews and Journalism 1969–1986* (Faber: London, 1987).
19. 9 October 1987, p. 17.
20. *Original Copy*, p. 29.
21. *ibid.*, pp. 109, 116, 120, 129, 134, 238.
22. *ibid.*, pp. 240, 241, 258, 267, 271, 274, 276.
23. *The Violent Effigy*, p. 144; *Thackeray: Prodigal Genius*, p. 175.
24. *John Donne*, p. 102.
25. *John Donne*, p. 14.
26. *Thackeray: Prodigal Genius*, p. 153.

27. *John Donne*, p. 9.
28. *Thackeray: Prodigal Genius,* pp. 155, 156; *John Donne,* p. 100.
29. *Thackeray: Prodigal Genius,* p. 158.

4
Media Dons II: Christopher Ricks

> Ricks is now by general consent one of the foremost critics writing in England.... Reading Ricks is liberating, as is reading Professor Carey.[1]
>
> The critic Eye, that microscope of Wit,
> Sees hairs and pores, examines bit by bit...[2]

With Ricks we move beyond the relatively enclosed, at times self-congratulating, world of Oxford and Fleet Street and enter that of an international élite, comparable in prestige and authority to the élites of computing, medicine or physics. Ricks is a representative of British criticism on the international stage. In American academic parlance he is 'a name'. He incarnates the professionalisation of English literary studies at its contemporary height. But Ricks, like Carey, and unlike the 'radical' critics with whom his work superficially contrasts, is determinedly a scholar of literature, not theory, though for this reason nonetheless a man of his time. In the practice of criticism, Ricks has like Carey taken advantage of the modern critic's access to media channels for the expression of literary views and with the growth of television and radio programmes in 'the arts', opportunities to do so have expanded. Ricks has thereby contributed to the sense in which punditry has become an integral part of the modern literary professional's package of necessary skills. But this is only one of the respects in which his career echoes Carey's. More formal parallels include: the production of a series of critical monographs which reflect a tendency to favour a criticism based both on the life and works of a major author, a body of editorial scholarship and a substantial collection of literary reviews. As far as this last is concerned, Ricks (who has written reviews for *The Listener* and *The New York Review of Books*), has worked as a colleague of Carey for *The Sunday Times*. As far as his editing tasks are concerned, Ricks (now employed in the United States, but having held posts in the Universities of Oxford, Cambridge and Bristol) has not been shy of the dull but indispensable labours of critical scholarship. One-time editor of the Oxford journal *Essays in Criticism,* Ricks has undertaken an extensive tour of editing duty. Of this, perhaps the most substantial outcome has been his standard edition of Tennyson's poems (1969). Ricks has acted as General Editor of the Penguin Critical Anthologies and Penguin English Poets, and of Volumes II and III of *The Sphere History of Literature in the English Language,* while overseeing a volume in the series of 'Twentieth Century Views' on Housman (1968) to which he contributed an Introduction and essay, first printed in *Essays in Criticism* and since reprinted in his recent (1984) collection: *The Force of Poetry.*[3]

Ricks is therefore the epitome of the modern professional critic with fingers in various pies and, given his current appointment in the United States, a stake in literary critical life outside the British Isles, something to which neither Carey nor the 'radical theorists' have appeared to aspire. But although he is in some ways a more idiosyncratic critic than Carey, with less of the latter's concern to appeal to the plain man, his criticism also focuses the extent to which, in the modern critical world, the professional life of the literary critic requires conformity to values that are at odds with the meaning of the term 'critic' in one not entirely dead sense of the word. This is a consequence of his solidarity with the academic world of which both are a part. But, where Carey is scathing or satirical, Ricks is touchy, and inclined to take a pernickety, donnishly disapproving and propriety conscious line with academic fellows who do not come up to scratch. This is one of the less attractive tones in his work. In a comment on Muriel Allott's note on Keats's 'And warm with dew at ooze from living blood!' he appears as the stuffy, slightly priggish, guardian of good practice and editorial taste; someone who knows how to behave: 'I think it not right of Mrs. Allott to annotate the last line with "An elegant periphrasis for the Indian maid's perspiration". (I think too, incidentally, that such summary critical judgements are out of place in editorial footnotes.)' Where positive comments are called for, Ricks, despite such occasional niggles, is freer than Carey in his tributes to fellow professionals, the writers of academic books like his own. In Ricks's comments on a series of books on Wordsworth's poetry, he reveals the professional reviewer's mastery of the choice and memorable compliment in the space of a phrase. John Jones's study of Wordsworth, *The Egotistical Sublime*, is a 'fine capacious book'. Jonathan Wordsworth's *The Music of Humanity*, meanwhile, is an 'excellent study', while 'another central study' is David Ferry's *The Limits of Mortality*. In C. C. Clarke's *Romantic Paradox* we find 'a spirited inquiry'.[4]

Given this solidarity, it is therefore not surprising that Ricks, in his own academic books, should reflect the formative tastes dominant in the academic world over the last thirty, forty or more years. His books range from *Milton's Grand Style* (1963) to *T. S. Eliot and Prejudice*, published in 1988.[5] Taken overall the books point to a sense of the history of literature that, while it varies in its choice of authors to discuss, is chronologically coincident both with the scope of Carey's criticism and with that of the 'radical' critics. The writers who are worth discussing belong to periods whose interest continues to be fashionably to the fore. Within these broad terms, the main difference between Ricks and Carey (and the 'radicals') is the time (above and beyond that which we might expect to be given by a critic who writes reviews of new books) Ricks gives to the twentieth century. A product of this is Ricks's recent study of T. S. Eliot, based in part on the T. S. Eliot Memorial Lectures given at the University of Kent. But although this work in some ways provides him with the ideal occasion to develop his highly personal critical approach, Ricks does not confine himself to dead twentieth-century poets, safely in the past. In *The Force of Poetry*, a series of essays published by Ricks in 1984, there is ample evidence of his twentieth-century tastes. Two analytical essays (very different pieces of work from the flattering 'puffs' that tend to form a large part of Carey's commentary on modern verse) are included on the modern poet Geoffrey Hill, whose art of poetry Ricks links with Eliot's: 'The maturing of Hill's achievement in an art of the parenthesis ... comes with Hill's remarkable rotations of what Eliot had sensed as the life lived within the contained breath and silent eloquence of brackets.' Carey's interest in modern poets tends towards the men who are the poets. Ricks's interest is often more technical in kind. The 'silent eloquence of brackets' is reminiscent of Larkin's 'something almost being said', or the 'nearly but not said' art of the anti-pun. It indicates Ricks's liking for a poetry (found by him mainly though not exclusively in the twentieth century) which contains hidden meanings or implicit suggestions and indicates Ricks's closeness to Eagleton's and Belsey's taste for the 'unspoken' aspects of literary texts. Ricks, more like them than like Carey, is concerned with squeezing out meanings of which the author of a text, though he may not be 'dead' (in the theorists' sense) may not have been conscious. Brackets are a way of saying something without actually saying it. Likewise, the hyphen, linking two otherwise separate words, allows Ricks to reflect on the at-one-ment, the bringing together, of separate things. In the same collection, Hill's poetry provides material for one of two general essays, on clichés and on lies. Ricks, himself wishing to avoid the cliché, sees clichés as a living part of the language: a source of energy and vitality, as in the words to Bob Dylan's songs. Here, a cliché is a power 'in the renovation of the state of the language'.[6]

But, with the exception of Ricks's work on the twentieth century (which he sees both in terms of living poets and, as what it now is, part of the history of poetry), his longer studies are concerned with poetry, written in periods that are widely researched, and which for historical reasons have come to constitute the cornerstones of post-war academic study of English Literature. Not that Ricks is always merely repeating the reasons for which poets in these periods have been thought important. He makes a significant, and within academic terms original, contribution to study of the seventeenth century in *Milton's Grand Style*. Compared with Carey's introduction to Milton,

Ricks's study has scholarly weight. (He uses, for example, readings and opinions of eighteenth-century editors of Milton.) Compared with Belsey's recent book on Milton, Ricks's has an evaluative, restorative purpose – such as Belsey would be likely to dismiss as beside the point, or outdated: 'to refute Milton's detractors by showing the kind of life which there is in the verse of *Paradise Lost*'. Ricks does not deny that Milton's poetry has faults: he turns to *Samson Agonistes* and to Johnson's criticism of that work to identify Milton's 'dead metaphors', a term he was later to use to suggest Johnson's own inability to reinvigorate the exhausted formulae of poetical language in his *Vanity of Human Wishes*. But Milton's syntax, he argues, can give drive and direction to his arguments. It is functionally tortuous. He sees Milton as master of syntactic fluidity: 'He achieves some of his finest effects precisely by leaving it possible for a word or a clause to look backward or forward.' Milton's puns are not the fault they have been taken to be. Wordplay in Milton 'insists on the derivation of a word, and so expels the bizarre or the fortuitous'. Milton's habit of using a word in the Latin sense is part of the art of the pun. In such details, Ricks offers an account of Milton's poetry that runs counter to Leavis's: 'It does not seem true that "the mind that invented Milton's Grand Style had renounced the English language."' Milton, rather, combined incompatible greatnesses. But in stressing the importance of language to the study of poetry in *Milton's Grand Style*, Ricks is also, of course, in alignment with a major trend in academic criticism that Belsey (and other radicals), no less than Leavis (as radical in his own way) would approve. This is his concern with rhythmical, syntactic, metaphoric and verbal qualities, the play of the sense across and between individual words that is to characterise his criticism for many years to come: '... Milton's style is still an interesting challenge to the verbal criticism which now seems one of the most important and useful ways of approaching literature.' The difference between Ricks and the 'new radicals' is that, while they insist that attention to language in literary criticism is a good thing on ideological grounds, Ricks actually attends – in his own practice, as did Leavis – to the language (particularly the diction) of poems.[7]

A second difference is that 'radical' theorists have insisted on the opacity of literary language, a concern aside from, and more important than, the human (despite the production of books which take particular authors as their theme, Shakespeare, Milton, the Brontës, etc.). Ricks sees the linguistic and human as linked. In *Tennyson*, the first of his two major contributions to nineteenth-century studies, language is again at issue (in a sense it is always the issue of Ricks's criticism). He holds a general critical line throughout the book: that Tennysonian mellifluousness has been too simply understood, too often regarded as external to the poet's deepest concerns. But the purpose of studying the language in this book is the light that it throws on the author, Tennyson himself. The study is author-centred. So in *Tennyson*, Ricks can allow (what the 'radicals' – in theory at least – would forbid) the features of a biographical approach. Ricks's biographical criticism is more evaluatively at one with his literary judgements than Carey's: 'one might say that the story of Tennyson's life until the publication of *Maud* in 1855 is *essentially* the story of his poetry, if by "essentially" one means that it is after all simply Tennyson's poetry which secures attention for his life.' Ricks writes in his Preface: 'Tennyson was not a recluse, but his essential life was the private life, and this made me decide ... that a biographical study could without falsification ... phase itself out.' Ricks uses the biographical matter to correct distorted readings of Tennyson's poems. He suggests in his comments on the 'Telemachus lines' in Tennyson's 'Ulysses' that if they seem wooden, this might be because 'At this stage of his life (perhaps throughout his life), Tennyson was not able to write with alert conviction about sons and fathers'. (We have been given a detailed account of Tennyson's relationship with his father by this stage of the book.) In another place, Ricks unites Tennyson's response to the facts of his own experience (the most single momentous event being the death of his close friend Hallam) with his response to other literature: 'Malory's Arthur, mingling loss and hope, called up Tennyson's Arthur. The death of Hallam created "Morte d'Arthur".' Ricks takes up the question of Tennyson's relationship with Hallam as it is expressed in his long elegaic poem, *In Memoriam*. Is the relationship a homosexual one or not? For Ricks, 'the reiterated metaphor of man and wife in the poem is sufficiently explicable in the simplest terms: that Hallam had been about to marry Tennyson's sister Emily'.[8] Perhaps, in this final example, Ricks, writing as vice-president of the Tennyson Society, is slightly forcing the point. He does not confront the question of why homosexuality in the Tennyson–Hallam relationship should matter, or why we should care, though he does wonder whether the issue has any bearing on the interpretation of *In Memoriam* itself. But the book's overall distinction is the way in which it succeeds in assembling poet and man as single construct, without simplification, and without melodrama. (The resistance to the theory of Hallam's and Tennyson's homosexual relations is a form of resistance to the melodramatic.) Biographical and verbal approaches are developed side by side: they check, modify and inform each other.

Ricks's interest in the verbal effects and consequences of literature is indicated by the fact that all his books are studies of poets, in whose work, it might be reasonably argued, the use of language is likely to be most intense, most concentrate. In a way that links him with an Oxford tradition (shared by Carey) of, wherever possible, positive appreciation, all his books (in general terms) defend the poets against hostile critics. At the same time, in what is in one sense a stricter Cambridge fashion, all act as forums for the exercise of a very self-conscious critical intelligence; a highly cerebral conception of the critic. Ricks turns to poetry in order to satisfy a love of intellectual distinctions and patterns, as in expressing one of his favourite ideas about language that it provides an 'axis': '... every device of the poet, every technical or formal disposition, is an axis and not a direction ...' The same distinction is there in the comment from an essay on 'Lies' from *The Force of Poetry:* 'What matters is that *I/je* does suggest an axis, an axis for egotism, its forms and pressures; which way the considerations then run along the axis is a different and difficult question.'[9] In this taste for applying to, and finding in, poetry, an abstract, almost mathematical, framework, Ricks may be considered one of the more 'difficult' of modern British critics. But Ricks is difficult and abstract, in a different way from the 'radical' theorists. While they (the 'radicals') aim to relate critical activity to a wider world of (largely political) ideas, Ricks continues to draw attention to the integrity and internal relationships, tensions and structures of the text itself. He thus comes near to being 'structuralist' in a non-current sense of the term. The effect is that Ricks's criticism is sometimes illuminating, but sometimes irritating. For those who dislike Ricks, the irritations he arouses may be seen as the result of a failure of proportion based on his fetishistic attachment to the pun. Ricks blows up, a hostile critic might say, minor artistic effects beyond their value. To this Ricks might reply that he is focusing attention on the concealed relations between local effects in the text and the life outside it. Thus, in the above essay on Lies in *The Force of Poetry,* Ricks values the pun because large cultural and ethical questions can be compressed into one little word. Small things have large significance: '... there is ... in our culture a central place for a pun which brings dishonesty up against ... not honesty or dishonesty – but an honesty testing situation.' The tendency to find general significance in small things is a characteristic of Ricks's criticism. Commenting upon Tennyson's 'Tithonus' in his study on Tennyson, Ricks is of the opinion that it is his 'most assuredly successful poem': '... at once quintessentially Tennysonian and yet with its Tennysonian felicities of sound made stronger and more poignant by its chill of silence, its desolated loss of that "strange song" which had once animated its world'. But Ricks continues:

> Given the pathos of Tithonus's plight, it invites wonder that the poem staves off self-pity. Again a skill in miniature – a pronoun – effects something not miniature at all. For to the withering Tithonus his past self is another person; the split is painful but free from self-pity because it is virtually unimaginable that so distant a past self is his self. Tennyson nets this by casting "I" as "he".[10]

In Ricks, a whole essay (or book) can turn on the double or various meanings (as he sees them) of one word as in *Keats and Embarrassment,* where Ricks brings together a complex interlocking pattern of ideas, and offers the idea that embarrassment, or the physical manifestation of embarrassment that appears in a person's blush is an explanation for Keats's preoccupations as a poet, and where bodily communication is associated in Keats's notoriously sensuous poetry with artistic communication. Thus Keats's poetry has been found embarrassing. But its effect can involve the embarrassing nature of powerful expressions of feeling, such as grief. The onlooker's embarrassment makes it difficult to sympathise fully with anguish. But in Keats, according to Ricks, this is a triumph of art. Not only has Keats left critics embarrassed, he was himself embarrassed, by for example *Endymion*. And yet despite his own embarrassment, Keats can show us what is good in the adolescent state. As part of this complex of associations, Ricks moves between Keats and life. Keats's insight when portraying Adonis asleep, we are told, springs from the fact that 'we are embarrassed either to sleep in public or to watch the sleeping, for instance in a train.' (The assumption is that embarrassment in such circumstances is a general experience, not just Ricks's.) Not only was Keats himself embarrassable, he was struck by examples of the wholly unembarrassable; such as that of an old woman in a dog kennel Sedan chair encountered during a visit to Ireland. But he was also freed from personal embarrassment (such as self-consciousness about his short stature) by the sight of immense natural phenomena, waterfalls and suchlike. The point about embarrassment in sexual or physical contexts is that feelings are mixed. There is an element of attraction and an element of repulsion. The mixture of attitudes in Keats and his readers is explored in relation to various examples of the sensuous: nipples, breasts, rich food, etc. Certain key words, like 'oozy', 'sluicy' and 'spongy' are invoked and dwelt on to suggest a physical duality. There is a fine balance of 'attraction and possible repellence'. To suggest this, Ricks quotes a long passage from Sartre on 'slime' and the 'slimy'. Everything is connected to everything else:

> What Keats values in poetry is its strange true kind of blushfulness; that it can both create a composed embarrassment and free us from the discomposures of embarrassment.

> Wine, too, stands oddly to blushfulness; it makes us less inhibited, less immediately liable to blush – then more liable to flush and more liable, if altogether unrestrained, to be precipitated into situations for which we do indeed blush now or later. It is for these involuted contrarieties that wine can truly be called "blushful".[11]

In the next sentence, it is not surprising to find Ricks quoting the author of *Seven Types of Ambiguity*.

There is no doubt that Ricks's appetite for puns has enhanced his appreciation of the writers he treats, even though we may feel sometimes that he is choosing to treat them partly because they happen to suit his critical method. Thus puns are praised in the study of Milton, where Ricks finds various meanings resonating in single words. A main reason for turning to Keats's poetry may be that 'Keats's mind, so alertly prefigurative, was especially liable to puns and portmanteaux....' Tennyson's *The Princess*, meanwhile, 'enabled Tennyson – as *Endymion* had enabled Keats – to experiment' and widen his ideas of linguistic propriety: '*The Princess* is full of covert puns, suggestions glimpsed between the interstices, "And watch/ a full sea glazed...": "glazed" seems to be precipitated by "watch", out of "gazed".' But Ricks's concern extends beyond the discussion of puns *in* writers, to a whole method whereby poets are studied by means of what is itself a protracted and conscious literary conceit or fancy, a witty affiliation of previously unrelated elements drawn out to the length of a book. In *T. S. Eliot and Prejudice*, Ricks's latest book, he again works by means of this to-ing and fro-ing of reciprocal association: 'Once you think about prejudice you are taken into a great deal of and about Eliot – into the nature and boundaries of his imagination. Reciprocally, once you think about Eliot, you are taken into a great deal of and about prejudice...' Again, a single idea, or concept is brought to the consideration of a poet, meditated at length, turned this way and that, inside and out. The relationship of the works of the poet to the selected leading idea is ransacked. There are boxes within boxes. Thus Eliot 'might incorporate and enact within his poetry a double vigilance: a distrust of prejudice, and distrust of the distrust of prejudice'.[12] But, though Ricks exhausts his subject, here no less than in his earlier studies, it is also clear that he regards himself as setting out to enlarge rather than diminish our conception of the poetical art. The purpose of the attention employed is to attempt to bring out, often, the grand, sublime and majestic effects of poetry, its grandeur – the explicit intention of Ricks's collection of essays *The Force of Poetry* where the title is taken from Samuel Johnson's famous remark in *The Rambler,* No. 168, on the invocation to the powers of evil and darkness made by Lady Macbeth. (The extent to which the collection lives up to its title has been disputed by reviewers.)[13] Judged as a collection, *The Force of Poetry* exhibits a broad chronological range and a sense of poetry as a whole, despite chronological gaps and a feeling that the essays included represent Ricks's idea of the important 'moments' in literary history with an eye to adjusting the balance. Thus there is an essay on Gower, but not Chaucer; on Marvell but not Donne. It is true that, throughout *The Force of Poetry,* Ricks's eye never seems very far from the page, a method which expresses the collections's theme: literature's quality of language; the nuances, multiple suggestions, ambiguities, shades of meaning and cross-fertilisation of phrases and words. But it also means that the poetry of earlier periods is brought into relation with a modern critical perspective. Ricks, as he confesses in his essay on Gower, is 'no medievalist', and the essay itself is controlled by a modern literary aesthetic, as are the essays on Marvell, Milton, Johnson and Wordsworth. In his search for 'the force of poetry', Ricks discovers rhetorical identity in historical difference (Marvell's 'self-inwoven simile . . . is at the heart of the achievement of a recent group of poets'). Treatments of a girl's age in Gower's *Confessio Amantis* 'are like the song at its best; in Wyatt, say, or in Bob Dylan, who sings (in "The Lonesome Death of Hattie Carroll") of the young assailant that he "had twenty-four years" but the assailed woman that she "was fifty-one years old" '.[14] Ricks's mode of attention to poetry is 'liberal–humanist' in the sense that there are, for Ricks, 'eternal verities' which enable him to conceive of poetry as one, an artistic unity from its earliest days to the present, and discussable within the terms of a single vision.

Even in his book-length, author-specific studies, Ricks's subjects can acquire enlargement and solidity from his touch, as when external attitudes to poetry and internal workings of the poetry are woven together. Thus Eliot's poetry is the victim of critical prejudice (by its critics); but has also been accused of prejudice (such as anti-Semitism), and so on. The one thing throws light on the other: 'Eliot is from the beginning preoccupied with prejudice because it constitutes an intersection of philosophy, psychology, politics, and art.' The study starts from details, personal intuitions and self-revelations, as when Ricks is discussing the famous lines 'In the room where the women come and go/Talking of Michelangelo,' and addressing the subject of how to pronounce foreign names: 'It is not for Englishmen to say Roma, and it is in its way handsome of us to say Rome; why, we even say Naples, those of us who would die rather than say Napoli.'[15] As ever, Ricks is a specialist on the little, nervous, rightnesses and wrongnesses of English usage. But *T. S. Eliot and Prejudice* can in a short space turn to questions of immense moral breadth and scope such as the nature of prejudice against Jews. Eliot is defended against the crude imputation of anti-Semitism (it is, for example, Ricks suggests, the Jews themselves, not Eliot, who are responsible for linking the religious with the racial). In Eliot's notorious statement that '... reasons of race and religion combine to make any large number of free-thinking Jews undesirable,' Eliot 'collapsed his thoughts, and made himself responsible for a paragraph which at once appals and palters'. But though at this point Eliot's critics may show prejudice, at others Eliot himself is surely open to blame: 'This is shameful,' is Ricks's comment on an apologia for anti-Semitic sentiment in an unsigned review. From prejudice against Jews the issue is then further broadened to an examination of the social, psychological and philosophical meaning of prejudice. Anti-Semitic attitudes, Ricks shows, represent a particular expression of prejudice's general laws and his analysis of the accusation of prejudice against Jews serves to reveal attitudes implicit in accusations of prejudice of other kinds, sexism for instance. And yet prejudice, of some kind, he argues, is also necessary: 'no understanding of anything is possible without predicates, preconceptions, and categorical frameworks.'[16]

With Eliot, of course, the American-born 'English' poet, Ricks, the expatriate critic of an expatriate poet, is finding an appropriate channel (flowing in the reverse direction) for his own transatlanticism. In turning to one of the twentieth century's most important and influential poets (in both Britain and America), he aspires to escape the shackles of national prejudice, and several things in the book, particularly the anecdotes and occasional slang, suggest that it is directed at an American as much as a British audience. But in the study of Tennyson, against whom Eliot was in verbal–poetic reaction, critical commentary (on the text) and external knowledge (drawn in from outside about it) are equally subtly linked. At times in the book, Ricks's addiction to wordplay does not help his case. For example, he is inclined to savour linguistic facility in detachment from the temper or feeling of Tennyson's poems; to find it, even when its discovery actually (though unconsciously) damages Tennyson. Thus, Ricks can criticise the *Idylls of the King* for its mannered and extraneous style and can write of Tennyson's borrowings from himself generally in his poetry that: '... they bring out the conflict which is often felt in reading Tennyson, the conflict between confidence in his extraordinary expertise and faint uneasiness about the extent to which the expertise is verbal or purely verbal.' But when Ricks comes to write of the lyrics integral to *The Princess*, where according to Ricks Tennyson achieved a height of linguistic confidence, and then focuses on 'Tears, idle tears', which he wishes to praise, he says that 'No poem of Tennyson compacts more of his deepest feelings with more graceful fluency'. Ricks's use of the word 'compacts' here confers an unintended artificiality, and externality, on Tennyson's achievement: feelings and fluency are forced together. The word implies the successful exertion of a willed external pressure which feelings and fluency tend by their nature to resist, so that, in this poem, they are not to be seen as *inevitably* one. Ricks, rather than adhere to his thesis (in defence of Tennyson's language) is conveying Tennyson's struggle for expression: the heroism of the effort which is reminiscent of

Eliot: to master the unmalleable. Ricks's account of 'Tears, idle tears', though one of the most enthusiastic single treatments of any single poem in the whole book, is nevertheless in some ways relegated (unintentionally?) to a generic or technical success: 'No lyrical poem in English gives so powerful a feeling of moving upon effortless rhyming while in fact being unrhymed...' But Ricks offers a searching analysis of many individual poems in *Tennyson,* and these are the more effective by virtue of the fact that, as in almost all Ricks's work, analysis of them is done 'on the page'. The strength of Ricks's method is the effort to relate critical perceptions to the evidence of the words; to pin them down. When this is the case, his analyses can lead to pointed considerations of the worth of the poetry under discussion. Overall, Ricks achieves the balanced judgement he requires: more is said in favour of *In Memoriam* than of *Maud,* more in favour of *Maud* than *Idylls of the King.* There is particular praise of Tennyson's poem of 1832 'St Simeon Stylites'. At its best, Ricks's critical wit is successfully harnessed to the aim he stated in the Preface to his *Tennyson,* to 'make an independent exploration of [Tennyson's] poetry, seeking to comprehend its special distinction and to establish distinctions....'.[17]

In *Keats and Embarrassment* Ricks's scholarship can, in the same way, 'function as criticism', in which respect, like *Milton's Grand Style,* Ricks is answering Leavis (with perhaps the implicit suggestion that Leavis was not scholarly enough). The rationale for the study is given in the Introduction: 'Dr. F. R. Leavis has spoken of the crucial critical question as "the relation between Keats's sensuousness and his seriousness"; the blushes are intimately part of his sensuousness, and I believe they are of great importance to an understanding of his seriousness.' Although in this book Ricks is going over some very well-tilled ground to mull over, as others have mulled over before, Keats's celebrated sensuous qualities and rich evocations of physical states, Ricks, by moving this way and that, around and about his text, establishes a succession of artistic touchstones by which Keats's poetry may be judged and described. Ricks weaves a cross-referential web, the associations established by scrupulous documentation and lavish quotation from the letters and poems. The literary is linked with the social and with Ricks's own observations on human behaviour, as in the perhaps rather strained humour of his remark that: 'Until quite recently, the young were discouraged from holding hands in public because it gave the middle-aged pains in the stomach.' Personal contributions are mingled with others from standard studies of Keats, and from other poets, such as Byron. The social–psychological stands at one end of the scale (as in references to modern studies of interaction ritual), the verbal and philological (as in Keats's uses of the word 'blush') stands at the other. On the one hand there is Darwin: 'No happy pair of young lovers probably ever courted each other without many a blush.' On the other, Keats's sense of the absurdity of passionately sexual scenes, his good humour, his 'robustness', 'the particular tone and temper of Keats's intelligence', the unique combination of qualities composing his greatness are brought out by contrast with the treatments of the same topic by others. In this instance, Ricks brings forward a catalogue of passages drawn from a comprehensive chronological range; from Chaucer, Marlowe, Dryden, Beckett and Byron. The examples chosen are to be seen as resembling Keats in the detachment implied by their manner. But they differ from Keats (and are like each other) in revealing coolness of various kinds. Chaucer's verse thus has 'cool translucency'; Marlowe's has a 'cool clarity'; Dryden's 'cool remoteness'; Beckett exhibits a 'glacial coolness'. The beauty of Byron who on the one hand is 'full of warm evocations of erotic life', derives from the 'coolness, from not raising the possibly torrid or hotly embarrassing any more than is necessary for a tacit recognition of its being elsewhere possible'. Keats, meanwhile: '. . . is one of the very few erotic poets who come at embarrassment from . . . the wish to pass directly through . . . the hotly disconcerting, the potentially ludicrous, distasteful, or blush-inducing'.[18]

At best, Ricks's method supplies the reader with a rich context of relevance – an elaborately documented setting or 'edition', and clearly owing a lot to some of Ricks's actual editions – in which the writings of any particular poet, Milton, Tennyson, Keats or Eliot, may be better judged and enjoyed. At worst, Ricks's method seems no more than an ingenious flourish where effects that are interesting but of passing importance become the key effects, all it is worth dwelling upon. When this occurs, Ricks's criticism (if not in the current ideological sense) is *de*constructive. The text disappears in the detail. Criticism then becomes almost entirely a matter of style. In earlier work, such as the study of Milton, Ricks's style can be vigorous, economical, sharp and incisive. He can strikingly deploy an adjectival or adverbial phrase which succinctly sums up an effect. This is also the case in *Tennyson* where Ricks criticises some of Tennyson's early work as 'grandiloquent cheer-leadings for poetry'. A later piece is praised as 'compactly miniature and glinting philosophical'. Often, a characteristically Ricksian half-slang adds an interesting touch: 'There were the early girly poems which Fitzgerald was to deplore . . .' But on too many occasions in his criticism, Ricks calls attention to his own style in a way that, though it seems intended to make us admire (as we do here), actually reminds us of its highly unattractive properties. Perhaps the least attractive feature of Ricks's style, as we have noted before, is his tone. This can be chill and tense, fussy, fastidious and occasionally supercilious. Sometimes it is enthusiastic and celebratory. At others, it suffers from want of warmth, the engaging qualities of critical manner which make one want to read on, and which include the reader in the critic's experience. Not that Ricks tends to forget the importance of generous responsiveness to the literature he examines. He can be sounding and rhapsodic. He often rises to expressions meant to continue to ring in our ears. He conveys at one point his richly pleasure-full response to works of literary imagination in the following terms: 'For the challenge which Keats's poetry most triumphantly contains is not a challenge *to*, but the challenge *of*, pleasure: the demanding challenge that a full and livingly imaginative apprehension of the pleasures of others cannot but make upon us.' By contrast, Ricks seems sometimes to be deliberately eschewing the kind of elegant variation of phrase on which traditionally acceptable and pleasing cadences depend. Thus we have a sentence like this:

> For the particular kind of half-convinced levity in those lines from "The Baite" sounds more like a Caroline poet than the innermost Donne, and the particular kind of half-convinced gravity in those lines from "The Calme" sounds more like the Dryden of *Annus Mirabilis* than the innermost Donne.[19]

Pretending not to try, Ricks ends up trying too hard.

Just as his criticism can become a matter of (at times unadmirable) style, so stylistic properties (of dubious worth) tend to dominate discussion of the authors he treats and to infect it. Thus Ricks's interest extends not only, as we have seen, to the pun, but also one further stage to the anti-pun, as in his essay on Stevie Smith in *The Force of Poetry* which shows Ricks's enjoyment of poetic complexity (and allusive subtlety) in outwardly simple, seemingly childlike forms. But as he describes the device, as when commenting upon lines from Stevie Smith's 'Night-Time in the Cemetery', Ricks cannot help punning in his own critical remarks: 'Stevie Smith's choice of the noun "pales" for the black railings has an inspired perversity: an anti-pun, it gives an idea just opposite to what it seemed meant to describe, and it pales into significance' [sic]. A slightly different definition of the anti-pun appears in Ricks's essay on Robert Lowell, in whom the device was a 'trademark'. In an anti-pun, according to Ricks, an alternative meaning is invited, and then 'fended off': '. . . whereas in a pun there are two senses which either get along or quarrel, in an anti-pun there is only one sense admitted but there is another sense denied admission.' An aspect of the art of the anti-pun (that not made explicit in a poem but nevertheless understood) underlies the essay in *The Force of Poetry* devoted to exploring different tones, intonations, and thereby meanings, in lines from poems by Larkin: 'Philip Larkin: "Like Something Almost Being Said" ': 'There is many a way in which things may almost be said. Absences, as in Larkin's poem of that title, make themselves felt.'[20] Our sense of the admirable acuteness of Ricks's attention to poetry may thus be modified by a fear that critical technique for its own sake is becoming too prominent, too intrusive, and is beginning to take over from or supplant interest in the poetry to which it is ostensibly applied. This is particularly the case when Ricks starts imitating in his criticism the verbal effects he observes in poets: compression of meaning (which the critic's business is to 'unpack'), turn of phrase, a quality of *multum in parvo*. Then, Ricks falls prey to a stylistic disease. As the reviewer in the *Times Literary Supplement* has put it, himself imitating Ricks, he 'ricks the language unnecessarily'.[21]

Ricks's concern with the pun, his own puns, recognition of puns (conscious, part-conscious, or unconscious in others, including the anti-pun) is a major symptom of this disease. The attention he gives to play upon words and the extent to which he plays upon words himself suggest a nervous energy, a critical compulsion, not always in Ricks's control. Ricks may thus obscure what he is often trying to bring out (as in his *The Force of Poetry*). In analysing a passage from Gower in an essay from this collection he writes that 'The word "gold" is tolled'. He notes of a line ending in Wordsworth: 'The sense of an ending is perfectly taken up with the sense of a blending.' Being sharp, or 'acute', can mean that Ricks can often descend to such jingles. A favourite ploy is to invert the adjective and noun, as in 'an authentic gracelessness, or a graceless authenticity', or the adverb and noun: 'Critics ... have found Beddoes very distinctly odd and very oddly distinct' – and so on. Coinages are common: Marvell 'does not subdue his momentaneous insight to the doled-out world of discourse'. Odd or striking words are another feature: '... with perfect equipollence ... the figure ... is retorted by the Body against the Soul.' Sometimes Ricks's clever spotting of semantic affinities, an ingenious semantic slide (even when intended by a poet) may be more intriguing than useful. ' "Car-dealers",' he comments on Geoffrey Hill's lines:

> Merovingian car-dealers, Welsh mercenaries; a shuffle of house-carls

are so nearly those other untrustworthy people who deal cards ...'[22] But, as anyone buying or selling a car would know, the term does not need the idea of sharp practice at cards to convey the behaviour of untrustworthy people. The assimilation is entertaining but gratuitous.

This example is taken from an essay in Ricks's *The Force of Poetry*. But the habit of attention, the critical focus, is a feature of all Ricks's criticism. It is the source of the reputation for brilliance that Ricks shares with Carey, and which makes them, though different in so many respects, two of a kind. For example, Ricks shows on one occasion how prepositions in Wordsworth's poetry inform the style of the critics writing upon him. They, the critics, rest the weight of their thought on distinctions prepositionally achieved. Of course, when making connections of this kind, Ricks can be joyfully agile and awesomely athletic. The links appear like magician's rabbits out of a hat. They make the structure of a typical essay or chapter by Ricks resemble that of a conjuror's stage performance, as when, in his study of Eliot, Ricks defines the expatriate state, the link between cultures and continents of both Eliot (and himself) in the role of the hyphen, the tiniest typographical detail. Different levels of meaning are suddenly brought together. Thus Pope's 'The Art of Sinking in Poetry' is invoked to illuminate Stevie Smith's 'Not Waving but Drowning',[23] with the recognition that the subject matter is the art; the art is the subject matter. Style is not just what a poet is writing within; it is what he or she is writing about.

In 'A Pure Organic Pleasure from the Lines', the former of two essays on Wordsworth in *The Force of Poetry,* the discussion revolves round a pun upon 'lines': lines as in 'lines/Of curling mist' and as in the lines of a poem. Ricks describes the effect as 'self-referring', as relating 'Wordsworth's delight in "the eternal Beauty" to his own beautiful lines which are here speaking'. Ricks's taste for reflexivity relates him to Empson (with whom he is grouped by Carey in his Inaugural Address to the University of Oxford, 'Wording and Rewording: Paraphrase in Literary Criticism'). In his *Milton's Grand Style,* Ricks attributes the position that Milton's poetry is sensitive and subtle and not just (as Leavis and Eliot had suggested) 'unEnglish' to Empson, who he numbers among those who believe 'not that Dr. Leavis's *principles* are wrong, but that his *tools* are few and inadequate'. Ricks here is offering a decelerated version of Empsonian criticism: 'Though the following pages owe everything to

Empsonian criticism, they try to slow down the process which in Mr. Empson is so agonizingly nimble.' Ricks differs from Empson in that he is not a poet (though he has written a warmly appreciative, amply illustrated and typically word-play-ridden, essay on Empson's poems in *The Force of Poetry*). But Ricks's emphasis is like Empson's in that it is the emphasis of an analytic critic specialising in dissecting figures and expressions in a way that, while it delights in intellectual challenge, may be sometimes unhinged from, and obscure, its larger points. Its brilliance can sometimes be tiring. Ricks's eye, like Empson's, is in Alexander Pope's term, a 'microscope of wit'. It moves over its subject to bring into focus tiny fragments of expression – little words in Wordsworth's poetry, the use of brackets, misquotations or imaginative mis-spellings. Ricks's element has become to an increasing extent in his criticism the minute. He fixes on the atoms of which poetry is made. 'Their attempts were always analytick: they broke very image into fragments...'[24] What Samuel Johnson said of the metaphysical poets can also be said, with some accuracy, of the literary criticism of Ricks.

In Ricks the critic is shamelessly the 'expert'. In the age of the specialist, he is the opposite of Carey's very British, vegetable-gardening, don-cum-plain man, aspiring without embarrassment to intelligence 'pure' and an interest (extraordinary for a critic who is not actually a creator of poems) in poetry as technique. The components of literary effect are reduced to their parts. In this way, Ricks's criticism, though it evinces a poet's interest in the resonance of language, is situated at the point where criticism gives public expression to, and becomes a mode of, modern intellectual life (as at times is more usually possible for philosophy or mathematics). Ricks thereby forms a bridge between traditions of modern British criticism and recent traditions of criticism in America and Europe (for which Carey seems to have little time) where criticism in many respects *is* the national life of the mind, though it need not be critical theory to be so. Carey looks down patriarchally from the pedestal of his professorial chair to cultivate the ordinary reader unprivileged to share the critical good life at the top. Ricks, in his chair, faces his fellow intellectuals at home and abroad and is content to be admired from below. Fewer compromises are made.

If therefore Ricks's literary criticism breathes in one way a more rarified air than Carey's (and operates on a more genuinely intellectual plane than that of the 'radical theorists'), it also ranges more widely through the totality which is, in the larger sense of the term, 'English Literature'. But this also means that Ricks is able to be, in one sense, more 'popular', less 'dated', than Carey, as in his discussion of Bob Dylan's poetry; though this, while it has a peculiar combination of fitness and irony for Britain's most eminent critic, dates Ricks in another respect. At times, Ricks's admiration for Dylan may seem too much a part of the necessary cosmopolitan pose, as the coy would-be humour of this remark may suggest: '... one might ... notice Dylan's dexterity with the phrase which is apocryphally taken as getting the Englishman into trouble, when he asks for an early call in the morning: "I ain't lookin' to block you up,/Shock or knock or lock you up." '[25] But Ricks is an enthusiastic reader of American writers. They stir his delight in the language, a delight far away from the more commonplace, academically fabricated, 'linguistic approaches' beloved of structuralist theoreticians and their mediators in Britain. Dylan gives Ricks a sense of the vigour of American English which stands as a linguistic and cultural challenge, as art not theory, to parochial English English and is vitally and creatively at odds with it. Eagleton advocates study of Dylan; Ricks (the establishment critic) actually carries it out. And it is Ricks who is the one actually to break down the barriers which hegemonically subordinate the non-literary to the literary, if we think of the range of reference Ricks brings to discussion of prejudice in Eliot, and where he can turn from Edmund Burke to *The Times*, or when commenting on the fatal errors that can result from misinterpretations of 'Tone', where he moves between Eliot, Dante, Shakespeare, Wordsworth, Lowell and the language of the modern courtroom at a trial for murder.

A second major difference between Ricks and Carey (and for that matter between Ricks and Eagleton or Ricks and Belsey) is Ricks's by comparison vital relation to the criticism and literature of the eighteenth century – itself a symptom of his cultivation of cultural connections with the 'Enlightenment' values of the United States, where the reign of Victoria has had less effect. In his essay on Milton in *The Force of Poetry*, Ricks is unusual in drawing attention to Milton's insufficiently recognised Augustan affinities. He stresses connections between Milton and Johnson and differences between Milton and Shakespeare. If Milton, according to F. R. Leavis, 'works from the outside' in the construction of his verse, this need not, claims Ricks, degrade his greatness as poet. What Ricks does not stress (though he might have) is the extent to which poetry of the Augustans is also a product of the abyss of the heart, and thereby resembles Milton's. Ricks, then, retains a conception of Augustan poetry in which externalities dominate. The Augustan poet Ricks particularly considers is Johnson, who is interesting to Ricks because he breathes new life into poetical clichés. He argues that Johnson's poetry, even his minor juvenile work (his translation of Addison's Latin poem 'The Battle of the Pygmies and Cranes'), gives vitality to old, dead, formulae and phases. But Ricks's analytical mode is the analysis of technique. Perhaps it is because Ricks is himself able to respond so positively to poetic technique that his criticism therefore fails to subvert (what for many would be negative) assumptions about Augustan poetry's concentration on surface effects; its over-concern, as some have argued, with style. But Ricks's interest in the eighteenth century nevertheless goes far beyond those aspects of eighteenth-century literature (valued by Eagleton) which might be thought to directly pre-figure modern (and Ricks's own) interest in aspects of literary technique. It is natural that Ricks, with his taste for technical concerns, should discuss the punctuation practices of Laurence Sterne. And his twentieth-century liking for Empsonian complexity (and 'wit out of season') is diametrically at odds with the powerful ideals of Augustan simplicity. But Ricks's criticism also involves restoration of eighteenth-century values precisely not fashionable today. Thus in Ricks's latest book, *T. S. Eliot and Prejudice*, Eliot's poem 'Animula' is said to have 'an Augustan weight of generality'. The title of Ricks's recent collection of essays *The Force of Poetry* is, as we have seen, taken from a significant moment in Johnson's *The Rambler*. In this same collection, when discussing a poem by Geoffrey Hill called 'September Song', about a holocaust death, Ricks brings in the moving words of a Johnsonian prayer. In his early book, *Milton's Grand Style*, Ricks had appealed to Johnson's judgement of Milton's poetry time and again, and he wrote that 'the eighteenth century editors are still in many ways the best guide to Milton.'[26]

Perhaps the strongest evidence of Ricks's positive relation to the eighteenth-century past is his high valuation, as a critical standard, of common humanity in literary works, and the ethical principles explored through it. Ricks appeals to literature as a matter of simultaneously human and moral concern: 'Can we praise and value works of imagination as we should praise and value behaviour? I think that we can, should, and do.' The assumption of a uniform emotional life directly available through the experience of one's own life informs Ricks's study of embarrassment in Keats (and is, like prejudice in Eliot, representative of his aspiration to find a universal term). And often Ricks can appeal directly to experience of what life is like: he defends Tennyson's *In Memoriam* against a hostile criticism of Verlaine's on the ground that: '... hearts may break with different causes and with different effects, and reminiscences may be precisely those memories which are not softened but made even more poignant by being humanized and localized.' The twists and turns of Ricks's analyses, on one level so much a matter of his obsession with technique, may on another level merely confirm the continuity of language with literary and human experience, itself the source of the common stock of poetical English diction and rhythms. So in discussing Keats's use of 'dimpled', Ricks switches from Keats to Pope: 'As shallow streams run dimpling all the way' (*An Epistle to Dr. Arbuthnot*), and then from Pope to Robert Frost: 'I found a dimpled spider' ('Design'). In this way further nuances in T. S. Eliot's reference to Michelangelo in 'Prufrock' are uncovered by invoking Dryden: 'But show shou'd any Sign-post-dawber know/The worth of *Titian*, or of *Angelo*.' Literature of different ages has common subjects. Ricks writes of Hill: 'All Hill's work is concerned, in a concurrence with Coleridge, with reconciliation.'[27]

From this it follows that Ricks's fascination with the technical aspects of poetic expression should reveal few *explicit* structuralist sympathies. In Ricks, as in Carey, the whole structuralist 'project', the whole movement of thought towards the view that criticism is or can be made scientific, is almost entirely ignored. Ricks does not profess to politics of criticism (though he may have one attributed to him, and it is hard to say whether the issue is affected by the fact that Milton, who he writes on, was heir to the English revolution, while Keats enjoys the status of 'Romantic'). Nor do sexual politics inform his work, although the accusation of sexism as prejudice is searchingly treated (if partly from the point of view of someone who thinks he, by virtue of the fact that he is a 'he', may be open to the charge) in *T. S. Eliot and Prejudice*. Only at moments, as in analysing various English and American uses of language, can a glimpse of his dismissive feelings be had: 'Those who believe that the bourgeoisie, or whoever, will oppressively claim that particular social arrangements are ineluctable reality are quick to put sneering quotation-marks around the word *real* ("real").'[28] Ricks is like the structuralists (who are themselves unconsciously like many eighteenth-century critics) in being interested in matters of technique, and in a broader way, 'The State of the Language' – the title of a recent collection of essays which Ricks has co-edited.[29] But his interest is not rooted in theory, so much as in the writings of critics who are themselves poets: T. S. Eliot, Philip Larkin and Geoffrey Hill. And Ricks's interest also owes much to his conjunction of, on the one hand, intellectual abstraction, and, on the other, Practical Criticism: the tradition of so-called 'close-reading' of poetry given currency by *Scrutiny*. Ricks takes the criticism of *Scrutiny* in his stride, without rancorous aversion or partisan praise. In general, Ricks, unlike Eagleton, sees *Scrutiny* as a contribution to critical wisdom, even though, if need be, Ricks can share a hostile critic's sense of the narrowness of the '*Scrutiny* view', to point out that 'The "un-English" of *Scrutiny* critics [when criticising certain kinds of syntax or diction] is always in danger of turning into the vague and apoplectic splutter which goes with *unBritish*.'[30]

The implication of this is that Ricks does not mind being unBritish (hence, perhaps, his interest in the language of American poetry as much as in the Latinate diction of Milton). But Ricks refers to *Scrutiny* with favour many times in his criticism, as he does to the criticism of *Scrutiny*'s editor, Leavis. Ricks begins his study of Milton, for example, with a survey of 'The Milton Controversy', instigated by Leavis. He takes Leavis's 'crucial critical question' concerning relations between sensuousness and seriousness as a starting point for his study of Keats. Ricks registers various differences with Leavis over individual poets and aspects of poets. He disapproves, for example, of Leavis's disapproval of Eliot's recording of *Four Quartets:* 'Leavis is signally uninterested in interrogating his own responses . . . Leavis animates a tissue of prejudice . . .' But this, reminiscent though it is of certain reactions to Leavis that aspire to a 'radical' view, is a sign that Ricks is taking Leavis seriously as a critic in a way that Carey, for example, does not. Regardless of these divergences on specific issues (where the particularity of the divergence is significant), Ricks is indebted to Leavis for critical criteria, the emphasis of his taste and aspects of practice. (He even seems to have adopted the Leavis habit of using footnotes, traditionally reserved for textual and factual detail, to make killing critical points.) In his study of Keats, Ricks turns to Leavis to support his sense of interrelations between moral behaviour in life and that in imaginative works: '. . . it is an essential strength of Dr. Leavis's criticism, disturbing though it may seem at first, that it can so unmisgivingly locate within the same world of human sympathies and human judgement an imagined adultery and an actual one, that of Anna Karenina and that of Frieda Lawrence.'[31]

On the whole then, Ricks, not less than Carey, has swelled rather than diverted a mainstream development of twentieth-century academic–critical taste. Ricks may be a member of the critical international élite, and *au fait,* as professional reviewers have to be, with the latest developments in the world of professional letters; but he has ploughed somewhat conventional seventeenth and nineteenth century furrows in the most sustained examples of his work. The only twentieth-century poet on whom Ricks has written a book (T. S. Eliot) is dead, and thus in a sense of the canon. Ricks never seriously questions Eliot's claims to continued attention by modern readers, any more than Carey questions the claims to continued attention by Eliot's poetical forbear Donne. Nor does Ricks consider the damage that Eliot's high reputation – which his own book must effectively extend – may have done to twentieth-century poetical styles. Despite (though in a way at the same time because of) Ricks's much greater practical and analytic interest than Carey in the living poets indebted to Eliot, like Dylan, Ricks helps Carey (and Eagleton, and Belsey) in hardening the bedrock of twentieth-century literary taste. He once more captures and modifies, but does not abandon, the tradition from Leavis. In doing this, Ricks may be regarded as an 'establishment' critic. And yet he has things in common with those 'radical' theorists, for whom (otherwise) his general position, and approach, is anathema. Ricks's intellectualisation of establishment criticism operates like the radicalising ambitions of 'radical' criticism in one important respect: it can exist without necessarily upsetting conventions of taste upon which it operates and seems to depend. Its tendency is academic in the sense of moving debate beyond a point where we think whether any particular writer might be considered to matter, or to matter no more. Therefore it is in a key sense of the word not 'critical', despite the fact that, unlike the 'radicals', Ricks is wholly unembarrassed by the need to use criticism to evaluate authors. Like Carey, he thinks in terms of 'great poems', 'the greatest poems', and success and failure, even when he is reasserting a traditional judgement, as in his Tennyson study: 'if the poems which figure in these pages are the traditional choices to the point of predictability, that is because in my opinion the traditional sense of what was most creative within Tennyson's achievement is a just one.' The success is judged in human terms: Tennyson has 'an unclamourous claim to the central humanity of a great poet'.[32] At a lower level, Ricks distinguishes literature that works from literature that does not. But his tendency to make criticism a tensing of intellectual muscles, and taughtening of nervous fibres (which has something in common with the 'radical' theorists' sponsoring of an intellectually more 'rigorous' theory), has become stronger as time has passed. There are, of course, many compensating attractions in Ricks's criticism. Any negative impression must be tempered by numerous local delights in Ricks's astonishing *coups de grâce*. But the danger is again that the critic comes between us and the work it is his business to expose; that in reading criticism, we are drawn in and away from literature. In Ricks's criticism, we see that when it is unmodified by critical motives of this larger kind, even the most professional–intellectual approach can begin to obtrude. Power and purpose become unhinged. Either the professional critic begins to live too exclusively within the terms of his separate professional world or, he leaves it altogether and we are left with an excessively prominent personality–critic, a mere 'media don'. For the reader of literary works (even when he is at the same time the student of criticism) the effect either way is impressive to the extent that it is counter-productive. The practice of criticism, in the important sense mentioned above, is annulled. Eagleton narrows an academicised version of post-Romantic *Scrutiny* taste; Belsey unconsciously reasserts and annotates it; Carey reinforces it while subjecting it to internal revisions which accommodate it to 'popular' values and Oxonian norms. Ricks expands its range, and extends its principles, to include a wider selection of twentieth-century poets. But not even Ricks, whose published writings suggest that he is perhaps alive to a greater variety of English literary periods than the rest, goes far enough to subvert it.

Notes

1. *The Times Literary Supplement*, 23 November 1984.
2. Alexander Pope, *The Dunciad*, Book IV, pp. 11, 233–4; *Poems*, p. 779.
3. *The Poems of Tennyson* (Longman: London, 1969). See also *English Poetry and Prose 1540–1674* (Sphere: London, 1970); *English Drama to 1710* (Sphere: London, 1971); *A. E. Housman: A Collection of Critical Essays* (1968); *Essays on Criticism*, XIV (1964); *The Force of Poetry* (Clarendon Press: Oxford, 1984).

4. *Keats and Embarrassment* (Clarendon Press: Oxford, 1974), pp. 118, 117, 118, 119.
5. *Milton's Grand Style* (Clarendon Press: Oxford, 1963); *T. S. Eliot and Prejudice* (Faber: London and Boston, 1988).
6. *The Force of Poetry*, pp. 307, 102–03, 368.
7. *Milton's Grand Style*, Prefatory Note, pp. 137, 68, 117, 1.
8. *Tennyson* (Macmillan Masters of World Literature Series: London, 1972), pp. 235, vii–viii, 126, 136, 126–7.
9. *The Force of Poetry*, pp. 342, 371.
10. *The Force of Poetry*, p. 383; *Tennyson*, pp. 132–3.
11. *Keats and Embarrassment*, pp. 13, 139, 202.
12. *Keats and Embarrassment*, p. 12; *Tennyson*, p. 197; *T. S. Eliot and Prejudice*, p. 78.
13. According to Bernard Bergonzi, Ricks's *The Force of Poetry* stands out as 'a work of enormous brilliance' (back cover, *The Force of Poetry*, quoted from *Encounter*). H. A. Mason, on the other hand, thinks the work, as far as it conveys the effect and value of poetry, does precisely the reverse of that which its title suggests, and believes that the highest compliment he could pay Ricks 'would be to suppose that he now wishes he had not collected his essays and presented them as *The Force of Poetry*'. 'The Last Straw,' *CQ*, **XIV**, 2 (1985), 132.
14. *The Force of Poetry*, pp. 1, 44, 24.
15. *T. S. Eliot and Prejudice*, pp. 110, 17–18.
16. *ibid.*, pp. 50, 51, 88.
17. *Tennyson*, pp. 311, 199, vii.
18. *Keats and Embarrassment*, pp. 7, 92, 62–8.
19. *Tennyson*, pp. 51–2; *Keats and Embarrassment*, p. 97; *The Force of Poetry*, p. 44.
20. *The Force of Poetry*, pp. 254, 265, 277.
21. *The Times Literary Supplement*, 23 November 1984.
22. *The Force of Poetry*, pp. 17, 116, 127, 135, 36, 41, 349.
23. *ibid.*, p. 253.
24. *The Force of Poetry*, p. 96; *Milton's Grand Style*, pp. 9, 21; 'Life of Cowley,' *Lives of the Poets* (ed. George Birkbeck Hill), I, p. 21.
25. *The Force of Poetry*, p. 429.
26. *T. S. Eliot and Prejudice*, p. 229; *Milton's Grand Style*, p. 13. For Ricks's Centenary appraisal of Johnson's achievement see 'Rescuing Johnson from Caricature', *Listener*, 13 December 1984, p. 13: 'This great man of his age, like Shakespeare he, too, was not of an age but for all time.'
27. *Keats and Embarrassment*, p. 94; *Tennyson*, p. 221; *Keats and Embarrassment*, p. 109; *T. S. Eliot and Prejudice*, p. 18; *The Force of Poetry*, p. 325.
28. *The Force of Poetry*, p. 438.

29. *The State of the Language* (University of California Press: Berkeley, 1980). (With Leonard Michaels.)
30. *Milton's Grand Style*, p. 33.
31. *T. S. Eliot and Prejudice*, pp. 182–4; *Keats and Embarrassment*, p. 96. In his Introduction to *The New Oxford Book of Victorian Verse* (OUP: London, 1987), p. xxviii, Ricks wrote that:-'The weaknesses and vices of bad Victorian poems are what Leavis judged them to be.'
32. *Tennyson*, pp. vii, 315.

5
Liberal Humanists I:
H. A. Mason

> In every age the task of the humanist is different, but the spirit is the same, for it is an aspect of all civilization to struggle for renewal by attacking inert ideas.
>
> The Classics are properly used when they enable an Englishan to become fully aware, that is, in his own idiom, of the aspirations to conceive life in ideal terms which are found in all attempts to make life civilized. This answer enables us to distinguish the mere Humanist, who, as it were, has the Classics in his head, from the true Humanist who has *translated* the Classics into the only form in which they can still live.[1]

The 'radical theorists'' caricature of 'liberal–humanist' ideals is most inaccurate in its necessary misrepresentation when critics on the 'opposite side' have brought human values most clearly to the centre of their work. The official 'radicals' are therefore unable to acknowledge the radicalism of humanist critics who have already reacted against the 'liberal–humanist' characteristics that they (the 'radicals') now appear to reject for the first time. But the literary history the official 'radicals' share with the critical establishment they do not share with the subject of this chapter. In a critical ethos dominated at every point on the political spectrum by professional literary studies, H. A. Mason proclaims himself amateur (in its original sense, i.e. lover). And, at a time when fashionable critics have urged critical revolution in the belief that they really are rejecting values of the past (and the 'eternal verities' that go with them), Mason has looked for inspiration (and literary renewal) back to the deepest roots of

European literature and thought. In turning to the past, Mason avoids the narrowly explicit emphases of modern criticism on politics and cultural studies. For Mason, political and cultural questions, while they are embedded in literature, are insufficient to subordinate or annex literary study. Answers to such questions are consequent upon the imaginative, intellectual and emotional totality that literature, in Mason's view, is uniquely fitted to convey. Mason is therefore one of the most persistently literary of modern literary critics. He everywhere defends literary values, *qua* literary values, against the attempted takeover bids of adjacent intellectual realms, including criticism itself. He consigns politics of all colours to the wings of debate. And it is perhaps for the explicit apoliticism of his criticism more than anything else that Mason fits the 'radicals'' stereotype of the old-fashioned (ideological unconscious, though in this case consciously unconscious) 'liberal–humanist' critic. But Mason's external credentials are also exceptionally strong. Mason was once an associate of Leavis: one of the original *Scrutiny* school, and contributed articles and reviews to *Scrutiny* in the thirties and forties. Since then, Mason has published a series of highly individual critical studies, explicitly and confessedly humanist in aim. At times these suggest the criticism of an even more cloistered environment than Carey's: Mason lives in the world of 'undergraduates' not students, and his conception of our 'English universities' appears unusually quaint (something that is perhaps attributable to the fact that many years of his life have been spent abroad). But Mason's critical works dispel the myth, propagated by the 'radical theorists', that 'liberal–humanism' may be either straightforwardly defined (and so dismissed), or that 'liberal–humanist' values may be understood as a synonym for 'conservative' critical views, a case of toeing a critical party line, however confidently it is imputed. In fact they point to the extent to which humanist practice (*and* theory – though the word loses the 'radicals'' conception of it in this context) may challenge the framework of received twentieth-century academic tastes. Mason's criticism is directed to (and in some of its effects achieves) wholesale subversion of the range of critical orthodoxies of his day, 'humanist' and 'radical' alike. Like the 'radicals', he is a critic both of literature and its place in his times. But for him (if not for them) literature is not in essence a university study, the preoccupation of a trained élite. It is, and was always intended to be, a common possession, potentially available to all.

Mason's publications in book form have emerged slowly but at regular intervals over the course of his career. Many book chapters have been given dry runs as articles in *The Cambridge Quarterly* (a journal started in the mid-sixties which, although in one sense extends the spirit of *Scrutiny* as a revaluation of the revaluation that *Scrutiny* itself performed, in another sense denies that spirit, in its questioning of particular *Scrutiny* judgements and criteria). Mason is an editor of *The Quarterly* and contributes regularly to it. Through this channel, and in the books that his articles go on to form, Mason has brought to the task of criticising English literature an extraordinary knowledge of its distant origins in the classical literatures of Greece and Rome. It is a fascination which divides Mason from Leavis, whose published interests were almost exclusively English. (It also effectively cuts Mason off as a critic from many readers who, while they might appreciate his approach, have little interest in, and no knowledge of, foreign literature in its original languages.) But, in Mason's writings, the classics (and European literature in general) are everywhere manifest, even in writings on English literature, and particularly in his unusual and original work on verse translations. It is at the centre of Mason's critical achievement that, in times of decline in classical studies at the academic level, his criticism constitutes a voice able to recreate the vitality of Greco–Roman literature as an active presence, directly and indirectly, in the substance of living literature in English, and thus in Mason's own terms, English life. From a similar inspiration, Mason has marked out for his times the key place in humane education occupied by English literature and literary criticism. No critic writing today seems to have explored more energetically why criticism is or is not worth spending one's life doing, or why literature bears an important relation to life. That it does is a conviction held consistently throughout Mason's writings. The whole force of his criticism is to suggest ways in which literature, and ideally if not in practice the discussion of literature, are wedded to the substance of living; how far they are from being privileged academic pursuits, reserved for those with special training and skills. But, to the extent that it does this, it is possible to see signs in Mason's criticism of his links not only with Leavis, but also with Arnold, whom he clearly admires, has learnt from and frequently cites. Mason himself is a Cambridge academic, and his questioning of academic values has caused him to form (as a kind of protective shield) an élite within an élite. It is hard to say whether this makes him more élitist or less. Arguably, Mason's concern with foreign and classical literature removes him, in part, from the field of vision of the modern British Common Reader he wishes to address. Yet no modern critic has pointed with more clarity to the contrast between the vitality of literature and the sterile conditions of its academic appropriation; the real cultural crisis of its takeover by university and latterly – in Britain – polytechnic worlds. Throughout his career, Mason has worked hard (as an academic scholar as well as a critic) to equip himself with knowledge and authority to justify this negative verdict on the critical profession. This has not made him a popular figure among members of the profession for whom the relation of literature to life is of less urgent concern. For many, the views of H. A. Mason can be dismissed as the views of an eccentric. As far as his critical ideals and ambitions themselves are concerned, nothing could be further from the mark.

'A central, a truly human point of view': this, subtitle to the Prologue to the first of Mason's major critical books, *Humanism and Poetry in the Early Tudor Period* (1959) sums up the aspiration behind all his criticism. Equally representative is the apparent disparity of scope within *Humanism and Poetry*. The issue is extremely large: what makes it worth bothering with literature. But the subject of the book, the literary and social history of the first half of the sixteenth century in England, is highly specialised. The disparity typifies Mason's literary concern, and expresses the relationship between particular and general that is a feature of Mason's desiderations elsewhere. This is caught in the manner and style of approach adopted in the Prologue to *Humanism and Poetry,* a Prologue at once very bold, yet unusually self-effacing. Mason is wrestling with all imaginable objections to his scheme, painfully conscious of being out on a limb, but comes out with a series of directly expressed, passionately felt, personal convictions. The Prologue, in this latter respect, forms a statement of faith. It is, at moments like the following, a classic humanist account of relations between literary criticism and literary creation:

> For if this is what we study literature for, if literature exists as experience, something we take in and in a sense recreate, it can never be properly described or handled at all with tools that do not belong to this order of reality. Literature, that is, cannot be thought of as something *totally* outside us, if, to side-step metaphysics, we are allowed to use the word 'outside' for the 'objects' we see with our eyes. If so, we must abandon the ideal implied in the word 'objective' as illusory. Our objects are unattainable without mixing ourselves with them. On the other hand, our objects when we study literature are not merely private moods. I shall not labour to *prove* that literature is sufficiently non-subjective for two people to be able to argue about it, that a given work is the same for two minds: I simply assume that the experience of ages that great poems are in a real sense the common property of mankind is not an illusion.[2]

Despite the exhaustive scholarship contained in the book, Mason modestly describes it as an 'Essay', and The Prologue to *Humanism and Poetry* is in fact Mason's 'essay on criticism'; the 'theory', informed by practice, which is reciprocally to govern his practice as critic in this and all later work. The above passage is representative of the Prologue's examination of the whole question of one's critical stance: what literary study is; the difference between fact and opinion; what experience of literature is; how study of literature differs from mere dilettantism; what marks out the great writer; what 'life' literature has. To explore these questions, Mason appeals to diverse authors, from Dr Johnson to Dryden to D. H. Lawrence and Henry James. These, in Arnoldian way, are offered as 'touchstones' to thought. They establish the scope of enquiry; the framework of experience and ideas to be appealed to in the book as a whole, which is, at the same time, a contribution to specialist study of the early

Tudor period. In this way, what is at first sight an unpromisingly detailed study of neglected and misunderstood areas of literature and thought (the first fifty years of the sixteenth century) achieves a direct modern application. This is because Mason's interest, though scholarly, is not confined to the scholar's (as modern academic life currently defines the nature of that role). It is interest, via the truth that scholarship in its limited way is able to reveal, in making human civilisation truly human. For Mason, scholarly enquiry (in this case into the early humanists themselves) is continuous with the ambition to establish afresh grounds for a humanist study of literature today. The founding conviction of the whole book is one Mason makes manifest in his procedure: that there is ideally no difference between literary scholar and critic. The dichotomy (as Mason's own scholarship sets out to 'prove') is a false one; as false as opposition between description of literary facts and expression of critical opinions, or the notion that, where literature is concerned, there is such a thing as wholly subjective, or wholly objective response. In offering this thought, Mason does not anticipate what Eagleton – in his theory – is later to claim: that every reading is reproduction of the text. Mason assumes that literary works, though they are individually felt, are not merely private experiences; and that experience of a given work, though not identical, can be sufficiently the same for two people to enable them to argue about it.

The book's first half is on the humanists, More and Erasmus. The second half is mainly devoted to the development of English poetry before, within and after the Tudor age. Special attention is paid to the place in English humanist tradition of Wyatt. In distinguishing between generations of early humanists, and identifying the spirit of true ones, the breadth of Mason's cultural and critical grasp becomes clear. Just as Mason sees ancient writing as indispensable to understanding the new, so literature and culture of the twentieth century are drawn in as means of feeling our way into literary conditions remote in time, thus: 'It would certainly help us in the effort to enter imaginatively into the admiration of the Humanists who read *De Fructu* to note how Henry James managed to admire Pierre Loti's book

Matelot.' For Mason, literature and culture, because they are human, and because humanity – regardless of race, gender or class – is one, constitute a unity of experience. Negatively this means that Mason, in commenting on the past, can simultaneously take a swipe at twentieth-century authors he does not like while appearing to lament a general condition:

> The prestige of literature, the honours to be won through literature, cause many people to write who were not intended by Nature for literature. In our day this has been said of Mr Stephen Spender, but it is common in all ages to find books which, like *De Fructu,* have no other *raison d'être* than the author's desire to be in the literary swim.[3]

A related consequence, this time with negative and positive results, is Mason's curiously digressive, perhaps often tortuous, way of advancing his case. Mason's habit, which must have tried the patience of many readers, is to circle an issue, drawing quotations and references in from far and wide, often from literatures in three or four different languages at a time. Of these, as Mason must himself know, most of his readers are bound to be ignorant, though he isn't. At worst, it seems a matter of trite donnish display, or an irritating failure to get to the point. And this surely, on various occasions, perhaps in some measure on all occasions, is all that it is. And yet the motive (if not always the effect) of this method is not always fetishistically academic, a bad dose of the mannered and exhibitionist ramblings internal to the Cambridge college system which Mason in many respects stands outside. Mason's wanderings enable him, in a simultaneously critical and scholarly way, to 'set' a richly informed context for critical judgement. In weaving this context, Mason invents various *personae* who then offer views that he then refutes. Sometimes he engages in little dialogues with these *personae,* so that judgement, when it finally comes, as it always in the end does, seems to have taken many things into account. At its best, Mason's process enacts the painful, halting, circuitous means by which critical judgement seeks to transcend the glib or the smart. It is part of the effort to allow literature life of its own and opportunity to speak for itself. While the function of the critic is to withhold his personal view, producing it at the last minute and often in the form of a throwaway or aside, the reader must read and respond to quotations (as well as the critic's own text) if he wishes to follow the line being pursued. Unless he does so, he will quickly become lost. As Mason develops as critic, he moves towards a critical address that is increasingly direct. Even in later, highly confident, publications, he is still, at times, painfully addicted to critical progress via the great circle route.

In *Humanism and Poetry* the critical method enacts an implicit message of the critical text. While striving to extend his standards, Mason, in his own writings, aspires to embody the standards taught by the subjects he treats: in this case the humanists themselves. In rising to their standards, Mason is aspiring to make values of the past continuous with those of the present – and not just a substitute for them. This follows from what is (to him) the perceived fact that they (the humanists) had, in their turn, reinvigorated the classics within the context of the deadening scholasticism of their contemporary Dark Age. And theirs, Mason hints, is in essential respects not too different from ours. The importance of the humanists for Mason emerges in the course of *Humanism and Poetry:* their place in helping us to appreciate the ability of English Literature (as part of the total literature of Europe) to mesh classical literature and criticism with its own, native, living concerns. Early humanists, according to Mason, exemplify this process. They show what can be done, and how one can fail. In his perception of the early humanists' success, Mason develops his own thoughts on the nature of classical translation (as well as translation from other languages). Mason's idea of translation is the guiding inspiration of the half of the book devoted mainly to Wyatt. For Mason, the great difference is between mere translation and *creative* translation, between an inert mode of contact with the past and one where old work is made significant for a new generation. When work is creatively translated, Mason believes, timeless qualities are reasserted by being re-imagined in modern (and simultaneously timeless) terms. *Humanism and Poetry* is then first of a series of connected enquiries that encompass, and unify, Mason's career to date. The centre of thought, a delicate one to which Mason continually recurs and adds, is the nature of the relations between past and present. Mason's idea of translation is built up bit by bit over the length of his book. It flows from examination of numerous instances of the form, compared and juxtaposed. Therefore it is not quite right to call Mason's idea of translation 'theory' in the theorists' sense of the word. While they apply theory *to* texts, Mason offers, rather, a succession of provisional, potentially modifiable insights, produced under the initial pressure of literary experience itself. How, Mason asks, do we gain access to the classics? '... we must supply the missing roots of the classical flowers from our own substance before the classical flowers will come alive. We must bring to the classics something corresponding to the spirit in which they were written before we can detect and enjoy that spirit in the classics.' What are the 'laws' of translation?

> ... comparative success in translation depends on something in the life of the translator's times, and a capacity in the translator to isolate and refine out of that 'something' a sense of 'absolute' civilization. But a translator's success is just as dependent on the contemporary poetry he can draw on. No translator can hope to rise very high – that is, to attempt a major classic with success – unless there is a contemporary literature which is nourished by and at the same time embodies the profoundest feelings underlying the way of life in the translator's day.[4]

The argument of Part One of *Humanism and Poetry*, and an aspect of Mason's interest in 'civilisation', culminates in examination of More's *Utopia*. The emphasis is not on ideas in *Utopia*, but wit, satiric-cum-mock-heroic combination of inextricable serious and comic strokes. *There*, we find, is an example of sixteenth-century humanism in vital relation to the classical past (and so *our* present).

Being 'humanist' therefore, in Mason's understanding, is precisely the reverse of what the 'radical theorists' are inclined to say that it is: it amounts to challenging conventionally sanctioned views. A function of the second half of *Humanism and Poetry* is to elevate into greater prominence the neglected field of Tudor verse translation. To do this, Mason turns to Wyatt. According to Mason, and contrary to what is in Mason's view the representative opinion of Wyatt's modern editor, Kenneth

Muir, 'Wyatt did not become a poet in the true sense until he abandoned the courtly lyric for something I should like to describe as translation.' Mason contends that in his courtly lyrics Wyatt reveals only the waning of the middle ages: he is not making it new. But it is different where Wyatt is basing his new poem on classical originals. Mason believes that Wyatt's 'Stond who so list . . .' can be seen as an essentially creative response to lines from Seneca:

> stet quicunque uolet potens
> aulae culmine lubrico . . .

Here, in response to the original, Wyatt has experience (perhaps, though we cannot be sure, bitter personal experience) behind him. And Mason sees this as something his language reveals. The poem's urgency 'comes out in the insistent, onward rhythm and the vivid phrases, such as *brackishe ioyes*'. It is thus on translation, unusually, that Mason rests his case for reconsideration of Wyatt's reputation as poet. Comparison between Wyatt's poem and its classical source and later versions of the same piece of Seneca by other English poets precedes Mason's general claim: '. . . I would claim that among Wyatt's translations are to be found most, if not all, his more interesting poems, for Wyatt used his original as a Mask or Persona, as a means of finding and creating himself.'[5] Wyatt is at his best when he is finding himself in critical-cum-creative response to writings of others. He expresses experience by sense of continuity with other poets in other times. His best poems thus affirm the existence and worth of the enduring humanity that does not change. This enduring humanity is Mason's test of Wyatt's work in *Humanism and Poetry*. It is also Mason's ultimate test of poetry in other criticism. It is what Arnold had called 'a central, a truly human point of view'. And it is what Samuel Johnson had called 'general nature'. Mason, as if to convey by his own practice the truth of their ideas, inherits the tradition perpetuated by both critics of the past.

We have seen that for critics in conscious reaction against humanist ideals, 'humanism' and 'common sense' may be regarded as essentially linked: two words for the same, mistaken, thing. But for Mason, whose humanism is explicit, the human is often exactly the quality that cannot be defined by stable 'common sense' views: hence Mason's admiration for one of the classical poets least sensible in this sense of the term – Juvenal: '. . . the pleasure we get from the opening of his poem [*Satire* 6] is derived in part from its airy disdain of common sense or earnestness.' At the same time, the appreciation of Juvenal is seen to depend on a sense of poetry that common standards of judgement are alone able to define. To 'understand' Juvenal's poetry in a sense that means anything to readers of poetry, the Common Reader, Mason would insist, has to be brought into being. And the interest of such a reader is what Mason's criticism of Juvenal seeks to engage, as in the essay 'Is Juvenal a Classic?' This was published in 1963 in a volume dedicated to 'Satire', the essay appearing in the series *Critical Essays on Roman Literature*.[6] As an essay, it reveals Mason's expositional manner at its most extreme. Long and wandering, and almost a book in itself, the essay takes the reader on extensive tours of Roman and English poetical worlds. It is called, self-effacingly, 'An Introductory Essay', and Mason intends it for non-specialist students of Latin (of which, among Common Readers, there must now be fewer than ever). It is, nevertheless, like most of the criticism of H. A. Mason, stocked with quotation. The idea is to treat Juvenal as a poet to be read, not as a 'classical text'. The assumption is that the most useful context for understanding Juvenal's satire, which is literature, is a literary one. The literary context Mason constructs comprises other poets and poems; those that inspired Juvenal and those Juvenal inspired. In the course of his essay, Mason steers this way and that between Juvenal, Dryden, Boileau, Shakespeare, Ben Jonson, Donne, Marvell, Oldham, Pope, Tennyson, W. B. Yeats, T. S. Eliot and T. F. Powys. All these figures are quoted or adduced. All, as *points de repère*, are woven into a seamless fabric of timeless values. Again, Mason's critical principle is enacted by the method employed. His mind moves freely through literature, past and present. The standard by which Juvenal is to be judged is communally achieved: Juvenal is the test of other poets' art; theirs is the test of his. On both sides, positive and negative points are made. Mason's comparisons *between* poets contain critical criteria *within* poetry itself.

In a lengthy preamble, Mason stresses the amateur status of his contribution to classical studies. He also asserts a main principle of his approach to critical activity: 'The principal object of this essay is to communicate delight, or to make faintly comprehensible what Dryden may have meant when he said of Juvenal, "he gives me as much pleasure as I can bear."' Mason starts by saying that no one really knows what Juvenal is like. Why exactly, therefore, should he be regarded as a 'classic'? He argues Juvenal has been mistakenly described as a moral satirist. In reality, Juvenal is not serious in moral terms. Instead, as Mason shows by a detailed account of Juvenal's debt to the epigrams of Martial, his art of satire is much closer to the art of shock. Juvenal, Mason claims, shocks the reader in order to delight him: '. . . his whole art consists in opportunism and the surprise effects obtainable from deliberate inconsistency.'[7] To this end, Juvenal revels in the obscene. The reason is not that Juvenal uses satires to conduct social or moral *exposés*. Even in Satire 3, he should not be seen as a commentator on his times: he has no interest in the vices of contemporary Roman life. His interests (Mason argues) are not social but literary: declamations function as literary criticism. Ultimately he is 'serious' in a different way. Mason's account of Juvenal, by insisting on the mysterious way wit, comedy, hilarity, cruelty and obscenity can all combine in 'serious' art, challenges tendencies to take art 'seriously'. It extends the principle Mason identifies and praises in the humanism of More's *Utopia*. And it is a further stage in Mason's development of the idea of humanism. Humanism is not always accommodated to modern standards of the humane or genteel. In Juvenal it is couched in wit designed to reveal things as they are. It thus represents frequently the opposite of such standards. Juvenal's realism is not social observational realism. It flows from tone; a play of mind shown in the clash between content and manner. And the 'chief ingredient in Juvenal's wit,' Mason argues, is *'the belittling remark in the style of epic grandeur.'* According to Mason, the effect is unlike the use of epic by later poets who were also classical translators: Boileau, Dryden and Pope. But it is clear, nevertheless (from comments like the following), that reading these poets has helped Mason to awareness of the quality in Juvenal's Latin: 'It is a complex effect, for it both mocks and belittles the epic style and raises the trivial or sordid subject only to let it fall lower than ever.'[8] In awareness of tone, Mason applies what he says the professional scholars of Latin have failed to exhibit: consciousness of the *poetic* substance of their material of study. He thereby prepares the ground for a claim pursued more widely in his criticism: that the best guide to classics of the past lies in works of poets who have translated them. Unless we are inward with poetry, as poetry, enjoying it to the full, meaning evades us. Mason raises the question, where poetry is concerned, of the kind of 'learning' that matters.

Hence Mason attends to imitators and translators of Juvenal. These are not only used to show Juvenalian spirit as caught by later writers. They also illustrate how later writers (such as Samuel Johnson) differ from Juvenal. Mason does not confine himself to English literature in the form of ostensible imitations or translations of the satires. Sometimes, passages from Juvenal have inspired art different in kind, and works not always true to the original: Mason cites a passage from Jonson's *Sejanus* to reveal Juvenalian qualities undigested. Even Dryden, who did direct translations of the *Satires* and in some ways comes closest to Juvenal, has missed his real spirit: 'What none of the English versions supplies is the harsh belittling sarcasm or contemptuous animus which Juvenal directs against his figures.' By examining first ninth, then tenth, then third, then sixth, satires Mason brings out Juvenal's incoherence as moralist: his lack of consistency. This, to Mason, is a freedom of reading Juvenal: 'Juvenal discourages the moral cataloguer in us and sets us free to follow the varieties of his wit.'[9] And the pleasure of following Juvenal's wit is a liberation of literature itself. Literature belongs in its own world and has an integral life: it is not reducible to terms external to itself, biographical, social or moral. It questions comfortable, appropriating assumptions of all these realms. The importance of classical literature for English readers, Mason says, is to challenge the terms of reference of a culture that, to the extent that it remains Christocentric, remains medieval. In this liberating sense Mason's 'humanism' is 'liberal'.

For Mason the common sense of mankind is subversive. As a critical standard, common sense is therefore likely to produce judgements exactly at odds with the received scales of English literary value that are based on a sense less than common, because the product of values that are culturally produced. In his criticism of Shakespeare, *Shakespeare's Tragedies of Love* (1970),[10] Mason's aim is again to realise a consensus. In the course of this work, he reports on the feasibility of establishing common readings of Shakespeare's plays. The objective is to transcend assemblages of personal views making up modern opinion in general and academic criticism in particular. The possibility sought is one where a genuine because text-based agreement about Shakespeare's plays, however rudimentary, can be had by different people: a *'common sense* about *main* things in the plays'.[11] For Mason, criticism of Shakespeare is at fault because it has too often tried to be 'new' without being fresh. Thus it is plagued by merely private responses and personal views. His complaint is not that criticism has not been subjective enough but too subjective. Common sense, the establishment of a sense that is held in common, is for Mason an effort to rise above individual opinion to truths that hold true for more than one mind. It is also an effort to show what *Scrutiny* critics, for all their achievements, signally failed to achieve: re-examination of the grounds of Shakespeare's pre-eminence in English. Therefore Mason aspires to read Shakespeare in the light of standards that by including, also question the modern. It is perhaps misleading to call these 'classical' standards, unless we acknowledge that it is possible for values to exist that do not belong exclusively to one age or time. It is, however, clear that Mason's own standards, at least, embrace the criteria of a period in English culture when the values of the classics of Greece and Rome came vigorously alive, and in so doing created contemporary classics which challenged Shakespeare's supremacy.

Mason thus subverts Romantic criticism of Shakespeare, itself a root of the unradical because still reverential treatment of Shakespeare by 'radical' critics. Mason is like the authors of eighteenth-century 'Prefaces' to Shakespeare in questioning the payment of uncritical homage; the tendency, among admirers of Shakespeare, to ignore for example negligent, hasty or wilfully contrived strokes or allow Shakespeare (as his friend Ben Jonson never did) the supreme place in English literature without full acknowledgement of faults. Mason's criticisms of Shakespeare will therefore seem like sacrilege to some, to others a breath of fresh air.

Yet Mason's *Shakespeare's Tragedies of Love* is still probably the twentieth-century's most decisive critique of nineteenth-century attitudes and approaches to Shakespeare. Mason drives home his attack by recalling otherwise 'superseded' responses to Shakespeare that the nineteenth century was reacting against. Thus he says that Shakespeare betrays time and again the rush and hurry of his drama's composition. An inconsistency in the plot of *Othello* seems '*proof* that [Shakespeare] began the play without knowing how it was going to develop'. *King Lear* shows evidence of 'Radical Incoherence'. To the same end, Mason plays down interest that grew up in the eighteenth century (and became central in the nineteenth thanks partly to the prestige of the novel) in Shakespeare's characters. Mason's commentary, anticipating Belsey's *The Subject of Tragedy* in one way, at odds with it in another, is a criticism of such interest. Characters limited to specificities of one particular set of events elude realities revealed by Shakespeare through 'general nature'. Thus the nurse in *Romeo and Juliet* is not important as an individual character; she is rather 'a vehicle' for various 'moments'. Mason writes of *Othello* that:

> I have assumed that my major effort towards an agreed account must lie in persuading many people that they have been indulging in a wantonly exaggerated interest in character, that they have assumed that every single personage offered a consistent character, that the play is a jig-saw puzzle, every piece of which is made up of 'character-material'; that, in short, the play is *exclusively* 'character in action'.[12]

But the radicalism of *Shakespeare's Tragedies of Love* is mainly expressed in repudiation of a practice reflected in 'radical theory': critical interpretation. Mason, by contrast, neither writes nor favours interpretative criticism (for example, that *Romeo and Juliet* can be understood as working out of processes of, say, Fate). Instead of interpreting Shakespeare, Mason sees, lives through and re-lives what happens moment by moment in Shakespeare's plays, to follow, as in *King Lear*, a play's 'central stream', even where this clashes with 'common sense': 'We must become fluid so that the play can take us out of our ordinary comfortable ways of thinking and feeling, seduce us into leaving both common sense and cleverness behind and make us enter into combinations that had never before presented themselves to anyone but Shakespeare.' Mason's concern is whether we agree what is happening, how we feel about it and whether, when we take individual moments together, they amount to a 'whole', a sense of each play entire. His Shakespearean readings therefore contrast with views of Shakespearean drama which predetermine the overall cut-and-dried coherence or unity in plays. As far as 'unity' is concerned, it is Mason (the humanist) who does the rejecting: 'When a great artist finds himself grappling with the ultimate causes of things he does not characteristically produce a doctrine of any kind.'[13]

The effect of Mason's trying to find, and failing to find, 'unity' in Shakespearean plays is the more compellingly to de-romanticise Shakespearean drama. The 'provisional hypothesis' of *Shakespeare's Tragedies of Love* is 'that it might be the special contribution of serious drama to relate love and death in significant wholes, where the whole cannot be significant unless we feel that life as a whole has been re-sourced thereby'. According to Mason, *Romeo and Juliet* fails to do this. Here, Shakespeare is revealed as opportunist, a verdict reached by comparing the play with its source. *Othello* also fails: '[Shakespeare's] lovers are lesser figures than he meant them to be.' Mason's account of *Othello* stresses comic touches in scenes between Iago and Roderigo; that Desdemona should not be seen as helpless or a wholly innocent party; that we should take Brabantio more seriously and see Shakespeare as not always in control of his plot. The main point is that Othello descends beyond fool to beast. Shakespeare, in showing us the triumph of evil, gives birth to a play we cannot bear. The verdict recalls both the seventeenth-century outrage of Thomas Rymer and the eighteenth-century anguish of Samuel Johnson when confronted by scenes in the play: 'Othello is much more like Macbeth than any other play, the main difference being the want in Othello of a steadying confidence in the possible goodness in the world. Othello is consequently sickening and unbearable.'[14]

In de-romanticising Shakespeare, Mason simultaneously revives elements of an Augustan poetic. In his analysis of *Antony and Cleopatra* and *King Lear* Mason notes moral ambiguity in Cordelia's plain speaking, and how early sympathy for Lear is offset by contempt. But the standard Mason recalls, and applies negatively to Shakespeare, is not one of Order. Mason is impatient with hackneyed metaphysical and psychological interpretations of the storm in *Lear* on human grounds: 'I am sick and tired of hearing people discuss Shakespeare exclusively in terms of order and disorder. I don't wish to deny Shakespeare his metaphysical aspirations, but I do wish to stress his human concern, concern at the level where human beings are still recognizable as such.'[15] Even so, he says, the central current runs not through Lear but Gloucester, whose physical sufferings (he is blinded not soaked) are immeasurably worse. When commenting on these central, deeply painful scenes (in Act III), Mason's style becomes tense and pointed, almost annotatory. The chapter becomes a series of short sections. Argumentative flow is suspended. Critical eloquence is curbed. Mason then operates from inside the experience produced upon him by the literary material in view. There is no room to theorise about it. When he comes to the end of the play, Mason rejects L. C. Knights's idea that 'we are still concerned with the inclusive vision of the whole'. Mason feels Lear's death makes 'sense of the play', but there is little obviously satisfying about the end. Whether Shakespeare is in full control, it is hinted, is open to question. Is it, in the end, a case of 'Radical Incoherence'? There is more than slight suggestion that Mason thinks that it is.

Discussion of *Antony and Cleopatra* is also dominated by

questions of coherence. The Antony of the play's beginning is not heroic but a fool, a clown. The description of Cleopatra in her barge, famed for poetic qualities, reduces human participation: it is a purple passage, not a view of Cleopatra we seriously consider. For Mason, the play fails as drama because dramatic realisation gives way to a feebler mode: narration. Antony's fall is not the fall of a hero, but something less. When he says 'Authority melts from me late', and reminisces on the past effectiveness of his words on Kings 'Like Boyes vnto a musse', 'we know that he never felt the moral bond involved in being the head of society': 'He is more like a retired Colonial governor, lamenting in Bournemouth or on the Riviera his inability to boss his European servants as he used to boss his "boys" of Africa.'[16] Mason wishes to explode the glamorous romantic myth of Antony's and Cleopatra's love. Thus he attends to differences between things shown, dramatically, and what we are told. Again, his judgement qualifies admiration. But Shakespeare is not demoted. The 'Shakespearean standard' (internal to literature) by which Mason measures plays, and to which he refers throughout his account but does not discuss, is *Macbeth*. Perhaps this is because of the relative concentration of *Macbeth*, its focused intensity compared with other tragedies. If so, this in its turn suggests how a criterion Mason is bringing to Shakespeare is satisfied by the most successful examples of ancient Greek tragedy. Mason's work on Shakespeare is at one with his studies exploring realisations and transmutations of Greek literary culture in England.

This is the theme of *To Homer through Pope* (1972), where Mason again appeals (this time via Pope) to eighteenth-century criteria designed to undercut the orthodoxies inherited by the twentieth century from the nineteenth. Mason therefore again goes over ground covered in his essay on Juvenal: scholars of Greek or Latin are not necessarily best fitted to know the classics in a way that they are worth knowing. Full meaning is reserved for the poets. Therefore, Mason concludes, modern English versions of the *Iliad* should be abandoned as 'too merely modern'. A better way to approach Homer is through earlier poetical translators.

However, in choosing to approach Homer through a particular translation, that of Pope, it follows that Mason must reject Arnold's conception of what is truly heroic in classical epics. This, in turn, is because for Mason, Arnold's sense of the ancient epics comes too close to admiration for Victorian 'noble' ideals. In Pope, Mason is seeking a path to Homer unobstructed by the legacy of values specifically Victorian. His interest includes very un-Victorian understandings of humanity in a work which is 'highly disreputable and profoundly ambiguous'. It includes fascination with the imaginative continuity between human and animal worlds, even at the point at which heroes turn into brutes; it embraces a human world spurred into action by naked wrath, *kudos* and prestige. It involves recognising parallels between life on earth and the life of gods on Olympus, with realisation that, in Homer's conception, the gods do not care. Their power is immense. They are almighty. But they can be pettier than the pettiest of mortals. In a sense, Mason suggests, gods in the *Iliad* are Homer's playthings, his inventions: 'like Shakespeare's fairies, they shade off into folk-lore.'[17] For Mason, it is not Pope but Dryden (who translated Book I of the *Iliad*) who captures with most success this dual vision of Homeric gods.

Mason argues that confronting Pope's *Iliad* means realising similarities between Homer's and our world, and the depth of the difference. Close affinities (such as moments of imaginative contact which exist in Homer's similes of animate and inanimate nature), must be balanced against its profoundly alien nature, evident in Homer's extreme detachment from his creations. Both Pope and Dryden have shown how dangerous and frightening a world Homer's can be. But they also bring out Homer's eternal nature, the essential principles which have not changed between Homer's time and their own, nor between their time and ours. Mason finds Pope bringing Homer's nature alive both for immediate contemporaries and future generations. To do this, Pope, according to Mason, trades local linguistic faithfulness to effects in the original to interests dictated by the larger structural affinities between Homer's poem and his own. He therefore at times imposes a contemporary consciousness on Homer (and enobles heroes and Christianises gods) to produce analogous parallels between gods and men. Unusually, Mason sees Pope's procedure as not just some mistake, a result of blind adherence to Augustan 'norms', but as deliberate policy carried out with eyes wide open, and one Pope made clear in notes to the translation. Mason again stresses the notes to explain Pope's renderings of Homer's scenes of inanimate nature:

> If Pope appreciated Nature in the raw as something separate from Man, he annihilated it in order to construct something greater, a Nature that formed a unity with Human Nature and a Human Nature thought of as something far more important than inanimate nature in the small or in the large.[18]

In some ways, Pope (in, say, filling out from himself details not there in the Greek text) was more sympathetic to Homer than we are, not less. In other ways, Pope's creative individuality was limited by translation: '... much in Homer's epic checked and thwarted his natural impulses as a writer.' Mason's case is that in translation, Pope was unable to be wholly serious as poet; 'serious' in for example the way poetry of the *Rape of the Lock*, his mock-epic, relates freely and availably to the *little* absurdities of life. For Mason, Pope's Homeric heroes, like Arnold's, are too noble-vague and lack intelligible vitality. Pope's mock-epic, paradoxically, is therefore the place serious feelings about epic are given full poetic embodiment:

> It is a pity that Pope did not realize that, if his translation of the *Iliad* as a whole was to become a real classic rivalling Shakespeare, he would have to be as seriously concerned with his epic theme as he was with Clarissa's, and would therefore have had to write in the style of his Clarissa rather than that of his Sarpedon.[19]

Mason believes we cannot appreciate epic, and therefore the *Iliad,* without our own conception of the heroic; a modern term of comparison. The translator 'must believe in a hero who at the same time appears like a modern hero and like what Homer writes about'. For this reason Pope assimilated his Homeric hero to contemporary ideals of the Gentleman, but thus cuts us off. But moments in the *Iliad,* both Pope's and Homer's (such as the episode of Hector and Andromache) have timeless human appeal. This is not, Mason claims, because they remind us of the brutality of the fighting hero's life in war but because of qualities literally closer to home. For Mason, Pope's version of this episode (as Dryden's) is limited in success: Pope sentimentalises the last parting of the Trojan hero from his wife. And yet, when this is admitted, Mason can contend that Pope's translation leads to the permanent heart of Homer: 'his humanity'. Modern prose versions, Mason decisively concludes, do not. Of the latter he writes: 'My verdict on these translations is as depressing as could be: they do not transmit any of the qualities that make the *Iliad* distinguished or deserving of our attention.' Mason's verdict on Pope's *Iliad* is that overall and at many moments it is a successful translation. Not perfect, but the best we have. Pope's *Iliad*, like his *Odyssey*, at least offers credible speech. Here is Mason's crushing comment upon a twentieth-century version of the classic meeting between Odysseus and Nausikaa in the *Odyssey*:

> ... at this place in the book I found Professor Lattimore's poetry actually *repulsive*. As a child and an adolescent the taste of the material from which tram and bus tickets were then made was not repulsive to me (unlike highly flavoured chewing gums) but monotonous in the long run and saliva-absorbent. As a hardened reader, whose critical writing first saw print in 1927, I have had to chew the literary equivalent of much devitalized cellulose and have so learned to distinguish the respectably mediocre from the ever-living and the completely dead.[20]

But a summary of this kind must inevitably crudify Mason's position, and cannot do justice to the complexities engendered by Mason's refusal to accept the simplifications of a criticism designed to accord with, or bring out, a 'doctrine'. The same must be said of any attempt to summarise his equally subtle and compact study *The Tragic Plane* (1985), which, excluding a lavishly (and poetically) annotated edition of Wyatt,[21] is the most recent of Mason's book-length critical works. Here, as Mason synthesises his past thinking on Shakespeare and Homer, his convictions bring him once more to the questions of eternal literary value that are bound to be provoked by attempts imaginatively to reach out to literary productions three thousand years in the past. In this new context, the independence and integrity of the literary realm are again stressed, as is the unsatisfactoriness of trying to account for literature in terms external to literature. The inherent difficulties, Mason implicitly and explicitly insists, have to be faced. In recent years the 'radical' critics have sought to 'demystify' literary study by making the literary experience less mysterious. Mason takes precisely the opposite line: ancient Greek tragedies, he claims in his 'Preface' to *The Tragic Plane*, only can be true, as true now as they ever were, if 'Tragedy is ultimately a *mystery*, a unique phenomenon which cannot be classified under any of the heads used in the discourse of philosophers, theologians, psychologists, Marxists, structuralists, or post-structuralists.'[22] But, although Mason is of the view that tragedy is mystery, there are nevertheless, he believes, general properties it is profitable to discuss, even if tragedy cannot be ultimately defined. Just as the spectrum of modern approaches to literary study prevents tragedy being seen as it is, so do the forms of discussing tragedy handed down by the professional scholars who represent an ideologically reverse extreme. For this reason Mason resists the 'historicist' approach; there is no such thing, he thinks, as 'tragic development'. The notion is a scholarly invention of the post-Darwinian age. For his own part, Mason grounds the study of tragedy on the response of the reader. Tragedy belongs and does not belong to art. Only in art can we luxuriate in tragedy. Tragic events in life can be too painful for art. Here, therefore, as in all Mason's major criticism, a careful wavering balance or poise in critical argument is preserved. He characteristically holds in tension thought tugging in opposite directions at once. Tragedy is a matter of unity and ambiguity; tragic figures are neither entirely Stoic individuals behaving regardless of Fate, nor mere representative ideas, deprived of human individuality. But they are not just individuals: tragedy involves a whole society. The tragic end seems a finality, and yet the end becomes tragic 'because the final event seems to have been *inevitable*'. But, behind these juxtapositions, this reasoned 'liberal' balance of opposing perspectives, Mason's thought remains radical. It does so even while exalting literature above central doctrines of politics or religion. When we are experiencing the world's greatest tragedies *'Christianity never happened.'* And tragedy is as fundamentally at odds with bougeois values. In this claim Mason, though he fends off Marxists, can explore tragedy by going directly to Marx, and to *Das Kommunistische Manifest*:

> What we have to face is the impossibility of having Tragedy so long as we live under a 'social contract'. If each soul in society is a well-protected metal sphere, entering into only selfish interests with every other metal sphere, keeping itself to itself, as we say, there can only be bumps or wars of extermination. Neither is tragic. To discover a society in which tragedy *is* possible, we have to return to Shakespeare and the Greek tragic poets. Not to their actual, historical societies, of course, for there exploitation and cruelty were as rampant as in the nineteenth-century world pictured by Karl Marx. What we should direct our attention to in the societies presented in their tragedies are the deep bonds underlying everything . . .[23]

In stressing these bonds, these principles of connection which underlie everything, Mason's humanism makes Marxist critics seem bourgeois.

That Mason has spent so much time criticising literature in its traditionally grandest modes reflects the sense in which his humanism is, indeed, 'liberal'. It liberates readers excluded from enjoying such forms. But Mason's is also a radical humanism (to use the term that Eagleton once used to describe Leavis). This appears in his total commitment to the task of elucidating the constituents and effect of particular examples of art judged in terms of the properties that art creates for itself. And just as Mason demands that literature be taken on its own terms – not as anything else using literature for ulterior motives: 'conservative' or 'revolutionary' politics, feminism, social history, linguistics, psychology or religion – so his own criticism makes it difficult to regard modern criticism as a mere department of the academic business world or media industry, the medium of the modern intellectual *poseur* or just another professional expertise.

And the spirit of Mason's definition of the critic is there in his critical manner. He can be devastatingly outspoken: 'No doubt I should instantly be challenged to name one other eccentric beside myself if I said that *we* have been longing for somebody to wring Edgar's neck.'[24] A long digressive passage of quotation and comment, going off in various directions, can suddenly be reeled in by a strikingly pointed and abrupt statement of what it has all been for: 'Dryden, then, I am claiming, makes it possible for us to feel that this is a great moment in a great poem.'[25] But Mason can be also absurdly guarded and oblique, particularly, though not exclusively, in his earlier work. Here is a prize example from his Juvenal essay: 'Surely it is not merely snobbish to call provincial the man who would direct us at this moment to consider whether Juvenal is not being all-too-autobiographical here?'[26] This tendency to put things in roundabout ways (in 'my Polonius fashion') has the excuse that it is produced by the isolation of Mason's critical stance, with the problem of not knowing to whom, quite, he is meant to be speaking. But if on occasion Mason's syntax can create a kind of protective cocoon, woven from anxiety, in relaxed mood Mason can be extremely funny. He is usually laughing, at least in part, at himself (Eagleton and Carey, also humorists, laugh only at *others*). Mason, often, creates for himself an affable comic *persona* and does a good imitation of the blundering scholar. Winding his way painfully forward, he can then apologise to readers for his slowness of pace. A favourite ploy is to cast himself as the unwitting and slightly incredulous innocent victim of his own outrageous views, patiently reiterating, in the face of the acrimony he detects is about to descend upon him, his grounds for thinking as he does. Elegantly refusing to bite back, he then talks as a parent would talk to a naughty but dim-witted child. On one occasion, Mason imagines Pope and Homer walking arm-in-arm through the windows of his study so that Pope can tick him off, in refined quasi-*Dunciad* eighteenth-century terms, for presuming to know Homer better than he does. Fancies of this kind are a major source of the humour of Mason's criticism. Mason takes pleasure in introducing himself into the context of his critical discourse. This he does with a human touch, and, usually, a half-comic parade of elaborate regrets for having imposed on the reader. To some extent, this is an aspect of his deliberate critical art; a pose. But it remains an attractive quality – a nice change from the usual run of self-important modern critical officialese. And it also signals the real humanity of the 'liberal–humanism' Mason brings to the critical act; a humanity that allows him, from time to time, to admit having altered views, or changed his mind. At a time when fashionable modern critics play up their 'commitment' or forge ahead from one book to the next in pursuit of their 'project', it is refreshing to confront a critic who seems capable of second thoughts. On reading an obscure unfinished Ph.D. thesis on the drama of Sophocles, Mason confides at a point in his latest book, 'I then came to see how mistaken I had been in the implied basic theory of my *Shakespeare's Tragedies of Love*'.[27]

Also refreshing is Mason's irreverent attitude to the conventional form, or forms, of criticism. Mason exploits all of the twentieth-century's standard forms: article, review article (given powerful currency by the practice of *Scrutiny*), essay and book. But Mason challenges the generic integrity of twentieth-century critical form. By this means he insists on the provisional nature of his printed thoughts. His essay on Juvenal is 'An Introduction'; his book on Shakespeare is subtitled 'An Examination of the Possibility of Common Readings . . .'; his 'pamphlet' examination of Wyatt's poems (*Editing Wyatt: An Examination of the Collected Poems* (1972))[28] includes 'suggestions for an improved edition' and is itself a lifetime's work; his own 'improved edition' of Wyatt is really a book, quite unlike any modern edition of any poet. Mason's work on Wyatt spans his whole career and illustrates, as we have seen Mason set out to show, the fruitlessness of the division between scholar and critic. Criticism, for Mason, though it gives point to scholarship, does not in the end supersede it. Labour is essential. Accuracy is all; as Mason personally demonstrates when he corrects hundreds of mistakes (on various levels of meaning of the word) in the Muir–Thomson edition. But Mason does more than merely suggest the need for painstaking attention to detail in establishing a text. He makes a large point about the qualities editing requires. These are more and less mundane than usually perceived. If editors must accurately transcribe their originals (a rarer talent than we might expect), they must also display imaginative participation in their text. As far as Mason is concerned, participation is continuous with the critical and with the creative act. The editor, like the translator of poetry, is guided by sense. He must be in tune with his author. He must, like the critic, live through poetry to know, with the authority experience confers, the best available readings. For Mason editing is not mechanical: it is re-creative; a kind of translation. Mason assumes that editions are published to be used. The same holds true of all his critical studies; hence the amazingly detailed indexes to Mason's books. These imply and encourage participating readership of the literature each book is about. Mason's criticism may therefore be seen as a series of experiments in critical form, and is characterised by variety of approach. No 'formula' is adopted. Nor in any does Mason attempt to exhaust his theme. The important thing is to establish a stance, as in *To Homer through Pope* where Mason suggests the *Iliad* entire by a series of, as it were, 'cuts' into the subject. His forms, like his manner, reveal a creator-*manqué*.

Consequently, Mason's relation to Leavis is not that of theory, but an appropriately critical relation. In terms of reading and taste, his criticism offers a radical (i.e. fundamental) challenge to Leavis. It therefore escapes the parochialism of modern academic criticism that Leavis's criticism, despite itself, has come to sustain. However, aspects of Mason's method as critic recall Leavis's criticism. In grappling with the internal features of a text, Mason searches, like Leavis, for essential moments, key passages or isolable lines which capture a sense of the whole. Mason's practice (as Leavis's) is to make points by comparing and contrasting one passage with another so that they 'illustrate' each other, not simply the views of the critic. But Mason more than Leavis has the scholar's feel for the ways poets tend to be indebted to poets and traces borrowings which, once assembled, assist critical judgement in a fashion that Leavis did not exploit. Compared with, say, Ricks, Mason is not a 'practical critic'; an exponent of the style of close analysis usually attributed to the *Scrutiny* school. Mason's method is at once more concentrated and narrow than the 'practical critic's' (on the level of the word), yet simultaneously broader. Mason's ability to concentrate attention is to be found in his investigations of various individual terms, whether English (such as discussions of the 'heroic' or of 'tragedy'), or foreign (as in analyses of ancient Greek words *kudos, ate,* and *harmartia*). But Mason's field of vision is wider than the 'practical critic's' in its attention to the passage, or extract. 'Homer's similes,' writes Mason, 'prepare us for seeing something that is true of the *Iliad* as a whole, and one of the central truths of the poem.'[29] While the passage may sample the larger material from which it is drawn, it is often not subject to the detailed scrutiny of a *Scrutiny* essay, nor is it 'analysed' so much as 'set', or deployed. Other passages (some even invented by Mason, or consisting of his translation of an ancient text) are then invoked as a foil, or 'control', like poetical extracts printed as notes to eighteenth-century editions of English or classical texts. As previously suggested, we are often kept in suspense about Mason's intentions. As far as possible the reader must reach conclusions himself. He must make independent contact with the passage or extract. For this reason Mason's use of quotation (judged by incidence and length) has to be great. It proportionally relegates critical *vis-à-vis* creative text.

The sources Mason takes his quotations from are extremely varied, surprising rather than obscure, and seem often strikingly appropriate once they are recalled (as where discussion of feuding in *Huckleberry Finn* is used as a means of approaching, getting inside, Shakespeare's conception in *Romeo and Juliet,* or where Browning's Duchess is used to suggest one view of Desdemona's behaviour towards men other than her husband). In these examples, the surprise comes from being made to appreciate affinities that exist between works from different periods, and which a more devoted 'period' specialist than Mason might be unready, or unable, to point out. By this means, Mason makes us see the works as concerned essentially with the same things, in a continuum. Thus critical standards they are subject to are also, it follows, the same. The classics of one period, and one nation, become a critical commentary on the classics of another. All are, in an extended sense of the term, translations. Therefore Mason's life-long interest in translation may be seen as related to his critical practice, itself a form of 'trans-lation' because it is a carrying forward to new life in the present literature and critical thought of the past. Pursuit of criticism for Mason thus becomes what Leavis (after Eliot) had called it: a 'common pursuit'. But in Mason 'the common pursuit' becomes a means by which individual attitudes dissolve in a larger whole. They are humbly asserted, not with the bold individualism with which Leavis asserted his own. The passages and extracts Mason assembles are reminders of his criticism's pre-Leavisian, Arnoldian roots. But they also denote effort to go further back still, to what Johnson had called the judgement of mankind. If Mason's criticism anywhere expresses a doctrine, this would be it. Quoting a passage from Johnson's *Preface to Shakespeare*, Mason finds 'a far more acceptable account of the relation of great literature to life' (than can be found in Aristotle):

> It rests, as Johnson makes clear in his critical writings, on a doctrine of General Nature. Ours is an age of insane worship of the particular and an insane mistrust of the general. I must therefore ... insist on the indispensability of this doctrine of General Nature. If there is no ideal norm of nature to justify the word 'human', then the basic words in our language have no reference.[30]

But Mason's taste has its bounds. It is clear that for Mason, American writing (the odd reference aside, and discounting Eliot, Pound and James) hardly figures at all. This is because what matters about English Literature for Mason is not that it is written in English; or expresses the 'Englishness' obnoxious to critical writers hostile to *Scrutiny*. Mason's concern, like Arnold's, is larger than literature in English, and it is in this latter respect that Mason has offered a comprehensive and coherent view of English tradition that stands as a genuine alternative to Leavis's. At a time when many English critics were developing thought on the importance of Donne and metaphysical poetry, Mason was drawing attention to values in the poetry of Wyatt (and its European links), a subject to which Mason has returned again and again. Thus Mason, by painting a different picture of English tradition, itself resting on a different idea and starting from a different place, has aspired to include with and in English literature the literature of Europe and the classics of

Greece and Rome. Translation, Mason's primary 'idea', is a product of this European vision, as is his sense of the relations between serious and irreverent thinking seeing and feeling. All Mason's major publications allude to the movement, as Pope called it, from grave to gay, from lively to severe. The points of reference in Leavis's criticism, as in Arnold's, seem earnest by contrast. Mason makes Leavis seem a critic of the last age.

While therefore Mason is concerned to offset *Scrutiny* readings of Shakespeare, he also aspires to refute arguments Leavis had personally advanced: for example Leavis's uncritical (as Mason sees it) praise of *Othello*. (In *The Tragic Plane*, Mason prefers the ending of the Greek *Women of Trachis* to the ending of *Othello*, 'placing' Shakespeare – in Leavis's sense of the word – in the light of the more ancient work.) Compared with the Greek play, Shakespeare's *Othello* fails to achieve the true 'Tragic Ending'. Mason says that there is characteristically something impure in Shakespeare's endings: 'It is always a sad falling-off in his plays when we have a double consciousness that now the chief actor is about to make his last, impressive, exit, and now the hero is going to meet his death. In such cases there is an inevitable impurity in our response.'[31] Not that Mason is arguing for a lowering of the art of Shakespeare's age in favour of another's. But he is more inclusive than Leavis, able to keep more areas of literature simultaneously in play. Repeatedly in his criticism, Leavis had raised the 'Shakespearean', and lowered the 'Augustan'. Mason raises the 'Augustan', but not at the expense of the 'Shakespearean', and certainly puts it no higher. It is unlikely that Leavis would have seriously disagreed with the following praise of Enobarbus's wit: 'When an age can command wit such as this, it is in a finer condition than that of the years following the restoration of Charles II or the early years of the eighteenth century.'[32] Or with this, from *To Homer through Pope:* '. . . I shall still contend that Homer's simplicity is grander than Pope's, and that Shakespeare's Great Creating Nature is greater than the Ideal Nature of the best Augustan writers.'[33]

The difference is that Mason is able to perceive a continuity between the Augustans and the Renaissance that Leavis and his followers could not. While, for Leavis, the great breakthrough (the revolution) in seventeenth-century poetry was made by Donne, for Mason the great poet of the early years of the seventeenth century was Jonson. But, even if Mason's taste for Jonson could be interpreted as the fruit of critical seeds Leavis had sown (in passing comments), Mason deviates decisively from Leavis wherever Leavis cooperates with, and consolidates, literary historical conceptions inherited from Eliot. In Mason's view, English poetry in the late seventeenth century did not undergo spiritual degeneration, 'dissociation of sensibility'. Instead, it achieved a fresh and more profoundly creative relationship with the poetry of the past. It rose to new heights. And this rise is seen not as a departure from Jonson's work, but continuation of its humane quality in the best examples of creative translation: just as Jonson's was itself continuation of the humane quality of Wyatt's. As in his essay on Juvenal, Mason rehabilitates a non-metaphysical value for 'wit'. Mason, whether he is writing of the 'lost art of the Augustans'[34] or focusing on an aspect of Pope that Leavis had ignored, brings the Augustan achievement in translation to the centre of a conception of English achievement which is simultaneously more-than-English. For Mason the Augustans pale in the face of the Greeks. But in rising to the Augustans, and to the classics in general, Mason challenges respect for the Romantic orthodoxy reinforced by Leavis, as by critics who have followed in his wake. It is by exploring so vitally the historical and permanent principles of the humanist ideal that Mason makes modern criticism more than a matter of radical intent.

Notes

1. *Humanism and Poetry in the Early Tudor Period: An Essay* (Routledge and Kegan Paul: London, 1959; second impression, 1966), pp. 262, 289.
2. *ibid.*, p. 3.
3. *ibid.*, pp. 34, 33.
4. *ibid.*, pp. 61, 65.
5. *ibid.*, pp. 178, 182, 185.

6. 'Is Juvenal a Classic?' *Arion*, **1** (1962), pp. 8–44, and **2** (1962), 39–79. Reprinted in *Critical Essays on Roman Literature (Satire)*, (ed. J. P. Sullivan) (Routledge and Kegan Paul: London, 1963), p. 138.
7. *ibid.*, p. 107.
8. *ibid.*, pp. 101, 102.
9. *ibid.*, pp. 115, 174.
10. *Shakespeare's Tragedies of Love: An Examination of the Possibility of Common Readings of Romeo and Juliet, Othello, King Lear & Anthony and Cleopatra* (Chatto and Windus: London, 1970).
11. *ibid.*, p. viii.
12. *ibid.*, pp. 69, 35, 60.
13. *ibid.*, pp. 170, 20.
14. *ibid.*, pp. 55, 160, 105.
15. *Shakespeare's Tragedies of Love*, pp. 195–6.
16. *ibid.*, p. 260. The discussion of *Antony and Cleopatra* is an amended version of *'Antony and Cleopatra*: Angelic Strength – Organic Weakness?' *Cambridge Quarterly*, **I**, 3 (Summer 1966), 209–35.
17. *To Homer through Pope: An Introduction to Homer's Iliad and Pope's Translation* (Chatto and Windus: London, 1972), pp. 94, 40, 56.
18. *ibid.*, p. 69.
19. *ibid.*, pp. 137, 156.
20. *ibid.*, pp. 127, 177, 186, 204.
21. *Sir Thomas Wyatt: A Literary Portrait, Selected Poems with full notes and commentaries and critical introduction* (Bristol Classical Press: Bristol, 1986).
22. *The Tragic Plane* (Clarendon Press: Oxford, 1985), p. vi.
23. *ibid.*, pp. 96, 36, 44.
24. *Shakespeare's Tragedies of Love*, p. 222.
25. *To Homer through Pope*, p. 57.
26. *Critical Essays on Roman Literature*, p. 138.
27. *The Tragic Plane*, p. 106.
28. *Editing Wyatt: An Examination of Collected Poems of Sir Thomas Wyatt together with suggestions for an improved edition* (Cambridge Quarterly Publications: Cambridge, 1972). See also 'Second Thoughts: Sir Thomas Wyatt and the Birds of Fortune: A Postscript', *Cambridge Quarterly*, **VIII**, 2 (1978), 191–6.
29. *To Homer through Pope*, p. 94.
30. *The Tragic Plane*, p. 101.
31. *ibid.*, p. 91.
32. *Shakespeare's Tragedies of Love*, p. 236.
33. *To Homer through Pope*, p. 72.
34. *ibid.*, p. 67.

6
Liberal Humanists II: W. W. Robson

> ... the cause of literary criticism – which I take to be the discovery of the truth about books.[1]

W. W. Robson is yet another university academic; like Carey and like Ricks, a Professor of English, and a fellow editor of the *Cambridge Quarterly* with Mason. In a serious but unambitious way he is also a poet. (A volume of his poems, *The Signs Among Us,* was published in 1968.)[2] Robson is not the celebrity that some of his more outspoken or publicity conscious academic colleagues have latterly become, but he has won wide respect and affection (partly no doubt for these very reasons) both in Britain and around the world. Perhaps it is a testimony to an irony in the modern academic profession of letters to say so, but one of the features of Robson's writing that distinguishes it from that of other critics discussed in this book is that, unusually for a modern academic, Robson clearly and unambiguously *loves* the literature which it is at the same time his professional business to write on, teach and discuss. His writing on literature is conducted in a way that combines literary passion, intellectual force and extensive but unostentatious learning in a mix which makes him one of the most communicatively successful literary critics writing today. At the same time he is one of the least sensational: his critical writings are exceptionally modest in manner and in tone, and implicitly play down the role of the critic. But one can see why Robson's criticism is sometimes disliked. His work clings doggedly to 'old' practices and ideas. At a time when 'radical' questions are being asked, Robson's criticism may seem stubbornly pitted against the modernity of modern criticism; reactionary, humdrum, plain or perversely antique, a summation of the values and vices of the 'liberal–humanist' don at his worst. Many features of the 'radicals'' caricature fit Robson quite well. Taken as a whole, Robson's criticism is diffident, judicious, cautious (in tone) and unapologetically wedded to the idea that literature is something which requires of us an open-hearted emotional response. His interests extend to writers as people, worth considering (sometimes if not always) as human beings who write. In his more recent critical work, Robson has specialised increasingly in addressing an audience sought both inside and outside the walls of professional academic life. This is because for Robson, criticism, if it is anything distinct (and the issue in Robson's criticism is opened for debate), is an instrument of *human* communication: it aims, however unfashionably, more to inform and to share than impress; but this is also the reason why anyone interested in the varied directions modern criticism can take, and the literature to which it is applied or from which it is derived, should regard the pages of W. W. Robson's criticism as Essential Reading.

Although Robson is a professional academic, his work is not at its best the direct product of specialist academic research. He is in essence an essayist. His criticism is shaped in an earlier mould. This is the case even in book-length studies such as *Modern English Literature* (1970).[3] This short, packed, helpful book comprises a series of miniature portraits of various twentieth-century writers. Where relevant, Robson gives an account of the movements to which the writers belong and, when appropriate, some salient biographical facts. At its centre, each portrait consists of a terse statement (a kind of monument or epitaph) to the memory of individual twentieth-century writers. Robson says what in his opinion are the best and worst things each writer has done, where they stand in the hierarchy of twentieth-century literary achievement as he perceives it and gives advice on how we might 'take' them. In responding to the requirements of the general reader, and to the needs of students wanting to know who the twentieth-century writers are, and where to start thinking about them, the book is a useful aid with an obvious educational motive. In this it resembles the more recent, more far reaching (chronologically if not critically) *Prologue to English Literature* (1986).[4] Both works suggest the sense in which Robson's criticism has a practical purpose and is, at least for part of the time, imaginatively attuned to the needs of the huge student audience on which the academic profession depends.

However the central texts of Robson's criticism, in some ways narrower, in other ways as broad, are two major collections of work which define the primary record of his critical reflection from the fifties to the eighties: *Critical Essays* (1966) and *The Definition of Literature* (1982).[5] These collections bring us to the centre of Robson's achievement in the form of recast or reprinted reviews. In creating reviews, Robson takes the *Scrutiny* approach: the review forms the core of an essay on the author or topic of the book under review. Now and again, criticism appearing first in review form is reset as an essay, with the original review portion kept intact. This reprinting and collecting of work designed for a different context has, needless to say, its dangers. At times we are conscious, in a way that intrudes, that the piece we are reading has been removed from the occasion which gave it its point, giving a piecemeal, tired and half-hearted look to the criticism. At other times (the majority) Robson's essay–reviews are self-contained: they have a life and form of their own. And always, Robson attempts a more permanent statement than is the rule in professional reviewer's reviews. In both collections, there are pieces which are purpose-built, even though others have appeared in textually identically, contextually variant forms (such as the written-up text of a lecture or talk). But whatever its source, in Robson's hands, the essay becomes the characteristic vehicle for his critical concerns. Robson resembles in some ways what used in the eighteenth century to be known as a 'general critic', interested in a wide variety of literary periods and kinds. The subjects of his essays are highly diverse; more miscellaneous than those of the writings of most academic critics who have established themselves as 'specialists in their field'. When, as here, the essays are collected together, the diversity is the more attractive to the extent that it is more apparent.

In Robson's *Critical Essays* (1966), as in the later collection which makes up *The Definition of Literature,* the essays, while they do not conform to a pattern, suggest a design which in turn reflects a conception of criticism, a certain habit of attention and activity of mind. The essays are both general and particular. The general essays serve as a critical preface or prologue to the rest which, taken as a whole, vary widely in substance and weight. Some are on whole works by one author; some on a particular work; some are devoted to part of an *oeuvre*. Some, where Robson is rising to the occasion, offer a sustained and intensive exhibition of modern critical reason at work. Others are in the nature of extended footnotes and convey the impression of a critic routinely performing the professional duties his employment requires. The conception of literary history, as far as one is implied by the collection's order of contents, is conventional enough – that of the Standard Authors. Initially, a number of twentieth-century critical issues are raised, and are then studied via treatment of a series of famous and less famous figures: Leavis, Eliot, Lewis, Auden, etc. We then jump backwards to the seventeenth century, represented by Milton, and seen through the medium of a twentieth-century critic of his work. From there we progress forward in time, with groups of essays on Romantic poets, Victorian poetry and the 'modern' period. A 'keynote' essay is printed at the start of the book: 'Purely Literary Values'. This brings into focus the central question, one which Robson takes up here and throughout his critical *oeuvre:* the possibility, and probable undesirability as far as Robson is concerned, of 'pure' literary study:

> The objection to the hypothetical aesthete, or the critical purist, is the same essentially as the objection to those who censor literature in the interests of a conventional morality. In both cases too much that we know to be vitally important to literature, as literature, is being handed over to an external judgement.[6]

The impurity of literary studies is brought out in all sorts of ways in the body of the book: in, for example, the account of the mingling of personal preoccupations with a response to Homer and Dante in the essay on Tennyson; in examination of the Byronic cult of personality as a component in Byron's artistic reality, or among the Pre-Raphaelite poets; in the consideration of 'the man behind the works' in the study of Kipling; in connections traced between man and moralist in the essay on C. S. Lewis; in reflections on the mergings of life and art in the essay on 'Wordsworth after 1803'; and in the last essay of the collection: 'D. H. Lawrence and *Women in Love*'. Here, Robson writes that: 'The work represents very often the writer's living-through of his personal problems and conflicts, as well as his more general preoccupations; while the life comes to take on the shape of a symbolic story or legend.'[7]

This thesis of 'impurity' is assisted by the 'miscellany' form of *Critical Essays,* also a feature of *The Definition of Literature.* Both hint at elements, present in subtle shades, of an Oxonian approach to literary criticism: one that insists on broader 'criteria of relevance' than 'words on the page'. However, a number of things in *Critical Essays* seem to belong to what might be described as the earlier phase of Robson's critical career. The piece on 'English as a University Subject' was originally delivered as a lecture in 1965 in the wake of the Robbins Report. As such, it seems more confined to its temporal context than Robson's work was later to become. It has dated more than pieces devoted to particular authors. But since Robson is talking about the critical ramifications of the institutional setting for English Studies – Eagleton's and Belsey's 'Eng. Lit.' – this is scarcely surprising. Robson is portraying an ideal: how things might be rather than how they are. But when we find him saying that the Oxbridge college is 'the microcosm of that intellectual and social community which must be assumed to exist, or persuaded into existence, in the larger world, if there is to be any real continuity in criticism, or literature, or any higher collaborative mental activity whatsoever',[8] it is difficult not to reflect on the utter remoteness of ideal and reality; the contrast between the noble thing Robson calls into being in his portrait and the inanity marking Oxbridge 'College Life' at the time he was writing his lecture, as today. In its reflections on English as a subject, the essay reveals what is found in both Arnold and Leavis: a complex interlacing of educational and critical thought. It is an eloquent testimony to the inherent intractability (the desirable impurity) of English in 'academic' terms. And it provides a classic statement of a rationale that is likely to have great use in the naïvely vocational educational climate of today: that which argues for the *critical* basis of English studies in university education (Robson does not say 'Higher Education'). The trouble is that the context has faded; the occasion has passed, a fact which blunts the interest of the essay. Troublesome, too, is the sense in which this essay is too introspective or parochial, too confidently uncritical of the assumption that the academic debates of Oxford and Cambridge are always going to be of vital importance to the rest of the world. Robson is not alive, in this essay at least, to the sense in which they are a joke.

The collection's author-criticism has more enduring appeal. One of the finest and in some ways most characteristic essays is that on the critic and popular Christian apologist, C. S. Lewis. Robson, in a fashion typical of his strength, brings out how a writer minor in the relative scale may be nevertheless complex and human. The subject demands the achievement of a poise, one no less difficult than when discussing a 'great author'. Robson is able to preserve this poise in this essay. Its essence is the simultaneous acknowledgement of good and bad in a writer which can, we are shown, have simultaneous existence within him. In the case of Lewis, this involves sympathetic treatment of, and affection for, the flawed moral and literary character of Lewis, inspired partly by Robson's personal knowledge of Lewis the Man – his biographical background. There is kindliness and decency in Robson's reminiscence of Lewis, the examiner 'apt extravagantly to over-mark the papers of a candidate whose views he disliked'.[9] But the authority of the essay goes far beyond the authority conferred by personal contact; that of the 'famous characters I have known' form of approach. Robson's talent is to suggest how the writer is connected to the Man, and to create in our minds a sense of the writer as whole: the Man in the Writer and the Writer in the Man. The immense care with which Robson approaches his subject is immediately apparent.

It is an essay giving meaning and substance to the now outdated and suspect word 'Judgement' as the description of an essential property of literary criticism. In many ways, Robson's judgement is strongly negative. He states clearly though sympathetically what Lewis, given his powers, is unable to do; how silly he can seem; how so much of what he writes is diminished by its propagandist intent. And yet the 'level' of the writer under discussion does not depress the level of critical attention Robson gives to him. To appreciate the 'theory' which dictates this practice, it helps to recall Robson's admiration for Samuel Johnson, where, in a succession of fine distinctions, Johnson had compared the characters of Dryden and Pope.[10] In his essay on Lewis, Robson offers a classical *comparaison* of a similar kind, in this case between Lewis and Chesterton. The comments on Chesterton here may be compared with Carey's sneers at the expense of Chesterton's gross body:

> They were both Christian apologists who reached large audiences, and they shared a point of view, at the same time hierarchical and democratic... As a critic, Chesterton was more original than Lewis, but Lewis with his greater knowledge and scholarship was more responsible; Chesterton was a journalist, not a scholar... Chesterton is too highly coloured, Lewis too richly flavoured... Lewis was totally free from what is bad in Chesterton... On the other hand, Lewis did not have Chesterton's artistic gift...

Robson's willingness to see the positive in the negative in Lewis comes out in such comments as this, on Lewis's supposed philistinism:

> ... what I have discerned as a note of philistinism may have been no more than an unfortunate manner of expression, into which Lewis was sometimes betrayed by his promptness to defend the common man and common things against the facile contempt of literary intellectuals.[11]

Characteristically for Robson, good and bad in a writer are different sides of the same coin: 'This boyish romanticism is responsible for some of Lewis's worst sillinesses; but it is also responsible for what was best and purest in his response to literature.' Two-edged judgements of this kind are typical. They come from a dual vision, an instinct for the irresolvably contradictory nature of literary figures and literary things. Robson's 'liberal humanism', like Mason's, is complex. The instinct for contradiction is seen in the tension, in the Lewis essay, between art and religious doctrine. This is taken up on a second occasion in two essays devoted to Milton. The former, on Empson's account of Milton's God, shows Robson's admiration for Empson the critic of Milton's style. The latter is a not very enthusiastic account of *Paradise Regained*. Relations between art and religion provide scope for Robson to make what we shall see is an important contribution to criticism: as critic of literature's moral effects. On this ground, however, Robson is not always as successful as he is in the essay on Lewis. His essay on *Paradise Regained* (1960) tries with some strain to make the best of the poem, finding, as Robson had found with Lewis, good and bad things together: 'A certain *uncritical* element in [Milton's] genius is at once his strength and his weakness.' The essay is also illustrative of Robson the Practical Critic, a role now left behind. In 1960, he could write of 'such unfortunate effects as the last line' of the passage ('To gain a Scepter, oftest better miss't' [II, 486]), 'with its clutter of dentals and sibilants, suggesting a particular intensity of spat-out or hissed-out contempt'.[12]

The most substantial essay in the collection is Robson's Byron as Poet'. It is also one of the most subtly argued. Here, however, Robson seems to be taking on a poet who cannot adequately be handled by Practical Critical means. Why, Robson asks, since modern studies of Byron's life do not answer the question, is Byron 'worth discussing'? Robson quotes George Santayana's remark, in a letter: that Byron 'did not respect himself or his art as much as they deserved' and suggests that for a great artist Byron's poetry, or some of it, was too easily achieved an achievement. The converse of Byron's self-abasement was his attitudinising egotism. This, as Robson points out, Byron was alive to, and himself condemned. The essay draws useful attention to Byron's letters, where Robson finds 'intellectual mobility' forming a contrast with so much of his good bad poetry. It is not so much that the poetry lacks ear. It lacks, Robson amusingly suggests, '*mouth*', and Augustan poetry's 'distinction of style'. But Robson also finds good phrases to suggest what is attractive in the poetry: its 'athletic buoyancy', its 'immortal velocity'. Less attractive, he hints, is the Regency note of 'aristocratic recklessness'. But Byron can transcend this: 'Perhaps the most impressive poem that Byron wrote,' Robson believes, is the little-known *Lines on hearing that Lady Byron was ill*. The triumph of *Don Juan* is 'a triumph of personality'. Byron brings together his real experience with his acted Romantic self. And so Byron unites in dialectic contrary the cultural forces bearing upon him: 'The Romantic and the Augustan come together with an air of momentary reconciliation.' Robson's concluding judgement of the poem is negative: '*Don Juan* is the work of a mature mind, but not one with an integral vision.' On Byron as a whole, Robson's conclusion is characteristically low-key and undogmatic. Byron, like Lewis, brings out the need for judgement that is more than textual (more than a case of 'Purely Literary Values') in the data it takes into account: '. . . at his best he leaves us with a heightened realization of the value of *personality* . . .'[13] It is another case where unqualified judgement is radically out of place.

The critical essays of *The Definition of Literature* (1982) are more uniform in their quality and scope, even though, in terms of the topics taken up, the collection at first sight seems oddly assorted. But the strategy or organising principle is the same as *Critical Essays*: general and particular are mixed. General discussions establish a conceptual framework for examinations of particular writers and works. These then constitute the collection's core. Stevenson, Kenneth Grahame (*The Wind in the Willows*), Tennyson and Robert Frost represent the creative subjects. Hopkins, Eliot, Richards and Winters make up the critics (of whom all are poets). To the extent that Robson's criticism, here as in the earlier collection of essays, is concerned with particular authors and particular texts, it may therefore be said to express hostility to theory. But introducing Robson's studies of particular works in *The Definition of Literature* are four freshly composed essays of what must surely qualify as 'critical theory': 'The Definition of Literature', 'On Liberty of Interpreting', 'Evaluative Criticism, and Criticism without Evaluation', and 'The Novel: a Critical

Impasse?' These essays, recalling issues such as the nature of critical evaluation, dealt with more cursorily by Robson in his 1957 piece 'Mr Leavis on Literary Studies',[14] represent an extraordinary achievement. They are especially notable for their 'grip': a discursive generality supported at so many points by reference to particular experience, knowledge, intuition and feeling. Between them, they take up the whole question of what literature is and what criticism is. They are complementary: one is on literature, one on criticism, one on a major modern critical problem (authorial intention), one on a modern *genre*. The positions articulated in different essays interlock. In the first, Robson concludes by preferring what he calls an 'honorific' definition of literature, 'which commits its user to decisions about value and quality'. This is matched, in the conclusion to 'On Liberty of Interpreting', with an appeal to 'freedom of judgment, of personal decision whether or not the writer has actually performed what he seemed to promise'. 'Evaluative Criticism', meanwhile, concludes by saying that: 'Criticism never decides anything. It is an argument. The argument goes on.'[15]

Essays on particular authors then embody these general convictions. The essays have in all cases been published before in identical form, or worked up from one or more (in the case of the Winters essay) earlier versions. Two, on Tennyson and Hopkins, were given as lectures. Assembled together, the essays gain from the awareness we have, thanks partly to the general essays which precede them, of Robson's complex integrity of thought: his sense of literature and criticism as a single subject, with a common centre. In each essay Robson enters an argument, or starts one. He engages in what Eliot called a 'durable debate'.[16] Each time, Robson sets out to contribute to the total thinking on the subjects and authors he treats. The general essays provide a theoretical basis to broaden the range of material worthy of serious critical consideration, a range that is then extended to practical purpose in the choice of the subjects in the essays which follow. It is an aim of several essays to show that works we commonly take for granted as supplying literary pleasure on a fairly low level, and perhaps dismiss as children's books, are not ordinary but literary achievements in the full sense of the term. These, on an absolute and not relative level, are 'complete' works of art. Robson reverses the idea that popular works remaining popular do so because they appeal to the lowest common denominator of taste. Their appeal, rather, is to be seen as a testimony to their high qualities; though they may not be 'high art'. Robson thus questions the idea that any work has any permanent right to greatness. Among the essays in the collection of this kind, the one on *The Wind in the Willows* is a masterpiece of delicacy, humour, seriousness, sympathy, humanity and control. Here the central characters, Mole, Rat, Toad and Badger 'embody keen psychological and social observation'. Robson's treatment is remarkable for its absence of condescension to the work. In some people's view, *The Wind in the Willows*, which Robson calls 'this beautiful work', is an example of sub-literature, not literature. Robson disregards the distinction, and recalls for us the poignancy, delight and moral significance of the book. The implicit question is: can something like this, which is so moving, was once so widely enjoyed and clearly is still so largely enjoyable, not be literature? But such an appeal is not the only basis of the case. It rests on the book's more than satisfying the usual generic criteria by which conventionally sanctioned great art is judged:

> *The Wind in the Willows* is unusual among English novels in working from as many as three centres (not counting the authorial voice). Many novels, of course, have a large cast of characters; but in how many of them can it be said that there are more than one or two characters who are both drawn from within, and at the same level of probability?[17]

But it is not only non-canonical authors that require restoration. In his essay on Tennyson, Robson sets out to revalue an author who, though once considered 'great', and widely admired, now suffers neglect.

When Robson comes to the poets notable as critics we can see that, in a variety of ways, he is continuing debates initiated in general discussions at the beginning of the book. Thus, thoughts on evaluation in literary criticism are brought to bear, to negative effect, to criticise T. S. Eliot's too crude pronouncement that

'The rudiment of criticism is the ability to select a good poem and reject a bad poem' (*The Use of Poetry*). Robson takes issue with this over-simplified insistence on the necessity of literary evaluation, revealing its openness to the standard objection to value judgements. He participates fully in (but does not quite identify with) the argument the general conclusion of which he is unable in the end to share:

> In any case, is goodness (or badness) an essence or quality at all? One might take the view that to call a poem good or bad is to do no more than give or refuse endorsement to the judgment that it possesses or lacks certain properties which happen to be held in esteem by the individual critic, or by readers in a particular literary period.[18]

Robson's skills in criticising the critic are shown to good effect in this essay on Eliot, as they are, again, in the concluding essay, on Winters. The latter is executed with extraordinary wit, a wit characteristic of Robson in being dead-pan. It succeeds, somehow, in touching two extremes: it is both lethal and affectionate at the same time. To catch the irony in the prose, careful attention is required. Robson quotes Winters's warning against saying that the best poets of our time deal with subjects which are most important for our time: 'Five hundred years from now the subjects which will appear to have been the most important will be the subjects treated by the surviving poets who have written the most intelligently.' Drawing breath at this point, Robson comments in the following, almost Gibbonian, vein:

> We must wait, then for A.D. 2473 to settle these questions. In the meantime, I will summarise the mature conclusions of this eminent critic and poet, after a lifetime of devotion to the study, teaching, and composition of English poetry. His definition of a great poet is a poet who has written at least one great poem. When he applies this definition, his list of great poets in English after 1500 excludes, among others, Shakespeare, Donne, Marvell, Milton, Dryden, Pope, Gray, Johnson, Blake, Wordsworth, Coleridge, Byron, Shelley, Keats, Tennyson, Browning, Arnold, Hopkins, Yeats, Pound, and Eliot. The great poets are Gascoigne, Greville, Ben Jonson, the Herberts, Vaughan, Churchill, Hardy, Bridges, Tuckerman, Emily Dickinson, Robinson, Stevens (in 'Sunday Morning'), Louise Bogan, Edgar Bowers, J. V. Cunningham, and

N. Scott Momaday. We note that of the seventeen great poets writing in English since 1500, eight were American.

Thus *Forms of Discovery* offers a drastically revisionary account of the history of poetry in English.[19]

If there is a difference between *The Definition of Literature* and *Critical Essays,* it is that, in the later collection, Robson is moving further in the direction of a non-specialist public for literary criticism. Whereas in 1966 Robson had merely kept in mind the 'possibility of a wider public of which they [the members of the professional academic audience for criticism] are a part', in 1982 addressing this public has become an explicit, a 'general', aim of the collection:

> My general aim has been to take conversation about prose and poetry out of the limited and specialised 'literary' or 'academic' world in which it so often takes place, and to turn it towards the broader world of thought which is shared by all reflective people, whoever and wherever they are.[20]

At a time of increasing intra-muralisation of literary studies, Robson has taken the opposite path.

But although the intended audience for Robson's criticism seems to have changed (or become enlarged) the 'personality' which comes through the criticism – on which its integrity depends – is consistent throughout. One of the most pervasive marks of this personality is Robson's critical 'manner'. It is a manner embracing an assortment of tones. On the one hand, Robson is deliberate, or deliberative: beyond most modern critical work, Robson's is characterised by the taking of pains. Self-searching effort sustains tireless arbitration. This is not always attractive. Occasionally, Robson's scrupulosity gives his criticism a ponderous feel. His essays, sometimes, take time to 'get going' or warm up. Some have a rather wearisome, critically reluctant air. On the other hand, the trouble Robson takes in putting together some essays produces pieces of rare beauty. The prose is haunting; the style taut, pithy and plain. At its best Robson's critical style is dense but not crabbed, simple but not flat. The expansive is combined with the brisk; flexibility with order. This manner corresponds with, and expresses, his method, or critical procedure. Sometimes, this can seem a matter of 'chat', donnishly cultivated conversation-in-prose, and genteel to a fault. At other times, it seems logically propositional, almost quasi-syllogistic, spare, formal, 'diagrammatic' unupholstered and unflowery. The opening of his essay, 'The Novel: A Critical Impasse?' is representative of this: 'The problem for discussion is this. There are two typical views, or theories, about the Novel – call them A and B.' The same directness is apparent at the start of the essay 'On *Kidnapped*': '*Kidnapped* is like *Treasure Island* in some ways and unlike it in others.'[21] Many of Robson's critical essays have a logical–formal basis of this kind. It is one with the calm objective point of view to which they aspire. All the essays move by reasoned stages. Sometimes, as in the essay on *Kidnapped*, the effect is assisted by the somewhat external device of numbered points marking similarity and difference between two texts. An essay's conclusion may be equally self-conscious. In the last paragraph of 'The Definition of Literature', Robson says he is going 'To sum up what this essay has tried to do.'[22] Robson, while acknowledging that literary study is impure, nevertheless tries hard to impose order on criticism's diverse and intractable inspiration: literature itself.

Robson's criticism may be ordered, but it is not cold. It is, occasionally, extremely harsh. But it is never superior to its subject. This is because Robson, in his relation to literature, is capable of a critical passion that would be regarded as weakness by some modern academic critics. At times, his formality acts as a foil for pungent expressions of personal, subjective, sensation: 'I loathe [Tennyson's] "The Lord of Burleigh" . . . I find the whole poem distasteful . . .,' he protests in his essay on Tennyson printed in *The Definition of Literature*. At another point in the same collection, this time considering Eliot's criticism, he is equally direct: 'This tone is insufferable.' Many Robsonian insights are like this. They are offered seemingly as they occur, tossed off or bursting through as conversational interjections, or, sometimes, as strokes of testimony conveying a powerful unargued conviction, or naked response. At such points, Robson can abandon the slow pace of mere argumentation for an uncompromising declaration of belief. There may be more than a touch of impatience present, as here (paradoxically), in his attack on the modern plague of rampant subjectivism:

> Nowhere is it so notoriously powerful as in the arts. It is often taken for granted that 'beauty is in the eye of the beholder', that if you think, or profess to think, that a pile of rubbish is more beautiful than Chartres Cathedral, you can't be wrong, because there are no rights and wrongs in the matter. The general question about value is of course much too large for me to go into here. This is a moment for testimony, not discussion. All I will say is that I regard subjectivism as wrong, and that I think its influence in every sphere of life has been poisonous.

The point could not be more emphatically made. It is an example of what Robson, in the Preface to *The Definition of Literature,* says (reasonably enough) he is going to do: to be 'as fully explicit as possible about the standards, criteria, and methods which I favour'.[23]

But, while Robson is explicit about standards, his essays do not attempt scientific 'proofs'. This is because they are, among other things, too various in direction. While general lines are laid down, discussion runs off in a hundred and one different ways. Robson's critical discourse may be understood as a series of exploratory probings of difficult (the most difficult) questions. Criteria are invoked, as in examinations of particular authors, but are constantly shuffled, tested, refined, modified or withdrawn. Different points of view are taken up, aired, considered and then set aside, temporarily, in a provisional way, or permanently disposed of. This is true, to take one example, of Robson's essay on Robert Frost. It is also true of the 1977 essay on Eliot's criticism.[24] Often, Robson's process resembles nothing so much as trial and error. Having identified the problem, he then seeks to solve it. Sometimes questions remain unanswerable and we are left only with questions. Sometimes, when we come to the 'ends', we are left an answer of sorts, which is really the question again. We have come round in a circle. The essay 'The Novel: A Critical Impasse?' ends in this way. Robson has been deciding whether or not the novel is seriously marred as a form by not being able to rise to poetry's highest effects. The answer is: yes, it is. But we are to imagine the argument going on after the essay's last sentence is reached. It is a conclusion in which nothing is concluded: 'Is there not something in Arnold's characterisation of poetry as the most perfect speech of man, in which he comes nearest to uttering the truth?'[25] In Robson, then, while criticism is always 'argument', his own criticism is never merely argument*ative*. He pushes no 'line'. But nor does he, to any serious extent, ramble or digress in the way that can so damagingly detract from the value of a critical essay or chapter by Mason. With Robson we always 'know where we are', and where we are going. Robson is incisive, forthright, and plain, but he is less acerbic than Carey, and there is nothing of Eagleton's critical campaign style, his urgent tone, sometimes frenetic combative manner or his drive. In comparison Robson's critical work is cool and relaxed. Robson speaks the language of critical toleration, not revolution. His critical voice is more reminiscent of civilised discussion ('conversation') between equals than that of an advocate pleading a cause, or a journalist writing a 'dazzling' review. In Robson, there is time for contemplation. Perhaps this means that there is an absence of 'attack'. At times, as in the study of *The Wind in the Willows*, it is true that argument takes second place to *evocation*. Here, Robson works through the story in chronological sequence, episode by episode. The shape of the book controls the shape of the essay which is modelled on the succession of narrative events, not the 'case' Robson is advancing. In the 1955 essay on Wordsworth's 'Resolution and Independence', Robson similarly 'goes through the poem'.[26] If on the one hand this makes him seem not argumentative enough, even slack, yet by retelling a story he can also recreate it in a moving way in our minds. In his essay on *The Wind in the Willows*, Robson successfully summons into being Grahame's world of imagination and symbol. And thus he achieves the object of his argument. It may be true that Robson's arguments are less aggressively pointed than they could be: Mason's criticism, by contrast, is corrective in tone and approach. But Mason's often has a target (the rest of the scholarly–

academic world) in view; Robson's usually has conciliation as one of its aims.

Locally, Robson is very pointed indeed. If his tone – usually if not always – is mild, he is not intellectually complacent: modestly and calmly, things are thought through afresh. By carrying forward his stated educational principles into the practice of literary criticism, Robson thus teaches the methods and habits of original thought. This 'teaching', however, stands at the opposite extreme from criticism which sets out to preach at, or convert, the reader. Thought may be taught, but the result is something the reader is left to choose for himself. Robson's means are often oblique: enlightenment occurs in the course of reflection, not as a 'lesson'. Robson, by working in and through the process of discussion, and by re-applying key terms and ideas to the particulars of literature itself, constantly redefines them. Meanings become explicit in a form serviceable both within and without the context in which they are made to appear and which gives rise to them. Here, for example, Robson supplies an account of what, in fiction at least, may be understood by 'style':

> The boy who likes *Kidnapped* better than some ordinary adventure tale is not interested in 'style'; but perhaps he intuitively appreciates that his preference for *Kidnapped* lies in Stevenson's superior ability to make the things happen that we are to understand to have happened. And once he has become conscious of that, he has learned what 'style' means.

At another point, Robson defines the tricky term 'Sentimentality': 'So far as I can see, it means the appeal by an author to a mood which for some reason we do not want to feel at the moment.'[27]

If clarifying such terms is one of the uses of criticism, then Robson's criticism is exceedingly useful; as is the consequence of the talent that Robson displays for encapsulating appreciation of a literary quality or effect, and pinning it down. Of Blake's successful poems, for example, Robson at one point writes that 'we do not merely hear, we see, and our seeing is not confined to mere visualization . . . since Blake's own seeing is an activity of the intelligence, manifesting itself in an almost clairvoyant power of notation of mental and spiritual realities'. (Critics have often valued this distinction between hearing and seeing: the comment recalls Pope's famous praise of Homer.) Equally, part of Robson's practice as a critic is the attention he gives to locating 'good bits' in a long or difficult work. Robson's quotations, if less polymathically varied than Mason's, are still varied. Sometimes a passage (or whole poem) may be quoted for purposes of internal analysis, comparison and discussion. At other times, quotations serve as samples of a longer text, or a whole writer's works. Reading the part brings the rest into mind. In most instances, Robson's quotations are self-contained. They have intrinsic as well as illustrative value and are there to be read in their own right. In this way, they show off not the critic, but the writer whose works they are taken from. Robson shares this gift for quotation with Leavis. The difference is that in Leavis's criticism it issues an indication of the essential or characteristic nature of an author or work, its key feature. In Robson it is used to show a writer *at his best*. He wants us to see where a writer may be most enjoyed. 'Whatever we may think of *Maud* as a whole,' he writes, 'it is surely impossible not to be moved by one part of it.'[28]

This comment is typical of Robson, who is rare among academic literary critics writing today in not being afraid to admit to being moved by a work. Not that Robson's criticism is ever embarrassingly soft, slushy, or tearful: he is not an emotionalist. Robson's characteristic manner is one of restraint and impersonality. He shares, he says, and his own practice confirms, Yvor Winters's 'dislike for modern irrationalism and emotionalism'. Nevertheless, Robson's capacity for feeling, particularly that of sadness or poignancy, his lack of evasive neurosis about feeling, whether his own or that of his authors, is strong, and boldly at odds with the pervasive will to make modern criticism more 'scientific'. Being 'moved' is a real and important 'value' in Robson's criticism. It complements and moderates the calm rationality which otherwise characterises his critical essays. It lies at the centre of their human appeal. And it is the source of a literary taste both catholic and distinctive. Willing to be pleased, it follows that Robson is widely read. It also follows that Robson is often drawing attention to works he would like more generally enjoyed but which criticism has missed: Byron's poem to his sister, Tennyson's *Locksley Hall Sixty Years After*, etc. But while here, as elsewhere in his criticism, Robson is expert at ekeing the good out of seriously unsatisfactory works, his realised taste is narrower than the generous spirit of his criticism would suggest. Quantitatively speaking, a large part of his criticism is devoted to 'canonical' work, in particular to the already well-travelled landscapes of literature (and literary criticism) of the nineteenth and twentieth centuries: Byron, Wordsworth, Tennyson, T. S. Eliot, etc. Robson, therefore, has made his major contribution to critical studies where for the time being there seems little to be said. Introducing this fact, however, requires it to be taken in context. First, it remains true that Robson is frequently a severely negative critic of nineteenth- and twentieth-century literary work, as in his treatment of the faults of Pre-Raphaelite poetry. Secondly, we do not feel that Robson approaches authors as a 'period specialist', confined to this favourite period; that he could not if he wished comment with authority on anything else. Robson is inward with literary thought of periods other than the one he seems to prefer. In his essay on T. S. Eliot's literary criticism, for example, Robson discusses, and reproves, Eliot's flirtation with 'neo-classical' literary ideas. The ideas (on the dramatic unities) are seen for what they are: of mainly historical interest. But they are presented in an informative way. There is no condescension: 'It has always been the trouble with neo-classicism that the more reasonable its propositions, the more they slide towards analyticity.'[29] There are, of course, many particular pre-nineteenth-century authors that Robson has deeply enjoyed, or been moved by: Shakespeare, Samuel Johnson and so forth, and Robson's essays contain a wealth of reference to literature of other nations and times. It is not only literature he draws from. Popular songs ('Frankie and Johnnie'), entertainers (Danny la Rue) and film directors (Alfred Hitchcock), are on occasion brought into play. This 'cultural breadth', if one sign of the characteristic scope of

Robson's literary taste, is one of the ways in which Robson makes a distinctive, critically original, mark.

Robson's *forte* lies in the realm of what might be described as 'middle-brow' taste. This may be seen as the effect of his positive response to literature or criticism (or a literary figure, such as C. S. Lewis) that he considers the critical establishment has not taken seriously enough. Often, it includes a writer historically recent, popular in his day, still popular but not fashionable, for example, Kipling. Robson refuses to overstate such a writer's appeal. The 'principal weakness' of Robert Frost, whom Robson praises, the weakness 'that makes for the most doubt about his claim to high poetic rank – is monotony'. *Treasure Island,* in the combination of good and evil qualities in the same person, has only 'a tinge of serious interest'. Eagleton attacks the very idea of literary greatness; Carey sets out to give 'great literature' broader commercial appeal; Robson brings out how immensely pleasurable, how deeply rewarding, very small things (or half-forgotten things) can be; how all worthwhile literature is not necessarily 'great'. And he shows that standards of 'great literature' are often narrowly conceived. Robson believes that the evaluations we make of literature are 'not self-evident, common sense, transparently obvious to the disinterested eye'. Evaluations have 'ideological implications', mostly unconscious implications which should be made conscious.[30] Robson wants works to be admitted as 'literature' that are ignored because of meaninglessly 'high', or exclusive standards: for this reason his work on Kipling or Stevenson superficially recalls Belsey's enthusiasm for Conan Doyle. But Robson is also the enemy of the 'radicals'. If Robson is interested in literature on a popular level, his appeal is to the culture of the common reader, not that of the mass. And within modern literature, his critical attention falls primarily on works that are now relatively distant in time. Robson seems more 'at home' as critic in the Victorian or Edwardian period than the immediate present, embracing without embarrassment 'bourgeois' authors or works which appear to endorse such things as English country life or values of empire. In his concern for unfashionable works, Robson wants to do justice to them as art. Though neglected, they form part of literature as a whole. And since English literature is one and indivisible, nothing, according to anterior standards, is off the agenda. Robson wrote in his early essay, 'English as a University Subject' (1965): '... we must try to imagine our subject-matter, English literature, as an ideal totality; to see the present in the past, no less than to see the past in the present.'[31] When Robson returns to the past to discover the present, he does not do so because he is concerned with 'period flavour'. He is explicit in the contrast between 'interesting Victoriana' and 'engrossing reading for its own sake'.[32] But, in reclaiming past texts, Robson is not a critic able to spot and salute talent among new writers. He admires the ability to do so in others and condemns those who, like Yvor Winters, have tried but failed. But Robson's claim to be going back to the past to say something about the present can seem too oblique, too shy. In the Preface to *Critical Essays* he gave the following reason for the absence from this collection of his critical work of 'any discussion of the creative work of writers now active': '... this omission is not due to lack of interest or concern, but to my conviction ... that critical study of the authors of the past can be one way – and perhaps the most appropriate way for someone occupied academically with them – of searching for insight into the problems of writing now.'[33] Robson's conception of 'Modern English Literature' seems somewhat safe in its critical package.

But Robson is not an apologist for the 'middlebrow'. In discussing it, he calls up – as in all he writes – a sense of *all* that literature is able to do. This is evident when, for example, Robson is discussing the poetry of Robert Frost and comparing him disadvantageously with Wordsworth: 'Sympathy and understanding are surely not enough for a great poet; there must also be this suggestion of the larger perspective, the wider and finer mind.' Paradoxically, comments like this seem rather to lift than to lower the poet who comes off worse in the comparison. Robson performs the important function, critically, of bringing readers on different levels together. *Treasure Island* contains art that might 'close the communication gap that exists at present between the serious novel and ordinary readers'. A work on one level is explained by reference to a work on another. Literature in one language or culture is brought to bear on literature in another. Things inside literature are illuminated by reference to other things, often but not always of literary interest outside it. All three dimensions of relation are present and interwoven in Robson's comment on a moment in *Treasure Island*: 'If Jim seems naïve here, in his assumption that pirates are always dirty, we might recall that no less a poet than Baudelaire was accused, by no less a critic than Henry James, of a similar error about "evil" in *Les Fleurs du Mal*!' Juxtaposition of this kind is the source of many surprises in Robson. Things which academic custom has led us to keep in separate compartments are brought amusingly and illuminatingly together, as when in the criticism of *The Wind in the Willows* Rat's description of the pleasures of boating are defined by reference to 'the secret of art as Immanuel Kant defined it: "purposeful purposelessness" '. The reference, in discussion of a 'children's book', to a guru of Western Philosophy, is perfectly serious. It is a serious critical account. *The Wind in the Willows,* in Robson's opinion, is 'art'. But it is characteristic of Robson to be alive to, and to suggest, the joke. It is one outcrop of an underlying mock-heroic element in some of Robson's critical work, a quiet wit that contrasts with Eagleton's overtly satiric asides. Bringing literature before a common standard works two ways. On the one hand, we take previously categorised sub-literary works more seriously. On the other, Robson exposes ways in which canonical 'respected' authors, like Dickens, are often no different from the low. The line between them is blurred. Of Toad he writes: 'We know that he is not the "incorrigible rogue and hardened ruffian" that authority finds him. This is too like Sergeant Buzfuz on Mr Pickwick's "revolting heartlessness and systematic villainy".'[34]

Robson, then, 'breaks down the barriers'. And there is evidence that, from as early as 1956, Robson has been trying to 'open up' literary studies, to include among other things more discursive prose. (See his 'Mr. Leavis on Literary Studies'.)[35] At the same time, Robson resembles Mason in his interest in the special problems that attach to the (now unfashionable) long poem (Mason on Pope's 'Homer', Robson on Byron's *Don Juan*).

Both have more time for the self-consciously poetic in poetry than most modern critics. Mason attends to the poetry of Pope; Robson appeals to 'The Present Value of Tennyson', where he writes: 'it is possible to separate, to some degree, what delights us in a writer's power of expression from the general pleasure and interest his work has to offer us.' Expression itself, for both critics, can delight. Both, however, subscribe to a fundamental conviction about the function of poetical expression. Robson describes it as follows, as the assumption from which his whole discussion of Tennyson is approached: 'The first essential excellence, something that is always a virtue in a poet, is effectiveness of communication.'[36]

The 'primary purpose of all fiction', Robson also writes, is 'to provide the reader with imaginative understanding of human nature, in ideal conditions for the exercise of that understanding.' No 'radical theorist', having said that, could retain his 'radical' credentials. Nor would it be seemly or advisable, in a 'radical' critic, to show quite the interest that Robson does in R. L. Stevenson's 'good boys' books'. (Where, after all, do the girls come in?) But in that phrase, 'the imaginative understanding of human nature', we find a summary of one of Robson's major principles as a literary critic: his reference, in particular judgements, to an idea of literature's moral value. Robson argues for the importance of this, and reveals its effects, even when he is discussing works not normally regarded as 'serious' literature. It can be stressed, as characteristically as ever, in analysis of Stevenson's *Kidnapped*. Behind the 'mask of a boys' story', Stevenson treats 'adult problems and pressures'.[37] In seeking to satisfy this interest, Robson has no particular code of morals in mind. He criticises C. S. Lewis as critic because 'from being a moralist (as any serious writer must be) he deteriorates into being a moralizer . . .'. According to Robson, the practice of criticism, when concerned with literature, is necessarily, and in an inevitable way, moral: 'Literature,' he writes in his essay of 1963, 'Purely Literary Values': '. . . is a fully human product, and a sense of the author as a whole may be indispensable to our pleasure and our understanding. Certainly we need a sense of proportion, and some degree of critical – not to say ethical –

conscience . . .' But Robson is careful, as always, to avoid overstating the case. Robson does not think that the 'teaching' literature offers is always self-evidently 'good', or benign: 'This full humanity in great writers can be the reverse of reassuring. It can even be frightening.' And in a striking and unusual essay on *Hamlet* Robson points to the power of Shakespeare to shock.[38] He does however believe that literature, when moral, can exert a power not to discomfort but to console. His attitude may be summarised by his own phrase 'moral delicacy'. What he means here can be judged by the values that he places it with: 'Humour, imaginative insight, moral delicacy'.[39] In an earlier essay, Robson had used the phrase 'moral poise'.[40]

Such qualities are often as apparent in Robson's analysis as they are in any book discussed by him. Robson's critical principles are not external measures, even if it is common to find Robson applying critical 'tests', and standing outside the literary or critical subject under discussion. But though general principles exist (Robson writes of one of Yvor Winters's remarks: 'There is no need to raise the question of "right" and "wrong" here: the first test is persuasiveness, or otherwise'), standards are not *wholly* external: 'Books should be judged by the standards which are appropriate to them.' 'Every poet is entitled to his own singularity.' But a poet must according to Robson do something more than merely express singularity: *In Memoriam* is Tennyson's greatest poem because 'A personal voice, while never ceasing to be a personal voice, becomes at the great moments of the poem the voice of all humanity.'[41] Literature, for Robson, is the medium conveying 'the voice of all humanity'. He does not ban, on grounds of principle, the biographical contribution to be made to understanding and enjoyment of any particular author, nor the biographical inferences to be drawn from literary works. And yet Robson's *caveats* about this are many; as he writes of the critical treatment of Kipling:

> And it is this personality-pattern, holding the work together, which must ultimately be the subject for any general criticism of Kipling. But this does not mean that the critic is necessarily concerned with biographical inference. For one thing, this is risky. We know very little of people, even when they are there to be

studied; and though no doubt Kipling was a "human case", like everyone else, it is surely unwise to interpret his art by evidence much of which must be fragmentary and conjectural, and which is anyway mostly available only in the artistic treatment Kipling gave to it.

On many occasions, Robson stresses the importance of separating Man and Art: Lawrence's *Women in Love*, for example, is to be found 'pointing a moral of its own, which is not the author's'.[42]

Robson's 'principles' are inscribed in his practice. 'Method' is too exclusively formal a term to describe this, conceding too much to a conception of criticism that Robson resists. What Robson is as critic, what he stands for or represents, is suggested less by the scale of his critical achievement over a range of 'major studies' than by how he proceeds in close and concentrated treatment of a particular thought, idea or work in a particular essay. It is then a question of quality of insight and of 'touch'. His meaning, or function, resides in the content of his 'intellectual manners', if that is not too prissy a phrase. For Robson, criticism is still to be regarded as a form of debate, or urbane discourse. It implies a human relationship between author and critic and between critic and reader. It involves being fair, as fair as possible, to all sides. Often it is a publicly tested and tried externalisation of internal dialogue. On the one hand, it involves reflection of a personal, sometimes intimate kind, as when defending a much criticised episode in *The Wind in the Willows* he writes: 'But this is not an occasion for argument, but for testimony. I find "The Piper at the Gates of Dawn" moving and convincing as a religious poem.'[43] On the other hand it is often very much a matter of argument; of weighing possibilities and probabilities. It is always a matter of fine distinctions between things like in some ways and unlike in others. Robson's criticism is adjudicatory: there is one side of the case. But then there is the other. Some people have thought this. Others have taken another, quite opposite, line. This is all part of a politely understated challenge to us, the readers of the literature and the criticism. What are we to think? It is Robson's distinction as a critic to keep this invitation perpetually open. His criticism is the antithesis of the sermon; the opposite of the lecture. It is a manner (inscribing a value) which rests on total eradication of stridency of tone. Robson's criticism is important for its personal 'note', a corollary of the interest he takes in authors as persons.

For Robson, 'author' also means 'critic'. He is one of the few critics writing today who have mastered the art of talking about criticism in a way which gives it its full weight, and which recognises its possibilities, as art. Through Robson, we become more deeply aware of the many, often contradictory elements, emotional, intellectual, stylistic, ethical, social, which come together to make a critic. Although this awareness is reinforced by Robson's own critical practice, criticism is also a persistent, explicit, theme of his work. Sometimes the exploration is overt and theoretical, as in his essay on 'Evaluative Criticism'. Sometimes he is writing, in practice, on other literary critics' practice, or theory, as in his essay on Yvor Winters; or on the criticism of writers (such as Hopkins) who are not primarily regarded as critics. Sometimes, when writing on a creative author he takes critical response to that author into account in the discussion, to say something implicitly about what criticism should or should not be. Much of his writing on creative writers is inspired by what he sees as the malaise of modern academic criticism. 'Something has gone wrong,' Robson writes in his essay on Robert Frost, 'when we find an intelligent critic writing like this':

> – his text being the poem 'Design', of which he is analysing the first line ('I found a dimpled spider, fat and white'):
> At first we hear the cheerfully observant walker on back-country roads ... The iambic lilt adds a tone of pleasant surprise ...

Robson concludes: 'Anyone holding an academic post must feel sympathy with this critic.'[44] The example, as well as the comment, may well remind us of Johnson's Minim.

It is typical of Robson to respond to this failed attempt at criticism in a tone which combines humour with the note of 'there but for the grace of God ...'. Robson's idea of what he is doing as critic is formed partly by his sense of where others go wrong. But among the influences that have made his criticism the way that it is, the presence of Johnson is hard to ignore. This ranges from the extremely general to the extremely specific. It includes Robson's unusually lively and very human interest in

Johnson's creative works, one beautifully expressed in his direct and poignant essay 'Johnson as Poet', printed in a 1984 collection of centenary essays.[45] Robson's whole approach to critical commentary is, in a sense likely to be widely agreed, Johnsonian. Johnson is there in the intermingling of directness and logic, dead-pan humour and emotional openness; in the methodological habit of constructing a judgement from elements of positive and negative views; in the way Robson has of bringing an overall sense of what literature is and what it is worth to discussion of particular authors and works. At the same time Robson probably quotes Johnson more frequently than any modern critic not having a specialist interest in his work. Robson is still able to *use* Johnson as literary critic as specialist writers upon him, mostly, are not. Robson may be concerned with a poet (such as Milton) on whose writings, in Robson's opinion, Johnson's criticism is difficult to better. Yet he also applies Johnson to the judgement of moderns. He invokes criteria that are 'Johnsonian' in the respect that Johnson has helped to give them a special currency, a particular 'charge', and therefore an ineradicable place in the enduring debates of literary criticism. Sometimes criteria Robson deploys involve a 'tilt' towards a characteristic emphasis in the criticism of Johnson, as in the two critics' common interest in the moral purpose of a literary work, an interest which now (in the days of Derrida and Lacan) looks out of date. But sometimes the use made of Johnson is quite explicit and particular: 'Johnson observes of Dryden that "he that writes much cannot escape a manner"; but "Dryden is always *another and the same*". This could hardly be said of Frost...' In his essay on 'Hopkins and Literary Criticism' Robson appeals in a more general way to Johnson's whole perspective on literature; his sense of its relative unimportance compared with religion. Robson's ability to use Johnson's criticism for purposes proper to modern literary discussion qualifies the relative influence of Arnold. It is part of Robson's whole practical contact with the renewing force of the past, one that is summed up in the pointedly Johnsonian allusion applied by Robson to the criticism of Eliot, and which applies equally well to his own: 'He does not offer new things, but enables us to see familiar things anew.'[46]

As critic, Robson is greatly influenced by the critics he happens to be writing upon: he often adopts the characteristics he praises. This is true of the substance of his quotation from a letter of Hopkins: 'The most inveterate fault of critics ... is the tendency to cramp and hedge in by rules the free movements of genius, so that I should say ... The first requisite for a critic is liberality, and the second liberality, and the third, liberality.' From the 'liberality' of his own critical approach, we can see why Robson should quote with approval Hopkins's remark in a letter to Bridges: 'I disapprove of damfooling people ... I think it wrong, narrows the mind...'[47] Robson refers to a wide range of modern critics, living and dead. He is polite to the modern North American literary critics, Frye and Trilling, but negatively critical (in his essay on 'The Romantic Poets') of 'the representative blandness, the detachedness, which seem to go with the excessive "intellectuality" of Professor Frye's writing'.[48] It would be difficult to overestimate the importance of T. S. Eliot, both as Robson's topic for criticism and as critical model. Eliot's formulations about poetry and about criticism have had a formative effect. By quotation and allusion, they are frequently cornerstones of discussion, or put it in motion. At the same time, Robson's attitude to Eliot is mixed. There is respect for his catholic taste in poetry and thinking about the nature of poetic creation; but there is irritation with his occasional bored superiority, the collapse of his later criticism into an exercise in diplomacy or, to take a particular instance, his tasteless, 'unworthy' descent into such things as thinking about poets' reputations in terms of the rise and fall of their poetical 'stock'. On balance, T. S. Eliot is more the subject of (adverse) criticism by Robson than an influence upon him.

The more important (perhaps most important) influence on Robson's criticism, as he is on so many of the critics discussed in this book, is Leavis. Robson, on many occasions, admires in poetry precisely that which Leavis has admired, and responds, sometimes positively, sometimes negatively, to what Leavis brings out. When talking about Leavis, Robson seems less detached than on other occasions, and Robson's early handling of Leavis's criticism (at one point directed against himself) conveys a combination of respect, sensitivity and willingness to disagree which have become the hallmarks of Leavis's most intelligent admirers, for whom 'Leavisite' seems too crude a term. Robson's later interest in Leavis is twofold. He has an academic interest (comparable to that taken in Eliot) in the whole question of Leavis's historical importance, and Leavis's intellectual and critical *milieu* (of which he is himself a part). Robson's critical attention to Eliot, Richards and Winters is, of course, an aspect of this interest. It coincides with Robson's attention to the creative literature of this chronologically and culturally increasingly distant critical age. The other main kind of interest in Leavis is both more pervasive and more direct. Leavis has set the agenda for what Robson has felt it needful to say. He seems, *inter alia*, partly to explain Robson's enduring concern with, and defence of, in his own terms, evaluation in criticism, as well as, for example in his earlier writings, interest in English as a university subject. In later essays Robson shows a more Johnsonian, less Leavisian, interest in the appeal of English literature to mankind in general. And Robson at the same time seems often (like Mason) to be trying to qualify the effect on a reading public of Leavis's tastes (if only by more consistently employing his critical standards). Robson notes with surprise that Leavis excluded Stevenson from his 'great tradition', while requiring a great novelist to have a profound concern with moral problems, which in Robson's opinion Stevenson has. Of course, Robson's criticism still bears the marks of the 'great tradition': he writes in the Introduction to *Modern English Literature* that 'Conrad is the only great artist in Edwardian fiction'.[49] Leavis, in Robson's criticism, is qualified not overturned. Robson's is a healing hand. His criticism is less tortuous, less idiosyncratic than Mason's. In intent, and in effect, it is less inconoclastic than Leavis's. It seems somehow less consciously at odds with the universe of fellow scholars and critics, more charitably comprehending of the fads and foibles of critical human nature. Something good can always be said. For many writers today, critical composition seems often the outlet for childish personal pride and petty self-display. Criticism seems to have supplied Robson with the ideal form and medium to express the combination of moral breadth and modesty of manner that constitute an achievement which may seem in other respects slight. But what is in, and behind, the pages that we do have of Robson's criticism is a tonic force for sanity in the modern critical world. And that is not a slight achievement.

Notes

1. *Critical Essays* (Routledge and Kegan Paul: London, 1966), p. 65.
2. *The Signs Among Us, and other poems* (Routledge and Kegan Paul: London, 1968).
3. *Modern English Literature* (OUP: London, 1970).
4. *A Prologue to English Literature* (Batsford: London, 1986).
5. *The Definition of Literature: and other essays* (CUP: Cambridge, 1982). Reviewed by Martin Dodsworth, *Cambridge Quarterly* **XII**, 2 and 3, 215–21.
6. *Critical Essays*, p. 7.
7. *ibid.*, p. 264. See *English as a University Subject* (F. R. Leavis lecture 1965) (CUP: Cambridge, 1965).
8. *Critical Essays*, p. 40.
9. *ibid.*, p. 73.
10. 'Life of Pope' (1781), *Lives of the Poets* (ed. George Birkbeck Hill), III, pp. 220–3.
11. *Critical Essays*, pp. 61–2, 65.
12. *ibid.*, pp. 72, 110, 101.
13. *ibid.*, pp. 149, 157, 160, 158, 163, 170, 175, 177, 188. The essay on Byron first appeared as *Byron as Poet* (Folcroft, Chatterton Lecture on an English Poet, 1957).
14. In *Critical Essays*, pp. 14–21.
15. *Definition of Literature*, pp. 18, 39, 56.
16. *ibid.*, p. 224.
17. *ibid.*, pp. 124, 142.
18. *ibid.*, p. 223.
19. *ibid.*, p. 255.
20. Preface to *Definition of Literature*, p. vii.
21. *Definition of Literature*, pp. 57, 97.
22. *ibid.*, p. 18.
23. *ibid.*, pp. 155, 226, 146, viii.
24. In *Definition of Literature*, pp. 168–95; 216–36.
25. *ibid.*, p. 78.
26. *Critical Essays*, pp. 124–34.
27. *Definition of Literature*, pp. 99, 149.
28. *Critical Essays*, p. 205; *Definition of Literature*, p. 163.

29. *ibid.*, pp. 258, 226.
30. *Definition of Literature*, pp. 187, 96, 55–6.
31. *Critical Essays*, p. 26.
32. *Definition of Literature*, p. 161.
33. Preface to *Critical Essays*.
34. *Definition of Literature*, pp. 186, 92, 87, 121, 139.
35. *Critical Essays*, p. 15.
36. *Definition of Literature*, pp. 156, 153.
37. *ibid.*, p. 117.
38. *Critical Essays*, pp. 58, 7, 11; 'Did the King See the Dumb Show?' *Cambridge Quarterly*, **VI**, 4, 303–26.
39. *Definition of Literature*, p. 115.
40. *Critical Essays*, p. 10.
41. *Definition of Literature*, pp. 261, 123, 152, 167.
42. *Critical Essays*, pp. 241–2, 284. For Robson on Kipling, see also Introduction to *The Jungle Book* (ed. W. W. Robson) (World's Classics: Oxford, 1987), pp. vii–xxx.
43. *Definition of Literature*, p. 131.
44. *ibid.*, p. 183.
45. *Samuel Johnson 1709–84* (ed. Kai Kin Yung) (Herbert Press: London, 1984), pp. 25–36.
46. *Definition of Literature*, pp. 188, 236.
47. *ibid.*, p. 205.
48. *Critical Essays*, p. 121.
49. *op. cit.*, p. xv.

7
Creators as Critics I: Ted Hughes

There is an element of unconscious arrogance in the poet-critic. I must explain at once that I do not wish to say anything against criticism of poetry by poets. On the contrary, I believe it to be the most valuable criticism we have. Poets can tell us things about poetry that only poets can know.[1]

What then of those modern critics who are not professional academics but creative writers themselves? In recent times, critics and creators have often found themselves on opposite sides of an imaginary fence. Criticism is seen as hostile to creation, and the critic is regarded as an enemy of the poet; paradoxically jealous of genius and a parasite upon it. This attitude reflects a deeper divide between the faculties of criticism and creation. It is the symptom of a culture historically combining an addiction to specialised critical pursuits with a romantically elevated (and Romantic-poetry-derived) sense of artistic mystique. In this view, creation is generally seen as a higher faculty than criticism since creation is making, criticism destruction. By the same token the creator, it is sometimes said, is not helped but fettered by the critic, his born inferior. The unsatisfactoriness of this distinction is due not only to the fact that critical study has tended to supplant literary in recent years. It also ignores the fact that creators, while not always critics, could not make art without first reading books (just as no one could paint pictures without first seeing them). From this it follows that the creation of art is necessarily – in some sense – the criticism of art, and that critical instinct, including self-criticism, is a pre-requirement of creation. Art, if it is to be art, will not happen without it. But it has also been argued that criticism is itself a mode of creation; that in recording or constructing experience, it qualifies as art. Literary experience is not 'real' experience. But it *is* experience (even when the 'experience' of literature is consciously denied by the critic), and therefore in a different way real. No one can be sure where criticism stops and creativity starts. For centuries, therefore, major works have survived simultaneously as criticism and literature. Creative writers have strayed into the territory of literary criticism. And many 'critics', in their turn, have also been poets, writing 'Prefaces' to their own poetical work (as did Dryden or Wordsworth). Sometimes, criticism has been *in* poetry, like Pope's famous *Essay*. Writers may divide attention between *genres* of criticism and poetry, as Sidney, Johnson, Arnold or T. S. Eliot, but write essays on literature in a form which is literature in effect (subverting *genre*). The subject of this chapter, Ted Hughes, is one of the latest in a long line of such poet–critics.

Hughes's criticism raises questions attendant upon all such criticism by poets, the principal one being that of the poet–critic's vested interest in his own creative work, and the danger that consequently exists of his submitting to a bias towards poetry that resembles his own. Poet–critics, for tactical reasons, may be especially hard, may have to be hard, on poets generationally antecedent to themselves. And being a poet, we may feel, a poet–critic will sometimes have too little interest in what he is doing as a critic to care about criticism – as criticism – to the extent that (as a critic) he should. Therefore it is sensible to regard the criticism of a poet with caution. But there is nevertheless a major reason for viewing criticism by poets as important. In theory at least, the poet is the 'expert' where poetry is concerned. As a maker of poetry, no one knows better the nature and laws of poetry's construction, or where this is faulty. The poet has a practitioner's authority, a professional's eye.

The writings of Ted Hughes have drawn little attention to themselves as literary criticism. It may therefore seem strange, here, to consider Hughes as a critic: only in recent years has evidence emerged of interest in his critical work as a separate but complementary achievement to his writings as a poet.[2] Partly, no doubt, this is because Hughes's criticism is hard to get hold of, or to view as a whole. The shape of most critics' work can be charted from key texts. Readily available, these are usually written within decorums of 'criticism' determined by the standard products of academic life. But Hughes's criticism is not marked in this way. This does not make Hughes less of a 'critic'. Turning to Hughes (the professional poet) from critical 'professionals' like Eagleton, Belsey, Carey, Ricks or the rest, can seem a breath of fresh air; like putting down on a different planet. One fact is soon apparent. He writes on poetry in a way that most modern writers on poetry, outside poetry, could not. As far as the reader is concerned, Hughes's criticism emphasises how much criticism, to matter, must *always* in some sense be in touch with the powers of a poet. He makes the habit of creation *seem* a necessary prerequisite, a prior qualification, for successful critical work. This shows startlingly in everything he says.

In individual interest and cumulative significance, Hughes's critical remarks are distinct from the miscellaneous, fragmentary or casual asides by an off-duty creative writer. And yet Hughes's prose commentary on art necessarily takes second place to his poetry. This is where Hughes's real development must be seen to occur. Hughes's criticism is essentially incidental to the major creative concerns of his career; an outgrowth from a centre that is in, and explained by, his poems. This makes the criticism of poetry for Hughes a peripheral pursuit, and explains why Hughes's criticism, if widely diffused through his work as a whole, is a farrago of fragments. Its nature is occasional Introductions, talks, transcripts of broadcasts or snippets in journals. Unlike most academic criticism, it is never concerned with one subject or author for long. There are no exhaustive 'studies'; no 'definitive' essays. It may also explain why his critical writings have not been collected, and why he has taken no steps to collect them himself. From this we may conclude that Hughes is too single-mindedly devoted to his poetry to warrant serious consideration as critic, either in theory or in practice. This view is in one sense supported, in one sense qualified, by Hughes's impressively prolific (but necessarily short-winded) work as a reviewer. The reviews of Carey or of Ricks present a popular face for their otherwise academic selves. Hughes's reviews function as a critical background to Hughes the poet: they assist in sketching his personal 'lines' and obsessions. If for Hughes reviewing was (and is) a useful source of financial returns, it has also offered him an apprenticeship in literary judgement, and a popular forum for the discussion of ideas, whether in his capacity as professional Yorkshireman, as a poet, or as both. Not surprisingly, many Hughes reviews reflect interests and preoccupations also to be found in the poetry. But they also suggest the beginnings of a critical talent that, perhaps because of the poetry's success, is more overshadowed than it deserves to have been.

The origins of Hughes's career as critic lie in the early 1960s when he worked as reviewer for the *Nation*. In 1960 he published reviews of Clancy Segal and Arnold Wesker. The following year, he began contributing reviews to the *New Statesman* with offerings, in 1961, on Tim Dinsdale (*Loch Ness Monster*), Alan Wykes (*Nimrod Smith*) and Joy Adamson (*Living Free*). The 'animal interest' was continued, in 1962, with reviews of Robert Froman (*The Nerve of Some Animals*), J. C. Lilly (*Man and Dolphin*), Sally Patrick Johnson (*Everyman's Ark*) and Alice Goudney (*Here Come the Elephants*). Slight though these are (and though hardly qualifying as literary criticism), they do nevertheless from time to time show wider interests breaking through. Thus animal life, for Hughes as reviewer as for Hughes as poet, provokes reflection on the nature of human existence: in this case modern human existence. We shall see that Hughes's large idea of human existence strongly motivates his criticism, as it does his poems:

> Our inter-bred, laboratory-coddled wits, displaced by automata from their essential services, grow more and more meaninglessly theoretical, more and more passive and infantile. Our brain case shrinks, our thyroid glands are going to sleep, our adrenal glands are withering, and our sexual organs and interests tyrannize over a vast psychic idleness or swarm of neurotic ailments.[3]

Animals, of course, are the subjects of some of Hughes's own best early poems. Hughes turned to the theme of poetry, and in particular modern poetry, in his (largely negative) review of John Press's *Rule and Energy*.[4] In some reviews, Hughes's poet's instinct and vision are not used in this specialist way, but to bring unusual light to bear on topics which fit dominant social and political emphases of the *New Statesman*. These were addressed, in Hughes's 1963 review of Philip O'Connor's book on tramps, with criticism, typically pithy and profound, of O'Connor's Jeremiah-like anti-competitive social vision and style: his ' "wild" prose, a crazy flying-machine pieced together out of psychologist's and sociologist's and phrenologist's jargon, and driven by an irate blast of rhetorical poetry'.[5] In the following year (1964), Hughes's fascination with animal life and the dimension of social speculation were brought together in review of Vitus Dröscher's *Mysterious Senses*. This describes, *inter alia*, a frightening Californian experiment on a colony of rats reduced to basic instincts of competitive power relations and exhibiting naked competition run mad. Hughes portrays this as a chilling, only slight extension of tendencies 'we can see everywhere in modern human society'.[6] Milton Rokeach, Louis MacNeice and T. C. Lethbridge were also treated in 1964, where Hughes touched on matters from poetry to the occult.

But though the majority of *New Statesman* reviews are mainly interesting in suggesting contextual patterns of thought and ideas behind Hughes's own poems, there are signs among them of an unusual critical voice, and moments which point clearly to Hughes's importance and qualifications as a literary critic. Perhaps the most extraordinary early review (and most ambitious) was of a fellow poet: that done in 1966 of Constantine Fitzgibbon's edition of Dylan Thomas's *Selected Letters*. While much of Hughes's review work up to this point is worthy primarily for light it throws on strands of his imagery and poetical themes, his essay on Thomas has self-contained critical power, a passionate engagement with its subject which gives it an importance all its own. The piece is still related to Hughes's work as poet, but in a different sense. It is not a matter of theme or subject, as in other reviews. Here it is a matter of Hughes's intensity of apprehension and his fellow feeling. Starting from letters, Hughes uses the occasion to explore layer by layer levels of Dylan Thomas as man and as poet. For the usual stock-popular melodrama of Thomas's external career, Hughes substitutes awareness of the inner drama of Thomas's personality, a portrait altogether less pitiful and altogether more powerful:

> In the series of letters to Pamela Hansford Johnson, where he first settles into his recognisable self, the free-for-all monologue occasionally reminds one of the dogfighting voices in possessed medieval women. The only time he escapes this facetious theatre are when he speaks about poetry – his, hers, or in general. Then suddenly we hear the voice that polished the voices, the demon stylist, a cold, severe, even ruthless sort of person, a voice of settled, radical judgments and godly self-confidence: slightly pedagogue, freezingly objective, aggressively, almost witheringly critical, almost sarcastic, nearly cruel. Clearly enough, an abandoned surrealistic or therapeutic torrent was the last thing Thomas allowed his reservoirs to become.[7]

In one of the last *New Statesman* pieces to be published in the 1960s (24 May 1968), we return to a more external sense of the relations between Hughes as reviewer and Hughes as poet. In this case the grounds are Hughes's anthropological interests. 'Lore Abiding' consists of reviews of a series of related editions: *Folktales of Chile, Hindoo Fairy Legends, The Glass Man and the Golden Bird* and *The Black Monkey*.

Hughes's work for the *Sunday Times* is significant in the light of the creative writing he has done in the form of narratives for children. Hughes sees profound issues at stake in literature 'intended' for children, and these are connected with Hughes's anthropological interest in elemental, instinctive nature, as in the nature of the human and animal instincts themselves. Hughes's *Sunday Times* reviewing started in 1962 with an introduction in the series 'A Book to Remember' to Saint-Exupéry's children's story, *The Little Prince*.[8] This was followed by reviews of H. G. Wells's *The War of the Worlds* (1962)[9] and in the same year two Introductions: one to *Tarka the Otter*, the other to *The Worst Journey in the World* by Apsley Cherry-Garrard, both printed in the *Sunday Times Colour Supplement*.[10] There were no more reviews for the *Sunday Times* until 1970, when a piece appeared on Iona and Peter Opie's *Children's Games in Street and Playground*.[11] But although, in many cases, the reviews for the *Sunday Times* substantially *reflect* important interests of Hughes, they are rarely able to suggest his qualifications as a literary critic. Moving from these to his reviews written for the *Listener* (the largest collection), qualities become apparent which cannot be accounted for purely in terms of Hughes's own art. These, done alongside his increasingly numerous broadcasting engagements, reveal signs of a critical commitment parallel with, but not necessarily subordinate to, main things in his work as a poet. In their general character, Hughes's reviews for the *Listener* reveal the extraordinary width of his literary interests, the relation between these literary interests and the interest he has taken in other cultural forms, and the broad historical sweep of his concerns. Reviewing for the *Listener* seems to have provided Hughes with the opportunity to explore as a critic his sense of the deep-fixed roots of humanity's idea of itself and to reinforce, in critical terms, the cultural dimensions which poetry (Hughes's own and other people's) requires in order to thrive. Hughes's first piece for the *Listener*, a review of C. M. Bowra's *Primitive Song*, was published on 3 May 1962. This was followed by an essay on Keith Douglas in the following month and a review of Robert Lowell in the issue of 2 August. A fourth *Listener* review appeared in October of the same year: of Alta Jablow's *An Anthology of West African Folklore*. The following year, in 1963, Hughes contributed to the *Listener* a review of three novels by Michael Baldwin, of Charles Anderson on poetry of Emily Dickinson, as well as reviews of *Folktales* of Japan and Israel. This was followed in 1964 by an essay on *Voss* by the Australian novelist, Patrick White.[12] 1964 also saw a review of E. O. G. Turville-Petre's *Myth and Religion of the North* where, in developing thought on the significance of Anglo–Norse mythology, Hughes launched an attack, telling from the point of view of his own poetry, on the over-Latinized nature of modern English language and imagination:

> ... one has only to look at our vocabulary to see where our real mental life has its roots, where the paths to and from our genuine imaginations run, clearly enough. It's false to say these gods and

heroes are obsolete: they are the better part of our patrimony still locked up.[13]

But although Hughes's momentum in these pieces is kept up by the passion of the poet, his prose remarks on poetry also represent an unusual way of talking about poetry. They thereby convey the deficiencies of a criticism that rests exclusively on academic examples of the form. This they do by Hughes's explicit and implicit understanding of what poetry is; the conception of the object under consideration that is reflected back by Hughes's critical remarks. In another review in the same year, Hughes is out to establish further contact with sources of feeling that for him are the more fundamental as they are found outside the familiar round of Romano–Christian literary tradition. Now, Hughes's subject is African writing, both traditional and modern. In his comments on Volume II of W. H. Whiteley's *Selection of African Prose,* Hughes, though he is clearly referring to qualities which he wishes to come through in his own poems, creates for the reader a powerful idea of African literature's distinctive energy and voice: 'Their [the pieces'] embryonic character, which is linked to the pervasive imitation of cheap European models, does not vitiate the vehement inner concentration of these narratives, the core of imaginative fury, fused with realistic feeling, that breaks out into effects of great force and simplicity.'[14] Other *Listener* reviews of 1964, such as that of Mircea Eliade's *Shamanism* and Idries Shah's *The Sufis,* signal Hughes's interest in the *Bardo Thödol* or *Tibetan Book of the Dead,* and reach out in yet more associative ways to non-Eurocentric modes of thinking and knowing. In all these ways, Hughes, as far as he is expanding the geographical and cultural basis necessary for the consideration of human society and the artefacts it creates, is moving with equal energy inwards towards something that comes to be affiliated with the essentially poetic, or the 'romantic'. A review of Pushkin's *Letters* (also from 1964) is also concerned with the inwardness of remoteness: this time it is that of a Russian with African blood, possessed of 'gloomy reservoirs of romantic feeling'. Hughes's last review for the *Listener* was on a topic nearer to home: I. M. Parsons's edition of First World War poetry, *Men Who March Away.*[15]

Hughes's *Listener* reviews reflect thinking that accompanies his efforts to reach beyond the surface of the modern Western European consciousness and society. They exhibit a critical sense of poetry connected to Hughes's in its assertion of inward intensity, and point to a taste for the primitive sources of Hughes's own cross-cultural creative projects (for example, his translation of *Oedipus*). But they also suggest the terms of a critical stance that is independent of his poetry. This is developed in other review work that Hughes undertook in the middle and later sixties (of which some was to find a North American market). Here again, the interests of a modern poet in other modern poets combine with the now characteristic Hughes mixture of the anthropological, the non-Christocentric, the primitive and the environmental. C. Day Lewis's edition of Wilfrid's Owen's *Collected Poems* was treated in the *New York Times Book Review* in 1964. In the same year (December), Hughes did reviews of *Heimskringla* and *The Prose Edda* by Snorri Sturluson and *Gods, Demons and Others* by R. K. Narayan for the *New York Review of Books*. A classic review–essay on Isaac Bashevis Singer appeared in the same periodical in April 1965 and in December of that year a review of John Greenaway's *Literature among the Primitives* and *The Primitive Reader*. In Britain, Hughes did a review of Mathew Hodgart's *The Faber Book of Ballads* for the *Guardian* and later, in 1972, a review of Carlos Castaneda's *A Separate Reality* for the *Observer*. One-off jobs include an essay entitled 'Myth and Education' for the first number of *Children's Literature in Education* and a review of Max Nicholson's *The Environmental Revolution* for the first number of *Your Environment* (Summer 1970), the latter an expanded version of a piece that had first appeared in the *Spectator* for that year.[16] But while, in all these pieces, Hughes's talents as critic are often arresting, they are also unsustained and dispersed. They lack focus and occasion. Thus, in his reviews, the distinction that Hughes is to reveal as a critic remains substantially concealed, a distraction from what is really interesting and important about him. When, however, Hughes assembles his thoughts in a single work his qualities as a critic seem suddenly to spring to the fore. One of the major triumphs to come out of Hughes's work in the sixties was what began as a series of broadcast talks on poetry, was published by the BBC and then finally collected, amended and brought together as the volume entitled *Poetry in the Making*. Here we find one of Hughes's most impressive contributions to date to the critical discussion of literary art.

From *Poetry in the Making* we suddenly see why being a poet can make you a critic. We also see why to be a critic (in other than the merely academic sense) you *have* to be a poet, in reality or imagination. With this book before us, all other approaches to the activity of literary criticism seem now hopelessly academic, in the sense of remote from objects of study, and therefore miserably beside the point. It helps that the book is as much anthology of poems as critical study of poetry. It helps also that it has practical, educational, purpose. For though limited in aims (it is intended to help children in efforts to find more honest and adequate verbal expression for observations and ideas), it collects more wisdom about poetry than the works of any number of 'professional' critics put together. The book benefits from the fact that it is a printed version of a succession of radio talks for the series *Listening and Writing,* done for the BBC Schools Broadcasting Department. A quality of talk is preserved in the style. It is straight kind of talk. Hughes's limpid prose conveys enormous confidence of grasp. He is neither straining to develop an original theory nor out to impress us with the sharpness of his mind. He simply knows what it is he is talking about. The fact that he knows comes over in everything he says. In the opening section, Hughes compares making a poem to capturing animals, a favourite occupation of his childhood and early youth. Making a poem, he suggests, is like making an animal your own. The poem is a living creature, with parts or limbs, body and spirit. The fancy serves to illustrate vividly processes of poetic creation in a way which, while conscious of the need to address the young reader, does not patronise or condescend. It renders the abstract matter of poetic invention and expression tangible and real. The book is not just therefore a classroom book for children, and Hughes seems to know this. By getting down to basics, Hughes finds ways of saying things about poetry that few adults would dismiss as stale or routine. Why is a poem like an animal?

> It is better to call it an assembly of living parts moved by a single spirit. The living parts are the words, the images, the rhythms. The spirit is the life which inhabits them when they all work together. It is impossible to say which comes first, parts or spirit. But if any of the parts are dead . . . if any of the words, or images or rhythms do not jump to life as you read them . . . then the creature is going to be maimed and the spirit sickly.[17]

As well as general discussion about poetic creation, commentary sections of each chapter function as introductions to Hughes's own poems and those of other poets, thematically arranged. The non-Hughes poems are usually modern, but not always, and include examples by poets from other periods, such as those by John Clare and Christopher Smart, or other countries, as those of Vasko Popa. With Hughes's remarks, the reader begins from a fixed point. And with each poem he then moves off in all kinds of directions, as the theme of each chapter is varied and developed, and as the reader, when he reads the pieces, explores for himself, prior to writing a piece of his own. Generally poems, and sometimes sections of prose, or prose–poetry (and tasks they go with), start simply, getting more complicated as the book proceeds. Hughes's commentary and poetry are reciprocally related. Poems vividly illustrate, or encapsulate, the general point being made. At the same time the prose equips the reader, in each instance, to 'take' poem or poems more fully. It puts him in the right state, or mood, to feel their impact, so the effect is experienced more sharply than with a poem on its own. A bit of autobiographical detail, never much, is used sometimes to set the scene for the break from prose to poetry. This happens just like a singer breaking into song. Here, in the chapter on 'Wind and Weather', we have Hughes explaining the source of what, when we read it, comes over as having both its own separate life and one made more vital by the scene we are made to picture to ourselves in advance by the poet:

On and off I live in a house on top of a hill in the Pennines, where the wind blows without obstruction across the tops of the moors. I have experienced some gales in that house, and here is a poem I once wrote about one of them. The grass of the fields there is of a particularly brilliant watered green, and the stone walls of the enclosures that cover the hillsides like a great net thrown over whales, look coal black. The poem is called simply: *Wind*.

This house has been far out at sea all night...[18]

By the time we get to the image of stone walls covering hills like 'a great net thrown over whales', we are already in the poem. So it both is, and is not, a surprise to find ourselves tossed about in the house like a ship out at sea.

It does not matter that the book is a children's book, designed to help children write. The advice is classic, practical advice just the same. The knowledge of how poetry and prose work, and how to make them work, is just as sound. Try to see things as they are; take in details; learn how to concentrate; try to decide what really interests you and distinguish it from your casual interests; concentrate on your subject and let the words take care of themselves: '... the words are the colouring of the work, which, in the order of nature, is last to be considered. The design, the disposition, the manners, and the thoughts, are all before it.' So wrote the father of English literary criticism and himself a poet, Dryden.[19] In the final chapter of *Poetry in the Making* Hughes, his modern successor, offers his own modern-day meditations on the relation of words to things:

> It is the same with all our experience of life: the actual substance of it, the material facts of it, embed themselves in us quite a long way from the world of words. It is when we set out to find words for some seemingly quite simple experience that we begin to realize what a huge gap there is between our understanding of what happens around us and inside us, and the words we have at our command to say something about it.[20]

Hughes does not write of the signifier as arbitrary, but claims it is inadequate. He does not say that language creates meaning; he says that it has meaning, and meaning of its own, but that we are constantly struggling, mostly without success, to make it convey the meaning we want it to have. However words try to subvert meaning, it is experience, searching for expression through them, which is the important thing. It does not matter one way or other if we give this thinking a name, 'subjectivist', 'liberal–humanist' or some other. Whatever label we stick on it, it remains fresh thought, hot from the anvil:

> Words are tools, learned late and laboriously and easily forgotten, with which we try to give some part of our experience a more or less permanent shape outside ourselves. They are unnatural, in a way, and far from being ideal for their job. For one thing, a word has its own definite meanings. A word is its own little solar system of meanings. Yet we are wanting it to carry some part of our meaning, of the meaning of our experience, and the meaning of our experience is finally unfathomable...[21]

But the critical strengths that are focused in *Poetry in the Making* also appear in Hughes's other critical work, as in the articles on poets that Hughes composed for the *Critical Quarterly*. Here again Hughes gains critical insight and precision from that which he is and knows as a practising poet. Of three articles written for the *Critical Quarterly* two are printed texts of radio talks broadcast shortly before. Two have further, later, destinations: as 'Introductions' to selections of the poets in question. As essays on poetry they convey the range and tones of Hughes's broadcasting voice, moving from the warmly appreciative through the delicately matter-of-fact to the awesome and terrible. Hughes, as poet, blends his feelings about a particular poet with his feelings about poetry as a whole: his accounts read as explorations of what poetry can be and do. As in the criticism of other poet–critics, elements in Hughes's positive critical appraisals of other poets at times fit his own. But his criticism, when Hughes is at his best, does not seem limited by the terms of his poetry, but rather contributes to the inwardness with which he is able to appreciate, and critically communicate, poetry other than his own. The first essay, published in 1963, is on Keith Douglas; and became the text of an Introduction to Hughes's edition of *The Selected Poems of Keith Douglas* (1964).[22] Here Hughes says things that a critic not also a poet could not say. Douglas's relation to the past, for example, is seen from the viewpoint of a fellow poet trying to be true to his times: Douglas's temperament 'is so wholly modern he seems to have no difficulty with the terrible, suffocating, maternal octopus of ancient English poetic tradition'.[23] As a poet, Hughes is assisted to appreciate the modern poet's (and Douglas's) historical plight. Hughes applies to Douglas a heightened awareness of the contemporary context for poetry formed by his own poems. Also heightened is the critically tactful acknowledgement of the unity of other poets' work. Often in these articles, poems quoted are quoted whole. Albeit that he is dealing with poems which are short, Hughes avoids lopped-off lines or truncated 'illustrations', and this conveys respect for the integrity of the poetic material. The piece concludes with a striking definition of Douglas's poetic language, where it is hard to believe Hughes is not also thinking the issue through for himself, and for the sake of his poems:

> It is a language for the whole mind, at its most wakeful, and in all situations: a utility general-purpose style, as, for instance, Shakespeare's was, that combines a colloquial prose readiness with poetic breadth, a ritual intensity and music of an outstandingly high order with clear direct feeling, and yet in the end is nothing but casual speech.[24]

Being a poet, Hughes can discuss poetry almost routinely, as an everyday event. Hughes's criticism of poetry is thus without the pretension or postures often required in academic criticism. Hughes's criticism of Douglas reveals a characteristic prominent in *Poetry in the Making*, as in the next *Critical Quarterly* piece, on Sylvia Plath (again taken from a broadcast talk): that is, Hughes's extraordinary way as critic of 'setting' a poem by comments he uses to surround it, like the frame of a picture. Hughes orchestrates his critical prose to create quiet, separate, space for the poem he is quoting, compelling us to attend. But this is done without false reverential notes, or any melodramatic sense of occasion. It occurs with an easy, almost informal, movement of mind, an implied 'now look at this' or 'now look at that'. The power of poems is felt more strongly because it is taken for granted. It is something we all ought to see, not just a matter for the specialist or connoisseur: 'Here is one of the earliest of them [Sylvia Plath's poems] . . . Here is an early one called "Sleep in the Mojave Desert" . . . The next, from about the same time, describes drifting in a rowing boat, over a still Canadian lake at nightfall . . .'[25]

Then there is Hughes's personal affinity (as poet) with particular poetical topics. In the essay on the Hungarian poet János Pilinszky (whom Hughes translated), Hughes turns from the delicate and beautiful to the harsh and bleak, a harshness and bleakness intimately related to Hughes's personal sense of the conditions that prevail in the cosmos, and his own way of expressing them: 'In Pilinszky's world, there is no way out. The simplicity, the iron on iron impact of his awkwardly simple language springs direct from his confrontation with what he takes to be the final condition of the sensual world.'[26]

Hughes's criticism gains from the fact that he is a poet in two main ways. The first is a matter of style: his 'poetic' way of expressing reactions. The second is his grasp of what poetry is. But the two are connected. To illustrate the grasp that is there in Hughes's critical prose we can turn from Hughes's periodical articles to the introductory essay. Considering the praise he gives to two poems by Emily Dickinson, 'the great American poetess', in his *Poetry in the Making,* it is not surprising to find Hughes publishing a choice of her verse in the following year. Hughes's Introduction to his choice of Emily Dickinson's verse is a short piece based in part on his earlier review of C. R. Anderson's *Emily Dickinson's Poetry* printed in the *Listener.*[27] The Introduction, five years later, is less rhapsodic than the review and gives the essential details of the poet's biography and the editorial history of her poems. The facts are the kind readers new to Emily Dickinson would need to know (for example that only six of her total output of nearly eighteen hundred poems were published in her lifetime). The Introduction is sympathetic in tone and successfully sets the scene for reading her verse. In so doing, it suggests an intimate emotional resonance between the poet and her poet–critic. What she is doing in her poetry, and why, is conveyed from the inside, and in language having simultaneously restrained and expressive power. This power is present at some of the most routine moments in the Introduction, as when Hughes is briefly describing Emily Dickinson's life at home with her father, of whom she wrote: 'His heart was pure and terrible and I think no other like it exists.' Hughes adds: '... but he had a large library, and it was perhaps through his concerns and acquaintances that his intense daughter eavesdropped on the world'.

This half-humorous image alerts us to the contrast between what is at once the domestic smallness of the poet's preoccupations and their enormous potential scope. It evokes the ability, unique to a poet, of making the global and intensely introspective coincide. Shortly after, Hughes captures, by choice of words and measured rhythms, the mysterious inexplicable moment of suspended animation which precedes a creative outburst in a poet:

> Around 1860, something decisive happened to Emily Dickinson. How far it was the natural point of maturation of many things in herself, and how much it was triggered by some outer event, is not known, though the possibilities have been endlessly discussed. But the effect was a conflagration within her that produced just about one thousand poems in six years, more than half her total.

These cool statistics about Emily Dickinson's 'total', and her rate of production, serve all the more to sensitise us to the effect of 'conflagration', the fire which caused so many poems to pour forth at once. Picking up this image of fire and combining it with thought of the intense girl, Hughes can then write of 'the crucible of her imagination' in which diverse forces met. The concentrated heat of this intensely personal imagination is seen as giving precise location at once to private passions of love and to the immense drama of national political and spiritual events.

Beyond this, Hughes finds Emily Dickinson making contact with the great impersonal world extending outside self (a poetical preoccupation of his own), and material reality. Hughes's prose takes on poetic characteristics at this point. In rising to the subject, his poet's realisations form themselves in expression monosyllabically simple: 'She never seems to have known quite what to think of it,' and rhapsodic: 'It was her deepest, holiest experience: it was also the most terrible: timeless, deathly, vast, intense.' Hughes follows Emily Dickinson in capturing presence in absence; recognition through incomprehension: '... she could make up her mind about nothing. It stared through her life. It stared out of every smallest thing and gave the world its awesome, pathetic importance. Registering everywhere and in everything the icy chill of its nearness, she did not know what to think.' It would not be hard to find lines in Hughes's poems echoing the movement of such critical remarks, or others in Hughes's modest but compelling Introduction. No one could read it without wanting to turn urgently to the poems it precedes.[28]

This power to invite us to read poems (in ways impossible to refuse) is among the distinctions of Hughes as a critic. Hughes's genius as a poet spills over to his criticism on the question of how poetry is created. Often, Hughes is talking about his own acts of creation. But his utterances have at the same time the potential to infuse how we think about creation in poetry as a whole (and for that matter creation in arts other than poetry). Therefore what Hughes says of his own work affects how we think of poetry written by others. This is in turn a product of how Hughes describes working up a poem: his (poet's) choice of language. In 'Ted Hughes Writes' (1957), printed in the *Poetry Book Society Bulletin,* Hughes represents the activity of making poetry as that of reconciling opposites; bringing violently opposed energies of heart, body and brain to temporary 'peace' in a poem. To capture this act, Hughes employs a musical analogy:

> The way I do this, as I believe, is by using something like the method of a musical composer. I might say that I turn every combatant into a bit of music, then resolve the whole uproar into as formal and balanced a figure of melody and rhythm as I can. When all the words are hearing each other clearly, and every stress is feeling every other stress, and all are contented – the poem is finished.

Here, Hughes is talking about his own poems. But eight years later, in a review of poems by Sylvia Plath, he repeats the image of words in poems being able not only to speak, but to hear each other speak, forming an independent community separate from the poet: 'The words in these odd-looking verses [*Ariel*] are not only charged with terrific heat, pressure and clairvoyant precision, they are all deeply related within any poem, acknowledging each other and calling to each other in deep harmonic design.'[29]

Hughes is therefore at his strongest when his wisdom about poetry has helped him understand what other poets have succeeded in doing and have failed to do. His limitations appear when he seems to be imposing upon other authors a private conception of, and interest in, the nature of art. This is the case when Hughes is writing of Isaac Bashevis Singer: 'Vision seems to be the right word for what Singer is conveying. The most important fact about him, that determines the basic strategy by which he deals with his subject, is that his imagination is poetic, and tends towards symbolic situations.'[30] Often, however, the point at which Hughes's strengths as a critic become limitations, or his limitations strengths, is difficult to make out. Much of Hughes's criticism, for example, is on modern poetry. But Hughes's framework of ideas is not special to modern poetry. Hughes writes on poetry aware of his personal relation, as poet, to a traditional background. And yet even then his approach is intensely personal, even where he is appearing to move historically outwards from the present and away from the moment of his own poems. For Hughes, the past is alive as a poetic community of which he is a part. Hughes can thus defend poetry as a spirit always under threat. In a 1962 essay on 'Context', Hughes suggests the poet's only hope is to have faith in his gift, even though this faith will be constantly challenged. While stressing this point, Hughes condemns as a diversion the tendency of poets to become preoccupied with social and political questions of their day. Such preoccupation (discussed with reference to the poetry of Wordsworth, Coleridge and Blake) is not only harmful to the work of the poet; it is unnecessary. Social and political change is guided itself by change in the arts. For an artist, the important thing is concentration on art:

> Damon, quoted by Plato, says that the modes of music are nowhere altered without changes in the most important laws of the state. Is a

musician to listen to his gift then, or study legislation? The poet who feels he needs to mix his poetry up with significant matters, or to throw his verse into the popular excitement of the time, ought to remember this strange fact...[31]

But, if in one way this suggests a narrowly anti-contextual and therefore constricted approach to poetry and criticism (that consonant with the *purism* of the practitioner), many aspects of Hughes's criticism are the reverse of narrow. Hughes does not regard poetry as reducible to text, severed from the author who gave birth to it. Hughes's 'theory' of criticism and poetry aspires to include the whole of the author's humanity in any consideration of literary work. This is made explicit in Hughes's review of the *Letters of Dylan Thomas:*

> Part of the comic effect is that it's always concealing something unusually serious – in the early years, his poetic gift, ambitions and ideals, and later on his struggle against the odds, the gruelling rearguard retreat towards the 18 straight whiskies. This is what makes these letters the best introduction to the way his poetry ought to be read. Everything we associate with a poem is its shadowy tenant and part of its meaning, no matter how New Critical purist we try to be. Yeats's life is not the less interesting half of his general effort, and one wonders what his poetry would amount to if it could be lifted clear of the biographical matrix. Quite a lot, no doubt. But how much less than at present! With poets who set their poetic selves further into the third person, maybe the life is less relevant. But Thomas's life, letters and legends belong to his poetry, in that they make it mean more.[32]

It is not true that Hughes can only appreciate poems by others which resemble his own. In the second of two interviews printed by Ekbert Faas, Hughes confesses to enthusiasm for the poetry of John Crowe Ransom. Hughes felt this strongly in the earlier part of his writing career. But he is prepared to defend it in 1977, when the interview took place. When in 1972, Hughes was invited to read favourite verse by Philip Larkin on a radio programme, he chose 'Absences', 'Going' and 'Days'. None of this poetry is much like Hughes. And yet authors who come under critical scrutiny by Hughes on many occasions reflect influences found in his poems. At one extreme, Hughes's interests extend to primitive literature. At the other, Hughes devotes a considerable proportion of his criticism to commentary upon poets of the twentieth century. Hughes knows the *milieu* of twentieth-century poetry from within. By no means all of Hughes's modern poets are British. As a reader and commentator on the modern poetical scene, he is transatlantic in reach. But his criticism also stretches beyond the mere English-speaking world to the poets of the communist *bloc*, and the lessons they teach to the human world as a whole. In seeking such lessons, and the directness and intensity that Hughes is able to locate in poetry as a necessary outlet for feeling, Hughes moves outside well-trodden critical ground in another direction: to writing for children. And Hughes, a one-time archaeology student, is not confined to literature: he embraces thought, music and a range of artistic forms from classical to primitive to oriental: as for example in his interest in *The Tibetan Book of the Dead*. As we have seen, Hughes's willingness to move between poetry and prose in his own creations (and the poetic-expressive qualities of his own prose) is reflected in judgements: 'Patrick White,' he can write, 'is the most exciting poet Australia has yet produced...'[33]

Hughes's imposition of 'self' on his subjects may be interpreted as part of the impulse to become one with them. Even in his reviews, Hughes works from imaginative positions coincident with his poet's. He seeks empathy with a subject who is both wonderful to contemplate and painful to contemplate, tracing the movement from his subject's source inspiration, vision or plight, through the stages of composition to the finished creation. He stresses, almost always, the great agitating, sometimes desperate, sometimes doomed power that resides in genius, and many reviews anatomise the precise functioning of this power. As he shows it at work, Hughes is not out to impress. He is not slick. The interest he reveals is that of sympathetic fellow feeling with those who engage, sometimes in seemingly hopeless circumstances, at the profoundest levels in the processes of art. Hughes speaks *for* the author he is writing about. He does this, not in competition with the author, or as a mediator, or interpreter, or demystifyer of the mysteries of art to an otherwise ignorant public, but with the assumed delegated authority of a member of the creative community to which both he and the author belong. This may occur even when, as individuals, the writers discussed are completely unlike him. It is nowhere more apparent than when Hughes is describing the man in the poet, as in his review of Dylan Thomas's *Letters*, where the poet's uphill, futile effort is poignantly caught:

> And the poetry which is, among other things, an escape from personality, was not to be written. The battle he fought with his steadily solidifying poetic style, pushing the adjectives for months at a time to and fro over those hundreds of worksheets, must be one of the keys to his demoralisation.[34]

He does it again when outlining the strange alien and alienated character of Pushkin. There is nothing to feel superior to in this portrait. We feel only the critic's, and our own, insignificance by the side of the subject:

> Often he gives the impression of being two people. At one extreme, his deeper self, is the sufferer, solitary, outlawed from mankind somehow, with huge, gloomy reservoirs of romantic feeling (he liked to think of his private monopoly of primitive African passion), susceptible to moods of oceanic desolation, an archaic, muzhik- or life-prisoner sense of the nothingness and boredom and mere playfulness of existence, a self that could pour its energies into poetry and women. This is the self of the early poems. But after the first painful collisions with an exceedingly caustic and political society ... the other self came to his rescue and took over the practical guidance of his affairs.[35]

Hughes's reviews are marked by a steady humanity. They stress the idea of a consciousness at odds with itself. By revealing the critical interactions which take place in the process of poetic creation, they convey deep respect for the common lot of artistic struggle and have nothing of the flip, easy dismissive wit of the literary journalist who stands outside it all.

And Hughes's reviews are remarkable in attempting to see poets in the spirit once recommended to the literary critic by Pope:

> Survey the *Whole*, nor seek slight Faults to find.[36]

As he wrote of Sylvia Plath:

> Surveyed as a whole, with attention to the order of composition, I think the unity of her opus is clear. Once the unity shows itself, the logic of and inevitability of the language, which controls and contains such conflagrations and collisions within itself, becomes more obviously what it is – direct, and even plain, speech.[37]

As often in Hughes's description of poets, the whole achievement is perceived as a clash or confrontation of opposite or discordant qualities resolved in the creative heat of poetry. In seeing poets as wholes, Hughes sees them as gathering together disparate and diverse parts of themselves and their view of reality into oneness individually distinct and unlike anything else: '. . . it wasn't in Thomas to negotiate or protect himself on this or any other front'.[38] Sylvia Plath 'underwent a poetic development that has hardly any equal on record, for suddenness and completeness'.[39] Often, Hughes writes of a poet bringing everything of himself or herself together in poetry, life and art, as Emily Dickinson did: '. . . it is in her verbal genius that all her gifts and sufferings came to focus'.[40] For Hughes, the ability to unite separate things, and separate worlds, marks the true poet. 'It is all there,' he says of Vasko Popa, the Yugoslavian poet, in a tone which is almost resigned to qualities about poetry it takes for granted: 'the surprising fusion of unlikely elements.'[41] This belief in fusion is not just a technical matter for Hughes. It is a whole way of feeling and seeing the force of what is. In the human being, inner and outer worlds are made to confront each other. Hughes resembles Mason in rejecting distinctions between 'objective' and 'subjective' perception. Subjective and objective exist as opposed dimensions of an essentially single vision:

> Objective imagination, then, important as it is, is not enough. What about a 'subjective' imagination? It is only logical to suppose that a faculty developed specially for peering into the inner world might end up as specialized and destructive as the faculty for peering into the outer one. Besides, the real problem comes from the fact that outer world and inner world are interdependent at every moment. We are simply the locus of their collision. Two worlds, with mutually contradictory laws, or laws that seem to us to be so, colliding afresh every second, struggling for peaceful coexistence. And whether we like it or not our life is what we are able to make of that collision and struggle.[42]

With immense eloquence, Hughes then extends this idea of the condition of 'being' that is proper to the human being to the condition of the artist. What was true of Dylan Thomas in particular ('In his life, the reflex of this [his] vision was a complete openness toward both inner and outer worlds'[43]) is true of the artist in general:

> So what we need, evidently, is a faculty that embraces both worlds simultaneously. A large, flexible grasp, an inner vision which holds wide open, like a great theatre, the arena of contention, and which pays equal respects to both sides. Which keeps faith, as Goethe says, with the world of things and the world of spirits equally.
> This really is imagination. This is the faculty we mean when we talk about the imagination of the great artists. The character of great works is exactly this: that in them the full presence of the inner world combines with and is reconciled to the full presence of the outer world. And in them we see that the laws of the two worlds are not contradictory at all; they are one all-inclusive system; they are laws that somehow we find it all but impossible to keep, laws that only the greatest artists are able to restate.[44]

Belief in fusion (it can, if necessary, be described as a theory) itself unifies Hughes's critical comments on art. It therefore enacts the precept he applies.

While seeing poets as wholes, Hughes also sees poetry as a whole. Individual poets are significant, but do not matter as individuals. The conception of poetry to emerge from Hughes's writings and reviews is born of a single effort. Poetry is advanced by many people in different ways. But it acts in one direction. This is what Hughes is almost always writing about. Each poet offers another opportunity to define, work out, work through or explore a poetic idea or ideal. And the idea, as often as not, is Hughes's idea of creation. Many of his judgements in some way express this idea, cross-fertilise in relation to it and draw sustenance from it. Poetry is conceived in 'ecstasy' (Sylvia Plath, Emily Dickinson); it results from an 'explosion' (Sylvia Plath), or 'conflagration' (Emily Dickinson, Sylvia Plath). It occurs when some form of musical harmony is achieved (Ted Hughes, Sylvia Plath). A system of internal relations must be established (Ted Hughes, Sylvia Plath). The poet is not necessarily in control of his or her insight or genius: 'She [Sylvia Plath] didn't quite know how to manage it [her genius for love]: it possessed her.' Emily Dickinson 'did not know what to think'. What comes out does so, when it comes, under 'pressure' (Keith Douglas, Sylvia Plath) at a high temperature (Emily Dickinson, Sylvia Plath), often in headlong flight, or part of a 'ruthless drive' (Laura Riding[45]). Singer possessed a 'creative demon'; Sylvia Plath a 'demonic spirit'. Dylan Thomas, like Singer, possessed a 'vision'. Thomas possessed a 'psychic openness'; Plath 'psychic gifts'. Hughes's ability to convey an intimate sense of how poetry happens is one of his criticism's major achievements. Poetry can happen because the individual poet makes it happen, through a fevered and frantic effort of will. Or, it can happen when the poet acts as an instrument by which means sounds are conveyed. Then, the source of poetry is outside him. It acts through him. Here Hughes is, talking about the poet's way of capturing the truth of what it is to be alive in the Universe:

> And the startling quality of this 'truth' is that it is terrible. It is for some reason harrowing, as well as being the utterly beautiful thing. Once when his spirits were dictating poetic material to Yeats, an owl cried outside the house, and the spirits paused. After a while one said: 'We like that sort of sound.' And that is it: 'that sort of sound' makes the spirits listen. It opens our deepest and innermost ghost to sudden attention. It is a spirit, and it speaks to spirit.[46]

Once, in an essay on drama, the poet–critic John Dryden said of Shakespeare that 'All the images of nature were still present to him'.[47] Hughes describes the workings of the spirit through the poet in terms that, while more melodramatic, are not vastly different: 'In all these, that lost spirit-being opens a door to a world of spirit – nothing else, it simply opens a door, and that other world is present. And it is as if the whole Creation were suddenly present.'[48]

Hughes's interest in having poetry startle or harrow readers is related to his taste for a poetry stylistically and expressively direct. Hughes wants poets to push routes through all that obstructs what he sometimes calls 'the Truth', and sometimes 'Nature'. Eastern European poets' inability to do anything about the political and physical circumstances surrounding their compositions 'has purged them of rhetoric'.[49] Laura Riding does what Hughes advises new young poets to do in *Poetry in the Making:* she turns her mind to things rather than words; she was 'essentially contemptuous of words'.[50] Vasko Popa invents words 'in total disregard for poetry'.[51] For Laura Riding ' "The poetry does not matter." '[52] The standard that Hughes revives in his criticism is that of simplicity. Hughes wants and likes poetry that is naked, even raw. But he is also attracted to a simplicity that is less brutal in kind. Of Keith Douglas he wrote in 'The Poetry of Keith Douglas': 'He is a renovator of language. It is not that he uses words in jolting combinations, or with titanic extravagance, or curious precision. His triumph lies in the way he renews the simplicity of ordinary talk.'[53]

It is, of course, only a short step from Hughes's taste to his own professed practice as poet. In an interview with Ekbert Faas in 1970, Hughes refers to his ambition of directness in writing *Crow:*

> The idea was originally just to write his songs, the songs that a Crow would sing. In other words, songs with no music whatsoever, in a super-simple and a super-ugly language which would in a way shed everything except just what he wanted to say without any other consideration and that's the basis of the style of the whole thing.[54]

It is consistent with Hughes's appeal to simplicity that he should account for his fellow poets' essential activity by reference to a single inspirational vision. This is because Hughes, while he is able to make wide-ranging excursions through the literatures and cultures of the world, is seeing the world in his own creative terms. Many of the writers that Hughes treats in his critical articles, reviews, essays or introductions are remarkable for negative affirmations. He embraces writers who are themselves prey to the pervading bleak nihilism of his outlook. He seeks and finds in criticism those who share conceptions of poetry as, and of, crisis.

Consequently, Hughes is not interested enough, critically, in the ways poets differ. Excited by poets' ability to capture and express great forces of universal destruction, he gives special attention to the poets who make these forces the subject of their poems. But sometimes, he seems to read this personal creative requirement *into* his appreciation. He thereby reasserts a conception of poetry that is historically specific. Hughes is an heir of the Romantics in his nostalgia for the culture of primitive societies, his impatience with Roman influence on English, and his reiterated devotion to choice aspects of the oriental and psychological exotic. He is stirred most by the drama, or melodrama, of the poetic psyche. Whenever he is talking about poets in the process of creating art, this psyche is the focus of his critical concern, the creative crucible in which elements of poetry are fused. The narrowness and the intensity of this vision level down Hughes's particular judgements. They diminish the difference between poets on different political planes. One of Hughes's best known pieces of critical writing was included in his anthology of Shakespearean writing, *A Choice of Shakespeare's Verse*. At the other extreme, Hughes's criticism is dominated by a private gallery of favourite moderns, of whom one was his wife. Hughes's criteria of judgement shrink the former and overinflate the latter. Hughes, however, is most convincing when fellow moderns are in view. With the special insight of a fellow practitioner, Hughes can point to the core, or centre, of a modern poet whose output may seem at first sight lacking coherence or sense of direction. Hughes, in revealing a single impulse or ambition at the root of a poet, can help bring poems alive. But Hughes's practice, while appropriate to the discussion of a relatively minor poet, is of less value when more needs to be taken into account. With the exception of Shakespeare, such poets are generally absent from Hughes's criticism. And even when writing on Shakespeare Hughes is concerned to find at the heart of the plays one theme, one motivation, one vision, unifying and interfusing all. It is interesting to see how closely this criticism reflects Hughes's idea of poetry as he practises it himself: 'His single fundamental idea, then, is the symbolic fable which nearly all his greatest passages combine to tell, and which each of his plays in some form or other tell over again.' In the interview conducted in 1977 by Ekbert Faas, Hughes said of his own work that:

... it is not the story that I am interested in but the poems. In other words, the whole narrative is just a way of getting a big body of ideas and energy moving on a track. For when this energy connects with a possibility for a poem, there is a lot more material and pressure in it than you could ever get into a poem just written out of the air for a special occasion. Poems come to you much more naturally and accumulate more life when they are part of a connected flow of real narrative that you've got yourself involved in.[55]

In talking about Shakespeare, Hughes may as well have been talking about himself.

As a critic, Hughes is therefore both too close to the authors he treats, and too far away. Too often, he is inclined to find mirror reflections of himself, whether he is talking about favourite modern poets, or moving in large and vague realms of the shamanistic and psychic, primitive folklore, magic and the literature of cultures distant in time and place. The authors discussed by Hughes are either immediately at hand or over the horizon. Perhaps this suggests that Hughes, while working to avoid the charge of English parochialism, is keen to keep tactfully silent about predecessors in English poetry who might, if thought on more, place Hughes's own work in an adversely critical light. Hughes minimises this latter danger by concentrating on the minor modern or the mythically remote. It is too personally interested a view to leave Hughes's critical authority unimpaired.

Notes

1. W. W. Robson, *The Definition of Literature*, p. 44.
2. See *Ted Hughes: The Unaccommodated Universe*, by Ekbert Faas, with Selected Critical Writings by Ted Hughes and Two Interviews (Black Sparrow Press, 1980). This volume was reviewed by Graham Bradshaw, *Cambridge Quarterly*, **X**, 2 (1981), pp. 172–78.
3. 'Man and Superbeast', *New Statesman*, 23 March 1962, p. 420. For an annotated list of Hughes's reviews and other critical work up to 1980, see *Ted Hughes: a Bibliography, 1946–80*, by Keith Sagar (London: Mansell, 1983).
4. *New Statesman*, 9 August 1963, p. 172.
5. *New Statesman*, 6 September 1963, p. 294.

6. *New Statesman*, 27 November 1964, p. 838.
7. *New Statesman*, 25 November 1966, p. 783.
8. 'A Book to Remember I: Ted Hughes Tells You About A Book Of Fantasy,' 'Introduction' to *The Little Prince* by Antoine de Saint-Exupéry, *Sunday Times*, 25 February 1962, p. 45.
9. *Sunday Times*, 24 June 1962, p. 29.
10. 16 September 1962, p. 18; 18 November 1962, p. 27.
11. 11 January 1970.
12. Review of *Primitive Song* by C. M. Bowra, *Listener*, 3 May 1962, p. 781; 'The Poetry of Keith Douglas', *Listener*, 21 June 1962, pp. 1069–71; review of *Imitations* by Robert Lowell, *Listener*, 2 August 1962, p. 185; review of *An Anthology of West African Folklore* by Alta Jablow, *Listener*, 18 October 1962, pp. 629–30; reviews of *A World of Men*, *Death on a Live Wire* and *On Stepping from A Sixth Story Window* by Michael Baldwin, *Listener*, 21 February 1963, pp. 346–7; review of *Emily Dickinson's Poetry* by Charles Anderson, *Listener*, 12 September 1963, p. 394; review of *Folktales of Japan* (ed. Keigo Seki) and *Folktales of Israel* (ed. Dov Noy), *Listener*, 12 December 1963, p. 999; review of *Voss* by Patrick White, *Listener*, 6 February 1964, pp. 229–30.
13. 'Asgard for Addicts,' review of *Myth and Religion of the North* by E. O. G. Turville-Petre, *Listener*, 19 March 1964, p. 485.
14. 'Out of Africa', *Listener*, 28 May 1964, p. 892.
15. Review of *Shamanism* by Mircea Eliade and *The Sufis* by Idries Shah, *Listener*, 29 October, 1964, pp. 677–8; 'Opposing Selves', review of *The Letters of Alexander Pushkin*, trans. T. J. Shaw, *Listener*, 1 October 1964, pp. 514–15; review of *Men Who March Away* by I. M. Parsons, *Listener*, 5 August 1965, p. 208.
16. 'The Crime of Fools Exposed', review of *The Collected Poems of Wilfred Owen* (ed. C. Day Lewis), *New York Times Book Review*, 16 April 1964, pp. 4, 18; 'A Hero's History', reviews of *Heimskringla* and *The Prose Edda* by Snorri Sturluson, and *Gods, Demons and Others* by R. K. Narayan, *New York Review of Books*, 31 December 1964, pp. 6–7; 'The Genius of Isaac Bashevis Singer', *New York Review of Books*, 22 April 1965, pp. 8–10; 'Tricksters and Tarbabies', review of *Literature among the Primitives* and *The Primitive Reader* by John Greenaway, *New York Review of Books*, 9 December 1965, pp. 33–5; 'Music of Humanity', review of *The Faber Book of Ballads* (ed. Mathew Hodgart), *The Guardian*, 14 May 1965, p. 11; 'Sorceror's Apprentice', review of *A Separate Reality* by Carlos Casteneda, *Observer*, 5 March 1972, p. 32; 'Myth and Education', *Children's Literature in Education*, March 1970, pp. 55–70; 'An Idea Whose Time Has Come', review of *The Environmental Revolution* by Max Nicholson, *Spectator*, 21 March 1970, pp. 378–9, and in expanded form in *Your Environment* (Summer 1970), pp. 81–3.

17. *Poetry in the Making: an anthology of poems and programmes from listening and writing* (London: Faber Paperbacks, 1969), p. 17. Cf. 'Capturing Animals' and 'Writing a Novel: Beginning', talks printed in *Listening and Writing* (Autumn 1961), pp. 16–23, 29–34. (Slightly different from the ones in *Poetry in the Making*.)
18. *op cit.*, pp. 33–4.
19. John Dryden, 'Preface to Fables' (1700), *Of Dramatic Poesy and Other Essays* (ed. George Watson) (1962; Everyman: London, 1971), II, p. 275.
20. *Poetry in the Making*, p.119.
21. *ibid.*
22. 'The Poetry of Keith Douglas', *Critical Quarterly* 5 (Spring 1963), 43–8; Introduction to Keith Douglas's *Selected Poems* (London: Faber and Faber, 1964).
23. 'The Poetry of Keith Douglas', p.44.
24. *op cit.*, p. 48.
25. 'Sylvia Plath's Crossing the Water', *Critical Quarterly*, 13 (Summer 1971), 165–7. (Revised version of talk broadcast on 5 July 1971.)
26. 'János Pilinszky', *Critical Quarterly*, 18 (Summer 1976), 79. (Corresponds to radio script for Radio 3 of 6 February 1976.)
27. *Emily Dickinson: Poems, A choice of verse selected with introduction by Ted Hughes* (London: Faber 1968); *Listener*, 12 September 1963, pp. 43–8.
28. *op. cit.*, pp. 10, 11, 13.
29. Extracts from 'Ted Hughes Writes', *Poetry Book Society Bulletin*, 15 (September 1957) and 'Sylvia Plath', *Poetry Book Society Bulletin*, 44 (February 1965) are quoted from Faas, pp. 163, 179.
30. From 'The Genius of Isaac Bashevis Singer', *New York Review of Books*, 22 April 1965, pp. 8–10 reprinted Faas, p. 177.
31. Extract from 'Context', *London Magazine*, 1, 11 (February 1962), 44–5 is quoted from Faas, p. 164.
32. *New Statesman*, 25 November 1966, p. 783.
33. Review of *Voss*, *Listener*, 6 February 1964, p. 230.
34. *New Statesman*, 25 November 1966, p. 783.
35. *Listener*, 1 October 1964, p. 515.
36. *Essay on Criticism* (1711) 1.235, *Poems of Alexander Pope* (Methuen: London, 1968), p.151.
37. 'Notes on the Chronological Order of Sylvia Plath's Poems', *Tri-Quarterly*, 7 (1966), 88.
38. Review of *The Selected Letters of Dylan Thomas*, *New Statesman*, 25 November 1966, p. 783.
39. See extract from 'Sylvia Plath', *Poetry Book Society Bulletin*, 44 (February 1965), reprinted Faas, p. 180.
40. Introduction to *A Choice of Emily Dickinson's Verse* (1968), p. 14.
41. 'Vasko Popa', *Tri-Quarterly*, 9 (Spring 1967), 204.
42. See extract from 'Myth and Education', *Writers, Critics, and Children* (ed. G. Fox *et. al*,) (New York: Agathon Press, 1976), reprinted

Ted Hughes

Faas, p.191. This extract is from a quite different essay from that of the same title printed in *Children's Literature in Education*, **I** (March 1970), 55–70.
43. Review of *The Selected Letters of Dylan Thomas*, *New Statesman*, 25 November 1966, p. 783.
44. Faas, pp. 191–2.
45. 'Laura Riding' (1970), Faas, p. 189.
46. See extract from 'Orghast: Talking Without Words', *Vogue*, December 1971, reprinted Faas, p. 190.
47. 'Essay on Dramatic Poesy' (1668), *Critical Essays* (ed. George Watson), **I**, 67.
48. Faas, pp. 190–1.
49. 'Vasko Popa', *Tri-Quarterly*, **9** (Spring 1967), 202.
50. Faas, p. 189.
51. 'Vasko Popa', *Tri-Quarterly*, **9** (Spring 1967), 205.
52. Faas, p. 52.
53. 'The Poetry of Keith Douglas', p. 46.
54. Faas, p. 208.
55. Note to *A Choice of Shakespeare's Verse, selected with an introduction by Ted Hughes* (London: Faber, 1971), pp. 181–2; Faas, p. 213.

8
Creators as Critics II: David Lodge

> How the writing of fiction can be combined with reviewing fiction and with teaching, analysing and theorising about fiction in an academic context is, I find, to many people an occasion of puzzlement, scepticism and even scandal.[1]

David Lodge is a quite different kind of critical-creator. He is a novelist and popular writer reaching readers with no interest in literature other than desire to enjoy it. At the same time Lodge is, or was, like every other critic discussed in this study with the exception of Hughes, an academic author with a university post. Lodge's own academic experience was gained unusually for a critic who is nationally known, at a place other than Oxbridge. But it has served as a mine of comic material for his novels; especially for those loosely situated in what is perhaps the most successful of all his targets for satire: academic life at the University of Birmingham. The entertainment value of the Lodge novels is beyond doubt, and they are widely enjoyed. But Lodge's creative work stands in a different relationship to his criticism from that which Hughes's bears to his. As a creative writer, Hughes is artistically at the centre of his times. By the test of art, Lodge has little if any significance and may not want it. And yet while Hughes's creative reputation has eclipsed his criticism, Lodge's novels have enhanced the esteem in which his criticism is held; they have made it more generally noticed.

The test of Lodge is the test of modern criticism in one of its most disarmingly 'charming' of forms. Lodge's criticism is read by many readers who would not normally consider criticism important. But Lodge's criticism is doubtless often read just because it is written by Lodge. And this fact reflects the importance of a wide, popular readership to the modern idea of the critic. There will be many readers of Lodge, and the criticism of Lodge, who will never have heard of other critics discussed in this book and would not read them if they had.

Getting and keeping this market has affected what Lodge has been able to 'do' as a literary critic. In particular, it has meant that to the extent that Lodge has succeeded in becoming a man of his times (novelist, journalist, academic, etc.), so much the less has he been able to stand outside them, or against them, as a critic. Lodge's criticism is once more symptomatic of the irony of the contrast between the ambitions of theory and the timidity of practice. But Lodge does not merely adopt the academic tastes of the hour (which he shares with other modern academics). His criticism is geared to artistic priorities more narrowly dictated by his practice as novelist. But this disparity is concealed by an atmosphere of bright-eyed discovery, self-effacing amiability and practitioner know-how. On the one hand there is nothing to disagree with because Lodge won't disagree. On the other hand if we persist in trying then we can't anyway, because Lodge is the creator and the rest of us aren't. Therefore as far as Lodge's critical writings 'come out of' his novelist's practice, they lack what critics who are not creators may have to their critical advantage: the necessary 'outsideness' of critical vision determined by terms of reference beyond those of one's own, self-invested, creative practice.

This is the case with Lodge's first substantial published critical work, *The Language of Fiction* (1966).[2] Here, as in so much of Lodge's literary criticism, Lodge reflects critically on the literary form he has himself practised with such popular success. His own novels make fun of academic thought, as of academic life. But now Lodge is in academically earnest mood and, here, academic values are preserved in an attractive, eye-catching and (for 1966) up-to-date critical package. Thus Part One, 'The Novelist's Medium and the Novelist's Art: Problems in Criticism', is devoted to the weighty theoretical concerns that have distinguished modern criticism of recent years. This serves as preamble to Part Two, which reflects the growing influence that linguistic studies were at that date coming to have on courses in English. Lodge accordingly provides a series of essays on the language of particular novels, chronologically ordered from Jane Austen to the twentieth century. Theory is put into practice. To this end the chapters of Part One are split into miniature discussions, representing various dimensions, or aspects, of the theme, each a few pages long. The effect is that of a thesis, and the book in its early stages is slow, even laboured, in movement. Authorities are cited, accumulated, juxtaposed and quoted, often at some length, and at every turn. The reader is from the beginning placed firmly in the world of academic debate. He is surrounded by voices of university life. What matters to Lodge (as novelist and as academic) is a question of *genre*.

It is one of the aims of Lodge's *The Language of Fiction*, and central to his argument, that debate about the nature of language must be shifted away from the poem and towards the novel. Lodge sees this as a movement away from a position he attributes to Leavis, who 'shared the tendency of most modern criticism to accord the language of the novel less importance than the language of poetry'. He sees as a mistake the common tendency to talk about novels in terms of their ideas. The language of novels, he protests, has a reality. Fictional language, he claims (analysing a passage from Jane Austen) is 'a special kind of language, language which is more than the transparent container of Ideas.' Likewise, 'plot' and 'character' may feature in discussion of fiction, but without language we would not know what plot and character were. Language is antecedent to both. Novels are made of words, as are poems. Poetry and fiction are part of a continuum and not essentially different. However, Lodge argues, the style of a work (poem or novel) is hard to talk about. Until the invention of stylistics it was not systematically discussed. And yet Lodge's interest in the language of fiction remains, at this date, literary interest, and thus non-scientific.

> ... one still feels obliged to assert that the discipline of linguistics will never *replace* literary criticism, or radically change the bases of its claims to be a useful and meaningful form of human inquiry.

It is the essential characteristic of modern linguistics that it claims to be a science. It is the essential characteristic of literature that it concerns values.[3]

And literary criticism, Lodge concludes, 'seeks to define the meaning and value of literary artefacts by relating subjective response to objective text, always pursuing exhaustiveness of explication and unanimity of judgement, but conscious that these goals are unattainable'. But though Lodge appears to be keen to provide an account of the problematic nature of literary criticism, it is clearly for him something to be done at arms' length, by marshalling 'approaches'. The effect is therefore to offer a less problematic, more simplistic conception of literary criticism. It is one that subordinates 'subjective response' to the matter of managing *thought:* 'Literary criticism will ... best perform its task by striking a balance between the approaches represented by Wimsatt and Ong respectively,' a comment which looks forward to interest in the plurality of 'approaches' displayed in Lodge's later anthologies of twentieth-century literary criticism. But in 1966 Lodge has not begun to think of 'working with structuralism' or to go as far in this direction as he was later to do. Here, in fact, Lodge's stress falls less on the multiplicity of available theories in criticism as on its most unstructuralist characteristic of all: 'In the last analysis, criticism claims our attention, not as sets of data nor as sets of conclusions, but as human discourse.'[4]

While therefore Lodge is keen to advance a criticism based on the observation of technical and linguistic features, he is still unsure whether, after all, it is not a matter of 'human discourse'. He thus tries to have it both ways. But much in Lodge's criticism suggests that he is able to have it in neither. On the one hand, he fails to offer judgements that are new in the sense that his own, independent humanity is fully engaged enough to offer fundamentally original evaluations. But nor is he sufficiently detached for his criticism to be directed by instincts other than those of the popular novelist and the modern academic. On the other hand, Lodge's desire to preserve the appearance of an open mind, an even, reasonable approach to critical analysis likely to put nobody off, means that he is unable to carry through his programme for a more technical, linguistically orientated criticism. For example, Lodge's conception of criticism as 'human discourse' is most fully worked out in Part Two of *The Language of Fiction* by two final chapters on Wells and Amis. The latter, particularly, perhaps because Lodge is writing here on comedy, is a lively (and human) analysis of the ins and outs of Amis's jokes, literary and cultural. There is doubtless exaggeration in the view that *Lucky Jim* 'sends one back to Fielding'. But Lodge gains credibility from being able to take us inside the problems of the literary creator. He gives us a creator's-eye-view: insight into why these words and not others are used. And yet he is always more eager for new thought than new judgements or responses. Part Two of *The Language of Fiction* gets down to details. But the effect of looking more closely at the language of fiction in earlier novels seems largely to be that of confirming critical positions these novels already have. 'Great' novels predominate. In Hardy, we are 'tantalized by a sense of greatness not quite achieved'. In James (*The Ambassadors*) we find 'a testimony to his greatness as an artist'. Laudably, Lodge gives attention to novels which do not compel explicit interest in language, in contrast to Joyce's *Ulysses,* which does. There are however few surprises in store. Despite interest in valuation, Lodge's new approach does not lead to new valuations. *Current* valuations yield evidence congenial to it. Lodge therefore consolidates the place in the canon of those novels he selects. The effect is to confine, by narrowing, grounds for admiring them.

The novelty of theory operates to disguise the fact that received twentieth-century tastes are served, not subverted. Part Two begins with an essay on the meanings of 'manners' in *Mansfield Park,* where Lodge dwells on the overlapping and balance of moral and social meanings in the novel. The starting point for discussion is the definition of 'manners' given in the *OED,* plus Lionel Trilling's definition in 'Manners, Morals, and the Novel'. The point Lodge makes (and supports by citing words to which 'manners' are regularly linked) is that in Jane Austen's novel, social behaviour has moral value conferred upon it. There is then a 'close connection of social folly with moral vice'.[5] This observation is not new, though the analysis is 'modern', in that it is conducted almost entirely within twentieth-century perceptions of the resonance and extension of the term. The effect is to set in concrete twentieth-century understanding of Jane Austen's fiction. And yet there is a differrence between Trilling's definition, which he quotes with approval – '[manners] are hinted at by small actions, sometimes by the arts of dress or decoration, sometimes by tone, gesture, emphasis, or rhythm, sometimes by the words that are used with a special frequency or a special meaning'[6] – and conceptions of the term's 'spread' in the hundred or so years anterior to *Mansfield Park*. Consequently Lodge misses the sense in which earlier definitions would place the term, and Jane Austen's use of it, in a different light. For example Rapin's account of *moeurs*, represented in the translation of Thomas Rymer (1674) suggests how much passion and fire, though now lost, is available for critical reclamation, (it would also suggest how often Jane Austen is satirising narrower conceptions of 'manners' in her own time, and why in the first place they were worth her concern):

> The sovereign Rule for treating of *Manners*, is to copy them after *Nature*, and above all to study well the *heart* of Man, to know how to distinguish all its *motions*. 'Tis this which none are acquainted with: the *heart* of man is an *abyss*, where none can sound the bottom: it is a *mystery*, which the most quick-sighted cannot pierce into, and in which the most cunning are mistaken.[7]

In Lodge's analysis, Jane Austen remains largely a novelist of decorum. Lodge, humane though his attention to language is, does not reach beyond the usual sources (of society and morality) that make her vocabulary 'subtle and exact'.[8] He reinforces the idea of Jane Austen's fictional limitations.

This is because, like other academic critics discussed in this study, Lodge's taste favours the terms of a Romantic tradition. Jane Austen's vocabulary is 'subtle and exact'. But then she is not a 'romantic', unlike Charlotte Brontë who is. So in the second essay of the series, on Charlotte Brontë's *Jane Eyre*, Lodge can say that 'the dominant energies and sympathies of the novel are on the side of passion'. Starting from this view, and a sense of the 'Romantic' influence on Charlotte Brontë, Lodge assembles references to fire. This procedure shows

Lodge's taste for tracing patterns in texts, and anticipates the conclusion he wishes to achieve. This, in turn, accords with the favoured interpretation of the novel and its pre-determined literary–historical placing. Lodge points out the 'lavishness of epithet in descriptions of fires which seems in excess of the demands of functional realism'.[9] Fire has symbolic meaning in the novel. Like other elements, it reflects and embodies inner states. From the number of references assembled by Lodge, he conclusively demonstrates the energies and sympathies of the novel as indeed 'on the side of passion'. But he does not address the problems raised by an art in which the values of passion, reflected in references to fire, are so explicitly and persistently expressed. There is no hint that *Jane Eyre*, in this respect, is too explicit, too coarse, too obvious. Lodge supplies what (academic) critical convention requires that he should.

The same can be said of the succeeding essay on Dickens's *Hard Times*, where negative judgements have for the first time to be taken into account. Rather than review the standing of *Hard Times*, Lodge shifts debate to an academic plane. The technique is to start by taking the novel as a work of one particular kind ('a polemical work'), and then consider the novel from a particular angle (that of rhetoric). Lodge takes exception to the criterion of 'life' Leavis used in his essay on *Hard Times*: he seems, from later asides, to believe that Leavis is referring here to social reality. But Lodge wants to defend Dickens against the charge that *Hard Times* is a 'crude travesty of... reality'. Therefore he substitutes specialist literary criteria of failure and success, moving attention from questions of the work's success to measures of generic definition, artistic means and authorial intention. Sometimes, he seems to be using the production of successful rhetorical devices as a criterion of success in art:

> ...where Dickens invokes the world of fairy-tale ironically, to dramatize the drabness, greed, spite and injustice which characterize a society dominated by materialism, it is a highly effective rhetorical device; but where he relies on the simplifications of the fairy-tale to suggest means of redemption, we remain unconvinced.[10]

Unconvinced of what? The effectiveness of the rhetorical device or the reality of the fictional moment it serves? We cannot be sure. Lodge surrounds discussion of the novel by a protective qualifying layer. He wishes to 'mediate', as he later described his intentions, 'between conflicting evaluations of the novel . . .'.[11] Therefore it is hardly surprising that the conclusion should when it comes sound 'balanced' enough, but be actually crippled by the terms of reference of the enquiry, and thus innocuous: 'If *Hard Times* is a polemical novel that is only partially persuasive, it is because Dickens's rhetoric is only partially adequate to the tasks he set himself.'[12] Perhaps it is pointless to ask, after this, whether Lodge thinks *Hard Times* much good. But by the detailed attention he gives it, Lodge actually appears to confirm (not deny) Leavis's estimate of *Hard Times*'s importance in Dickens's work. The methods and criteria of criticism may have altered (or become more specialised). Valuations they produce have not.

This is because the basis of *The Language of Fiction* (as of Lodge's criticism as a whole) is not evaluative but interpretive. Lodge is not always uninterested in value in novels, and can claim (evaluatively) that Wells's *Tono Bungay* 'is a much better novel than it is commonly supposed to be'. Lodge expresses explicit preferences in his criticism from time to time, but his explicit interest in criticism lies not in how texts should be judged, but how 'read'. Hence in *Jane Eyre*, 'The instinctive, passionate, non-ethical drive of Romanticism towards self-fulfilment at whatever cost, is held in check by an allegiance to the ethical precepts of the Christian code and an acknowledgement of the necessity of exercising reason in human affairs.' Hence concern with fairy-tale analogies in *Hard Times*. And hence discussion of various 'interpretations' (by Liddell, Van Ghent, Holloway, etc.) of Hardy's *Tess*. In his attention to language, and rhetoric, and 'voices', Lodge is either seeking new interpretations of novels, or, alternatively, new illustrations, the latter issuing in accounts of what, artistically or linguistically, is 'going on' in them. Therefore in attending to the linguistic and rhetorical riches of novels Lodge institutionalises them, buttressing their status as texts for academic study. Ability to yield to academic enquiry becomes then itself a kind of 'worth'. Hence, 'The way in which James, in the river-scene [in *The Ambassadors*], disperses the vision, and modifies the style, on which he had lavished such loving skill, is a testimony to his greatness as an artist.'[13] James's greatness as artist is taken for granted. All the critic has to do is to find reasons for showing it may be.

It is consequently easy for Lodge to seem undogmatic and detached, even though he isn't. He sways characteristically between assertions of the need for criticism to take a more technical approach, and reminders of its human value. This is the case in Lodge's collection of essays entitled *The Novelist at the Crossroads* (1971). Although this is a less unified work than *The Language of Fiction* the opportunity is still taken to draw essays together under thematic 'heads', each in a different way exploring possibilities of fictional prose: 'Fiction and Criticism', 'Fiction and Catholicism', 'Fiction and Modernism', and 'Fiction and Utopia', discussions (mostly revolving around three or four key texts by different authors) which are sandwiched between the title essay and a long concluding chapter, or 'Part', entitled, neutrally, 'Crosscurrents in Modern English Criticism'. The authors considered are less 'mainstream' than those of *The Language of Fiction*. They represent a more personal choice: William Burroughs, Muriel Spark, Hemingway, Beckett, Updike, Graham Greene, etc. Otherwise Lodge is reworking ideas, and in some cases returning to writers (such as H. G. Wells) examined before. In this respect *The Novelist at the Crossroads* reflects the characteristic spread of Lodge's interests, and his favourite way of going about literary discussion. The work is also typical of Lodge in striking a disarmingly personal note. Lodge can begin with defence of the virtues (and support for future successful continuation) of the realist novel: 'I like realistic novels,' he admits, 'and I tend to write realistic fiction myself.' The idea of the realist novel then inspires him to humane defence of humanist values. The belief such novels support is that 'We are conscious of ourselves as unique, historic individuals, living together in societies by virtue of certain common assumptions and methods of communication....' Lodge then links this attitude to creation with a humanist attitude to criticism. In 'Crosscurrents in Modern English

Criticism', Lodge writes of 'the ongoing debate criticism must be'. And in the essay entitled 'Waiting for the End: Current Novel Criticism', he spells out his credo in these terms: 'Literary criticism, like any other highly developed intellectual discipline, cannot entirely dispense with jargon; but since its subject is human eloquence it has a responsibility to maintain as much continuity as possible with human discourse.'

This stress on the human discourse to which criticism is related recalls one strand of *The Language of Fiction*. But also represented is the other side of Lodge's conception of criticism; one that, while it points back to Lodge's technical interests, also looks ahead. This is to develop in proportion to Lodge's interest in formalist and structuralist analytic modes. And so far as it expresses his sense of the place of language in critical enquiry, it diminishes the sense in which Lodge is willing to take personal human responsibility for his literary judgements. Lodge explains this sense in his essay 'Towards a Poetics of Fiction: An Approach through Language': ' . . . my position is that all good criticism is a response to language – that it is good insofar as it is a sensitive response – whether or not there is any explicit reference to language in the way of quotation and analysis.'[14] Yet at this date (the chapter was first published as an article in *Novel* in 1968), Lodge is not seeking a comprehensive explanation of the art of the novel: 'We . . . cannot ask the critic to tell us the "whole truth" about a novel.' But what starts as a move against expecting too much from the critic becomes a justification for the critic saying little or nothing at all. This is because for Lodge, the only way a work of criticism can transcend the partial is to duplicate the literature with which it is concerned. And this, of course – he concedes – it obviously cannot do: 'Criticism does not – cannot – aim to reproduce the work it contemplates.' Lodge is therefore bound to conclude that critical discourse 'cannot avoid being partial and selective' and must inevitably revert to defending a specialist critical approach. Criticism cannot be other than specialist, and should therefore not try. 'There is no satisfactory total account of a work of literature,' Lodge says, 'except the work itself.'[15] Lodge does not ask why anyone should want from criticism a 'satisfactory' total account of a literary work (when they can have the work itself); who the account would satisfy, or what the satisfactions would be. While exalting criticism, Lodge simultaneously confines our sense of the power and interest criticism might have.

The same reductive linking of criticism as a specialist activity to its (necessarily) limited responsibilities, is reflected in Lodge's selection *Twentieth Century Literary Criticism: A Reader* (1972).[16] This edition is still widely used, reflects Lodge's work as a university teacher, and has surely done much to stimulate student interest in Criticism, despite the fact that one of the most challenging and influential twentieth-century critics is unrepresented: apparently, Leavis refused to allow Lodge to include any of his work. Otherwise, the selection is as impressively ample in scale as it is narrow in conceptual range. It offers to the student and general reader means of becoming quickly *au fait* with the recent history of critical ideas. The volume consists of selected passages from a variety of critics and theorists, British and foreign; choice extracts from a comprehensive catalogue of 'big names'. The contents are arranged in three different ways: chronological order, according to form or topic, and according to method or approach, in which respect the edition is itself a critical response to criticism. As such, the edition reflects a conception of modern criticism interpreted through a range of 'approaches'; a supermarket selection from which student or reader can choose. But the criticism and selection of texts is less varied than the scope of the enterprise would appear to suggest. Most of the contents suggest an image of criticism (and sense of its function) equated to theory. Even creative writers are caught theorising about literary problems. This image of criticism is strengthened by Lodge's placing at the head of his selection, 'to serve as a general introduction', M. H. Abrams's chapter: 'Orientation of critical theories'. It is therefore on theoretical grounds that Lodge, in the Foreword, can cheer on criticism's growing importance as quasi-literature 'in its own right'. The practical use of criticism, Lodge now feels, is looking increasingly out of date: 'In our era, criticism is not merely a library of secondary aids to the understanding and appreciation of literary texts, but also a rapidly increasing body of knowledge in its own right, and a primary vehicle for the values and ideas of the literary imagination.'[17]

Lodge sets out personally to contribute to the 'body of knowledge' in *The Modes of Modern Writing* (1977). Here, for the first time, Lodge attempts to engage in a sustained way with a collection of broadly structuralist perceptions of literary thought. According to his Preface (a contracted version of an earlier article), Lodge had embraced the intellectual 'movement' of structuralism as he recognised its 'rapidly growing influence and prestige', and because he is 'predisposed to be sympathetic to a formalist and linguistic approach to literary criticism'.[18] At the same time, he is unwilling to go all the way. He still insists on the strongly practical nature of his interest in formalist method. *The Modes of Modern Writing* therefore zig-zags between theoretical discussions and examinations of particular authors and texts. It is true that in invoking various modes of modern writing, Lodge, despite his technical ambitions, conveys a love of twentieth-century literary forms suggestive of the enthusiastic reader rather than formalist scholar. It is an activity portrayed as a world in its own right, one that is fresh, various, comic and profound. But although the work has 'modern writing' as the ostensible central concern, where particular texts are considered, the study falls short of its title. This is because it is dominated by fictional prose: the creative medium of Lodge.

In Part One ('Problems and Executions' – executions being a pun), Lodge treats 'Realism', and, given 'the inherent ambiguity of all human report . . . the ultimate impossibility of "realism".' Realism is explored in relation to fictively differentiated texts: reportage, realistic novel, the surreal, etc., tied together for examination by a bizarre common theme: that of execution or capital punishment. But as a unifying topic – a constant term beside which variant modes of modern writing emerge – the theme is in dubious taste. The effect is unpleasant and sensationalistic. The repeated doses of capital punishment repel rather than instruct. The object, no doubt, was to gain the reader's attention. But the impact rapidly fades, even though we are warned against dwelling on content (the preoccupation of the 'realist' novel) rather than form (that of the modernist).

Lodge's aim, after all, is now to discern formal properties. *The Modes of Modern Writing* is meant as an extension, of a technical and theoretical kind, of the formalist side of Lodge's ambitions in *The Language of Fiction:* 'What is needed is a single way of talking about novels, a critical methodology, a poetics or aesthetics of fiction, which can embrace descriptively all the varieties of this kind of writing.'[19] The conception of criticism as 'human discouse' has now moved into the shade.

In pursuit of this scheme, Lodge, as in *The Language of Fiction*, wants a linguistic approach made towards writing 'normally approached via content, via the concept of imitation', albeit one more 'catholic' than that of Barthes and followers who 'instate' one kind of writing at the expense of another'. The key to the lock Lodge finds in Jakobson's 'binary' distinction between metaphor and metonymy, which he attempts to refine. The object of the exercise is to classify writing according to these two basic types. We are also to see connections between speech and writing. Lodge compares the difficulty of modern writing to the problem of a patient suffering from aphasia searching for words. Laws apply to visual and verbal expression alike. Plays and films can be metaphoric, or metonymic, or can mix the two.

There are two difficulties with this scheme: one its applicability to literature, particularly the kind of modern literature Lodge wants to bring to the fore; the other is the problem for Lodge of supplying a clear definition of his terms. For example, the metaphoric and metonymic are sometimes two ends of a scale whose intermediate points are illustrated by various accounts of executions, or modes of describing place, from encyclopaedia entry at one extreme to description of London in Eliot's *The Waste Land* at the other. At other times, metaphoric and metonymic are distinct types of text, inherently different, so that it is possible to speak, as Lodge does, of 'metonymic text'. But this distinction hangs on how we are 'likely' to take them; on the probability of receiving them in a particular way. The difference is not after all inherent: it depends on the readers. Thus *King Lear* and *Paradise Lost* are written in a metaphorical mode because 'We are not likely to interpret [them] as literal reports of the real.'[20] Books we are likely to interpret as literal reports are *Emma* and *The Old Wives' Tale*. Lodge's recourse, ultimately, is to the authority of the reader the technical analysis is meant to have called into question. Lodge's confidence in his chosen method dissolves, and he wavers. Applying the concepts of metaphor and metonymy to actual texts only exposes the inadequacy of the concepts.

Lodge glimpses this in one way (hence his resort to the reader's response). But in another way he does not, and ploughs ahead; at which point *The Modes of Modern Writing* declines from an ambitious attempt to account for all writing, at least all fictional writing, to an exercise in labelling texts. Criticism is reduced to an act of categorisation in which the value and importance of the texts are off the agenda. Thus Lodge uses 'metaphoric' and 'metonymic' in Part Three to identify or classify particular works the essential critical decisions about which have already been made. Joyce's development, we therefore learn, is from 'metonymy to metaphor'. *Dubliners* is at one end of the scale; *Finnegans Wake* at the other (a point brought out through Joyce's games of verbal association). *Ulysses* stands somewhere in the middle. It is 'a realistic or metonymic fiction ... with a mythopoeic or metaphorical structure'. Gertrude Stein, meanwhile, 'oscillated violently between the metonymic and metaphoric poles'. In Hemingway, 'an apparently metonymic style is made to serve the purposes of metaphor'. Lawrence's style 'had to be essentially metonymic in structure ... though the meanings he groped after could only be expressed metaphorically'. Virginia Woolf, like Joyce, develops from metonymic to metaphoric, and escapes the form of the realistic novel. In the thirties, 'there was a pronounced swing back from the metaphoric to the metonymic pole of literary discourse'. In the forties, 'the pendulum of literary fashion swung back again – not fully, but to a perceptible degree – towards the pole we have designated as ... metaphoric'. But Lodge is stumped by postmodernists' work: '... it would be difficult to show that their work, considered *collectively*, has any bias towards one pole or the other'.[21] Metaphor and metonymy thus serve the purpose of cult critical terms from the past, Wit and Judgement, Nature and Art, or in Dick Minim's case, Nature and Learning. He too was *au fait* with the smart imported 'binary' critical language of his time, and set out to explain everything through it: 'Of the great authors he now began to display the characters ... His opinion was, that Shakespeare, committing himself wholly to the impulse of nature, wanted that correctness which learning would have given him; and that Johnson, trusting to learning, did not sufficiently cast his eye on nature.'[22]

The Modes of Modern Writing does not therefore discover the comprehensive framework that Lodge desires. Lodge's critical valuations are reinforced, and placed beyond challenge by a critical method in which evaluation is ruled out.[23] In *The Language of Fiction*, Lodge had been committed to 'humanist' decisions about value and quality. Robson was to argue for an 'honorific' kind of definition, 'which commits its user to decisions about value and quality'.[24] Lodge's definition (in *The Modes of Modern Writing*) suggests no such commitment:

> ... literature is an open category in the sense that you can, in theory, put any kind of discourse into it – but only on condition that such discourse has something in common with the discourse you cannot take out of it: the something being a structure which either indicates the fictionality of a text or enables a text to be read as if it were fictional.

The mysteries have increased, not diminished. Thus literature now possesses a 'something'. And this something is 'a structure'. Perhaps the definition is easier to grasp if taken with one of Lodge's examples: Boswell's *Life of Johnson*. Boswell's Johnson, writes Lodge:

> ... becomes something like a fictional character, and his *Life* is read as if it were a kind of novel – though without ceasing to be a biography: we read it on two levels at once, as literature and as history, whereas most other biographies of Johnson are merely history, and conceivably superior as such to Boswell's.[25]

But the example reveals only the trouble with the definition intended to embrace it: fiction and historical accuracy are too simply opposed. Fiction exists on a different 'level' from history. But the opposition, the language of levels, makes it more difficult than ever to feel the interdependence of fiction and truth that makes literary works (like Boswell's *Life*) true and historical works literature.

Lodge perhaps realised that *The Modes of Modern Writing* was a failed experiment, because he turned onto a different tack, and the remainder of his dealings with structuralist thinking are less earnest. Lodge escapes the implications of the theoretical impasse of *The Modes of Modern Writing* in *Working with Structuralism* (1981). This represents a return to the looser 'collected essays' form of *The Novelist at the Crossroads*. It is not so much a rejection of theories, but a sideways move to an altogether lighter, less specialist treatment, now directed largely at a student market. Here Lodge is showing others how theory *might* be applied. The funniest statement on *Working with Structuralism* is perhaps Carey's remark, in his review, that for Lodge working with structuralism is rather like 'Surviving with Sciatica'.[26] The collection's spirit, as Carey observes, is a matter of making the best of it all, accommodating structuralism, not because Lodge has much enthusiasm for it, or is a structuralist himself, but because it is there. We cannot ignore it and it will not go away. Therefore let's see what we can do with it – if anything. To this end, *Working with Structuralism* is a mix of loosely connected essays of formal analysis, not-so-formal analysis and entertainment. And only about half the essays are structuralist in the technical sense. In two, Lodge discusses literature in the light of two visual media: cinema and cartoon. But apart from structuralism's 'reading' of cinema, and treatment of popular forms as texts, it is here largely a 'cover' bringing together representational modes. And even in dilute form it can lead Lodge astray. For example, Lodge tries to picture the bird in Hughes's *Crow*, relating him to 'the anthropomorphic animals and birds of Walt Disney and his imitators'.[27] The objection to this procedure is not that the suggestion is wrong, or necessarily fruitless, but that Lodge ignores the point that *Crow* exists as a *sequence* of poems, powerful by eluding picture-fixing imaginative habits, regardless of Hughes's response to Baskin's sketches of 'Crow'. Lodge's 'structuralist' approach skirts the principal textual feature of the poems. Missing, too, is the sense in which cartoons compared with *Crow* are more than visual texts. What about speech bubbles in the printed variety; or sound track, dialogue narration and music, of those in animated form? In three otherwise conventional essays on Hardy, structuralism ensures only that discussion is kept up to date. By a structuralist framework, fresh gloss is given to an otherwise old-fashioned scholarly concern with fictional form (pastoral, etc.). But although structuralism flavours the analysis (the odd reference to Hillis Miller or Barthes) it is not a basic ingredient of the dish. Structuralism does not override Lodge's resurgent humanistic interest in the pleasure, pain and instruction of personal literary experience. Lodge describes Hardy's *The Woodlanders* as 'the powerful, absorbing and haunting work of fiction it is'.[28] For Lodge, structuralism now turns out to be a handy but dispensable tool of humanist practice, not a wholesale replacement for it.

Even in the section entitled 'Applying Structuralism', Lodge's approach is one of all-seeing professorial generosity, not proselytising zeal. Lodge preserves the impression of an open mind. He warms to structuralist tenets he is happy to borrow but not happy to own. On the one hand he wishes to move with the times. On the other he wonders whether he should. The result is a peculiar mixture of caution and 'radical' ideas. In 1966, in *The Language of Fiction*, Lodge's position was relatively clear. Discussing Michael Riffaterre's 'Scientific Stylistics', he pointed out that 'The paradoxical relationship between the formally fixed artefact and the necessarily variable human responses to it is one of the grounds for asserting that literary criticism can never be a science.'[29] Lodge here echoes Lawrence's famous remark on criticism in his review of Galsworthy. He quoted the same passage in 1970 in 'Crosscurrents in Modern English Criticism', printed in *The Novelist at the Crossroads*. But now reservations appear: 'A good way of determining any critic's principles,' he commented, 'is to get him to read this passage and to note when he stops nodding approval, or starts shaking his head.'[30] In 1981, in *Working with Structuralism*, Lodge is even less sure, denying from the outset that criticism 'can never be a science'. He quotes with disfavour Lawrence's 'Literary criticism can be no more than a reasoned account of the feeling produced upon the critic by the book he is criticising,' and his attack on academic criticism: 'All the critical twiddle-twaddle about style and form, all this pseudo-scientific classifying and analysing of books in an imitation-botanical fashion, is mere impertinence and mostly dull jargon.' In *Working with Structuralism* this provokes Lodge to defence, albeit rather half-hearted, of Lawrence's target: 'But I would maintain – and I think most academic literary critics would share this view – that if the critical account is to be, in Lawrence's word, "reasoned", it must involve the classifying and analysing which he dismissed so contemptuously, and even a certain amount of jargon.'[31]

It is not surprising that most academic critics would share Lodge's view, since in his own terms they are 'academic' – which is Lawrence's point, and if applied to Lodge would rule him out altogether as a literary critic. The fact Lodge equates reasoning in criticism with classifying, analysing and jargon, if only 'a certain amount', suggests that to work with structuralism, Lodge is prepared to bend over backwards a long way in its favour. But perhaps this is not the effort it seems. For a new force, structuralism supports some very traditional critical habits. Literary taxonomy was satirised as long ago as *Hamlet*. But, for Lodge, working with structuralism means taking it seriously all over again, as a basis for the 'new' structuralist 'challenge'. Lodge shares with enthusiasm the new-world optimism that surrounds taxonomy. All is progress in this particular field. Total fulfilment is near at hand: 'we are now, it seems to me, within sight of a truly comprehensive taxonomy of fictional form at this level [that of tense, person, speech and indirect speech in fictional narrative].'[32]

In an analysis of Hemingway's short story 'Cat in the Rain', Lodge assembles a varied array of readings. But in common with other parts of the book, the story only matters as a peg on which theories and approaches are hung. Lodge employs a formalist distinction between the *fabula* and the *sjuzet*, as in the succeeding essay on Dickens's *Hard Times*. (This is designed to complement Lodge's earlier essay on the rhetoric of *Hard Times* printed in *The Language of Fiction*.) In *Working with Structuralism* the object is to show what a structuralist critic would have said, were he discussing the story. Lodge entertains the approach though it is unclear how far he is himself willing personally to go along with it. He is not a structuralist critic. So at times we feel that Lodge is conceding very little indeed to the practical value of approaches he so painstakingly sets forth: 'Here,' he says of the Hemingway story, 'it seems to me, the structuralist notion of language as a system of differences and of meaning as the product of structural oppositions can genuinely help to settle a point of interpretation.' At other times, though, it is hard to distinguish between what Lodge thinks and the attitude of his imagined, composite, structuralist *persona* (a *persona* extrapolated and constructed partly from Lodge's summary of structuralist thought and partly from other structuralist critics). A clue to his sense of the crassness and irrelevance of much structuralist thought appears in the slight undercurrent of humour that comes through his doggedly long-winded analysis of 'Cat in the Rain'. Here, occasionally, the voice of the comic academic novelist seems to be heard. Lodge is adept at turning his academic experience to good account as a joke. In an apparently serious analysis of connotative meaning in the story's opening paragraph, Lodge's handling of the story takes on a form he must have seen time and again in his work as a university teacher of literature students – the page of typical bad lecture or tutorial notes:

> *There were only two Americans stopping at the hotel.*
> Americans opposed to other nationalities: index of cultural isolation.
> *They did not know any of the people they passed on the stairs on their way to and from their room.*
> Index of social isolation and mutual dependence – vulnerability to breakdown in relationship.
> *Their room was on the second floor facing the sea.*
> Culture faces nature.[33]

This *appears* to be serious. But a knowledge of the wit that twinkles in the novels would lead us to suspect it may not be, and that Lodge is not working with structuralism but playing with it. (The same is true of the later chapter, 'Oedipuss, or, The Practice and Theory of Narrative', where Lodge analyses, from the author's perspective, the draft of a rejected radio play script of his own.) And yet, if he is playing with structuralism, at least for part of this book, he seems strangely in awe of it all, wishing he could think like that, and sometimes succeeding.

But the humour of *Working with Structuralism* is largely covert. From the collection of essays published under the title of *Write On: Occasional Essays 1965–1985*, the commitment of Lodge's whole enterprise as a critic is called more crucially into question. In *Write On* Lodge's talents as a humorist are allowed full play, and it is therefore Lodge's liveliest collection. Among the brief essays and reviews, less than half are autobiographical; the rest are 'critical'. *Write On* is aimed at an even more popular market and in the hope that it will 'interest or amuse readers who know me primarily as a novelist'. Apart from the perhaps predictable essay on Joyce, published for the first time (and containing an account of Joyce as an inspiration behind Lodge's own novels), the collection brings together pieces that Lodge has previously written for a varied range of newspapers and journals. Among these are the *Tablet, The Church Now, New Society*, the *Times Higher Education Supplement*, the *London Review of Books*, the *Listener, The Guardian* and the *Observer*. Royalties from the book, we learn from the Foreword, are to go to the charity CARE. *Write On* offers a tour round Lodge's personal and literary preoccupations over the last twenty or so years, and a background to his productions. This includes an account of his childhood, education and religious influences. Much time is devoted to Lodge's favourite topic: his own literary efforts, the whole human interest story of what being a novelist, journalist, critic and essayist is really like, right down to the level of domestic life. (The Tailpiece to the volume describes in a homely way how Lodge went about buying a piece of sculpture for the garden.) A measure of self-absorption is apparent in this: that of a writer conscious that his mark has been made, and willing to satisfy the curiosity of his many readers and fans. Its glimpses of private life stand as a kind of rebuke to those modern novelists (like Graham Greene, for example) who play the recluse. On the other hand an apparently self-deprecating humour runs through it, and it is, in many ways, a confessional book about the novelist's failures and shortcomings, personal, literary – and pedagogic. One of the most comic and acutely observed moments in the autobiographical section comes again from Lodge's experience as a university teacher. His account of why seminars in Higher Education are almost always a flop is beautifully, if painfully caught. It suggests a critic who, whatever the worth of his creative work, is used to figurative expression, and readily finds it. The group dynamics of seminars, he says, are all wrong:

> A kind of unspoken, instinctive pact of solidarity exists which inhibits them [the students] from arguing with each other as freely and vehemently as they do outside the classroom; so that occasionally one feels, as a teacher, rather like a soccer referee who, having blown his whistle for the kick-off, finds the players disconcertingly reluctant to make a move and is reduced to dribbling the ball himself furiously from end to end, scoring brilliant goals in undefended nets, while the motionless players look curiously on.[34]

In the critical section of *Write On*, modern literature and criticism predominate. And as we might expect from the famous author of *Changing Places* and *Small World* there is a stronger than ever sense of the 'American connection', with essays on Mailer (the second of which, a review of *The Executioner's Song*, continues Lodge's analysis of descriptions of capital punishment in *The Modes of Modern Writing*), Salinger, Fitzgerald, Truman Capote and Lardner. Among the British authors discussed are the 'Movement' writers, Martin Amis, Graham Greene (again, a long study of his work appeared in *The Novelist at the Crossroads*), William Golding (in whose latest novel, as Lodge if anyone would know, the author gets the American touches quite wrong) and D. H. Lawrence. All are novelists, or writers of 'faction', raising again the inexhaustibly fascinating issue (to Lodge) of how fiction is real and reality fiction.

But fiction is too dominant a concern in the criticism of Lodge. Its dominance blunts his critical edge; as does Lodge's critical style, 'the lucidity and conversational ease which is one of the strengths of British criticism at its best'. ('Bourgeois Triangles'.) Readable though it is, his style is more engagingly fluent than suited to convey the intractable contradictions that constitute a critical response. It is a style in which difficulties of thought can dissolve away or be smoothed genially aside. Coming from the novelist's pen, the criticism has many colourful spots. For example there is the description of arguments in the 'structuralist debate' going on above everyone's head 'like dogfights between supersonic jets high in the stratosphere, while the civilian population goes obliviously about its business below'.[35] But in its easy available manner, its variations of tone, Lodge's criticism rather gives the impression either of a man going stylishly through the motions of academic criticism, or laughing at them, than someone committed to the pursuit of critical truth. To various aspects of modern theoretical criticism Lodge is, from time to time, 'committed', as in the early *Language of Fiction*, and even more strikingly in the more abstract sketches of *The Modes of Modern Writing*. At other times, he seems to be feeling how foolish it all is; the required modes of academic criticism seem not to come easily to him, and an effort is needed to rise to the appropriate, suitably professional, critical stance: thus in the opening of *Working with Structuralism* Lodge has to work himself up, reluctantly in a way but gamely enough, to a position from which he can take a properly academic view ahead. Even then, Lodge's humour breaks through, and he seems increasingly to realise what is comic about the academic criticism he himself writes. But the jokey approach (as in the punning titles of many essays) is a form of disguise. And it sometimes appears that Lodge is playing out, almost as a character in one of his novels, a professional, half-serious role for himself as critic. It is, however, then when Lodge is most entertaining, as in the short, witty essays, anecdotes, and stories of his most recent volume *Write On*. As an entertainer, Lodge has enormous appeal. There is an anti-assertive, undogmatic and open self-effacing quality in Lodge's criticism which is divertingly attractive and good-natured. This is suggested by such things as the conscientious good-willed attempts to apply personally reinterpreted aspects of structuralist theory, first with serious intent and then in a more light-hearted way, and without much sense of its burning personal importance for him. Structuralism for Lodge lacks the political pungency and wider social dimension that we find in Eagleton and Belsey. It is yet another 'approach', another opportunity to insist on the importance of language and form in literary study. Taking it up seems somehow the right thing to do; the thing that a dutiful and sensitive modern academic, conscious of the needs of the students he teaches, should be doing to stay in touch with his times. But, of course, Lodge also writes satire on his times, so it is hard to stay serious for long.

A critic able to challenge the orthodoxies of his times, to match interest in novelty of theory with an urgent and serious desire to renovate taste Lodge is not. His criticism works within terms of the given. And this is connected to Lodge's role as an illustrative, descriptive and explanatory critic. He takes other people's ideas (as, for example, the distinction between the 'contemporary' and the 'modern', or between 'metaphor' and 'metonymy'), and shows how they work; how they can be made to apply. In the same way Lodge adapts or borrows methods terms and distinctions of others in a conscious, open and deliberate manner which supplants interest in the work under critical examination with the critical procedure applied to it. As we would expect of an editor of an anthology of *Twentieth Century Literary Criticism*, and latterly *Modern Criticism and Theory; A Reader* (1988),[36] Lodge has a battery of procedures ready to hand: 'I believe,' he says in *The Novelist at the Crossroads*, 'we can profit from criticism using radically different approaches from our own.'[37] But this apparently attractive neutrality obscures the narrowness of taste his criticism displays. Lodge is not finding the detachment that criticism requires. He is evading objections to his very undetached relation to literature as a practitioner. Thus Lodge plays down personal convictions on matters of value. He does from time to time ask questions of value, and feels the need for them, such as the provocative: 'How successful is *Hard Times*?' But the question is quickly converted to a matter of *genre*-scholarship ('what *kind* of novel [my italics] is *Hard Times*?). The answer (to this particular question) is typically tentative: 'we should perhaps be more impressed by the degree of . . . success than by the novel's imperfections.'[38] No one could actually argue with that. It is not untypical of Lodge's conclusions to be less exciting than the openings of his essays have led us to expect. They can sometimes fade into truisms rounding off the essays to which they are attached. Thus 'Fire and Eyre: Charlotte Brontë's War of Earthly Elements', which explores the novel's imagery and symbolism of fire, ends with the following:

> In the war of earthly elements, in preserving a precarious equilibrium between opposing forces, Jane Eyre finds the meaning of life. Day is welcomed because it follows night, calm because it follows storm. Fire is a source of warmth and light, but it is most keenly enjoyed when snow and rain beat on the windows.[39]

Is that 'the meaning of life'? If it is, we hardly need the foregoing essay to affirm it. Nor, in the flatness of these statements, does it seem consistent with the impression of the novel the essay intended to convey.

Lodge, then, shows Jane Eyre (the character) finding the 'meaning of life'. And 'life', according to Lodge, is the legitimate subject, or raw material of the writer of fiction. It is, in fact, the centre of the controversy between 'modern' and 'contemporary' writers: 'Life, to the contemporary, is what common sense tells us it is, what people *do:* go to school, fall in love, make political choices, get married, have careers, succeed or fail ... To the modern, Life is something elusive, baffling, multiple, subjective ...' But life, though it may be the source of art, cannot (according to Lodge) operate as its test. Lodge is opposed to 'life' as a standard of critical judgement, even when the art in question invites a comparison. Taking issue with Leavis's criticism of James's *The Ambassadors*, he complains that: 'Whether James displays a sense of what is valuable and significant in living, and whether he demands a disproportionate effort from the reader, are questions that can only be answered in a spirit of religious witness.'[40] For Lodge, who is a Roman Catholic, a fact which supplies material for the social comedy of some of his essays, 'life', according to this theory, usurps the instinct to keep literature in its place, to be dealt with by literary standards.

In practice, however, Lodge's standard often is 'life'. Reviewing Lawrence Lerner's aim to 'compare the values of ... three writers – their human, not their artistic values', Lodge states that he takes 'the opposite view of critical priorities'. The logic of his appeal is convincing enough: that critical standards must be appropriate ones. Thus the critic, he warns in *The Novelist at the Crossroads,* 'must avoid the cardinal error of judging one style by criteria appropriate to another'. It is easy to see why this needs to be said, particularly in the context of a discussion of varied twentieth-century experimental styles. Perhaps, however, this sensible *caveat* does not quite explain why so much of his criticism is devoted to literary form; to the attempted construction of an all-embracing 'poetic' defined in *The Modes of Modern Writing,* and to taxonomic distinctions. On the one hand, Lodge is always trying to analyse literary works with literary tools. And his principal tool is language. Therefore the 'serious' mission of his criticism may be seen as an effort to demonstrate the relevance of language study to literary criticism. Books are made of words. Words are therefore the central preoccupation of literary critics. But even in focusing on language, Lodge would claim that he is only redressing a balance: '... in recommending an approach to the novel through language I am not seeking to deny or sever its connection with "life", but merely asking that the crucial role of language in presenting life to us in literary fiction be adequately recognised.'[41]

Lodge's criticism is not very technical or specialist. Despite his structuralist experiments (and a much more old-fashioned attachment to matters of generic convention) many of Lodge's judgements are ordinarily human. In practice, Lodge comments all the time on the life in the fictions he reads and critically discusses, for example the account of underworld Brighton in Graham Greene's *Brighton Rock.* And the 'life' he *appears* to approve (and find in modern literature he admires) is human experience in the large. He likes *Ulysses* because Joyce goes beyond what 'purports to be a story of Dublin folk ...'. For Pope, Nature and Homer were the same. For Lodge, the appeal of *Ulysses* is to do with the narrative's 'mythical dimension'. But this is just a version of what Johnson, when he praised Shakespeare's 'life', called 'general nature': '... the actions of Bloom, Stephen and Molly are not merely consistent with and expressive of their individual characters and historical situation, but re-enact (or travesty or parody) the wanderings of Odysseus and

and the actions of *his* family and acquaintance.'[42] Lodge's impatience with 'life' in criticism can be interpreted as impatience with attempts to imitate the surface of life (at a particular place and in a particular time) characteristic of the naturalistic novel. In the 'Preface and Acknowledgments' to *The Novelist at the Crossroads* he writes that one of the many and various conditioning activities of literary criticism is that: 'One has an insight into a text, or one disagrees with someone else's interpretation, and one feels a human need to communicate these things.'[43] Lodge can readily abandon technical criteria, as when he writes in a chapter on Evelyn Waugh:

> It seems to me that there comes a point in every reading of a novel when the writer either commands our assent or he does not – and if he does, then the holes or flaws in his work become less perceptible because our attention is fully occupied in the collaborative task of extracting the maximum amount of delight from what he *does* give us.[44]

But while there is no doubt that Lodge takes 'delight' in the works he discusses and that, as a producer of books, he is also an enthusiastic consumer, enthusiasm is inspired by a relatively narrow range of literary works. For all the generosity of approach, and the 'liberal' manners, of Lodge's criticism, only two *genres* are really discussed: the novel and criticism itself. And even where Lodge is revealing his interest in the way criticism is done and laying down various criteria for success, as in his essay 'Waiting for the End: Current Novel Criticism' in *The Novelist at the Crossroads*, his advice, as here, may be very routine (not to say banal): for example that jargon is sometimes necessary, but it is sometimes obtrusive; that passages need to be related to their contexts in order to be fully understood; that the quality of a critical book emerges through its critical style, etc.

A more seriously disabling consequence of Lodge's work as a critical reviewer is that it focuses attention almost exclusively on twentieth-century criticism, and is thus as *notably* unexpansive in chronological range as it is generically specific; as in his two students' editions of critical extracts, and 'Crosscurrents in Modern English Criticism'. Lodge as modern critic may therefore be seen as a critic of the modern literary scene, or to be more specific, the modern academic literary scene, that of the well-known 'names': Hillis Miller, Roland Barthes, Frank Kermode, etc., or the obscure, specialist commentators on particular texts or features of texts. Leavis, who quite frequently appears, is sometimes introduced to be rapidly dismissed (though seems important enough to have helped stir Lodge to extended disagreement in both his essays on *Hard Times*, as in the one on James's *The Ambassadors*). This is because Lodge blames Leavis for ignoring the language of fiction (leaving, of course, the field open to him). Lodge pays an elegant tribute to Leavis's influence in 'Crosscurrents in Modern English Criticism': Leavis and *Scrutiny* 'have left an indelible mark on cultural life in Britain and the Commonwealth'. However, the trouble with Leavis's work is that it does not square well with Lodge's impression of what modern literary criticism is mainly about: 'It is not an achievement that can be reduced to a number of seminal ideas, because Leavis is not a deeply original thinker, and has, out of strong conviction, deliberately avoided the field of literary theory.'[45] But there are many occasions in Lodge (no more a deeply original thinker) when we recognise him echoing critical habits, turns of phrase or distinctions given currency by Leavis. Thus, in 'The Rhetoric of *Hard Times*', the earlier essay, Lodge comments unfavourably on a passage of personal description that: '... the character is read *before* we are given the appearance. It is as if Dickens has so little confidence in his own imaginative evidence that he must inform us, over-explicitly, what conclusions we are to draw, before we come to the evidence.' Examples of Leavisian 'rhetoric' are common in Lodge. Thus the hearth-fires in *Jane Eyre* 'have an obvious function in contributing to that effect of concrete particularity which is a staple of the novel form'.[46] On the precise verbal criteria Lodge holds dear, he is more Leavisian than he may be willing to admit. But as Lodge himself says, wisely enough, Leavis's 'style and tone have proved fatally easy to imitate without maintaining the pressure of Leavis's kind of intelligence and sensibility'.[47]

And, whenever Lodge puts a foot outside the twentieth century, it is almost always to discuss novels. But Lodge does not spend much time on the early European origins of the novel, and rarely returns to writers in centuries prior to the nineteenth. Lodge's criticism is fixed at the modern (and specifically English-modern) end of the scale. Though there are mentions, there are no exhaustive treatments of Tolstoy, Flaubert or Stendhal. All the sample texts used in attempts to apply structuralist theory are taken from twentieth-century works written in English. Admittedly, the range of fictional material offered by English (and American) literature within this period is extremely wide, as is Lodge's interest. His two particular favourites may however suggest evidence of a personal (religious–doctrinal) slant. One is Joyce (a major basis for his 'modernist' interests). The other is Graham Greene ('among his own generation of British novelists it is difficult to find his equal'.)[48] As we have seen, Lodge has published pieces on a range of other novelists, of greater and lesser importance: Jane Austen, George Eliot, Thomas Hardy, Evelyn Waugh. (Greene and Waugh are Catholic novelists, as is Lodge.) But it is not his treatment of any particular novelist which distinguishes Lodge's critical interest so much as his untiring concern with the Idea of the Novel, the general form or theory of which each novelist can, in his or her different way, offer a fresh particular expression.

Of all the critics examined in this study, Lodge is the one to which students of literature will perhaps be most frequently 'sent'. The available ease of his prose, his seemingly undogmatic approach, make him a natural choice. Hughes exhibits the positive as well as the negative values that flow from criticism written by critics who are themselves writers: Lodge exposes the delusions of the view (which Hughes's writings show to be not wholly deluded) that it is necessary to practice in order to judge. The lesson of Lodge's case is that criticism by a creative writer requires a detachment that is easily lost, or may not be sought. It is not enough for a critic to be close to the art he creates. Without disinterest, the difference between the modern and the new is obscured. Originality is no more a consequence of specialising in literature of the modern age than in the literature of the ancients.

Where critics have exalted *themselves* as 'radical', it is there, ironically, that critical freshness of the kind necessary to renew the literary taste of the time is not to be found. And not only is it not found; its absence may be concealed. When concealment takes the form of an explicit 'radical' label, it is perhaps not too hard to spot, and thus, by the 'radicals' ' own method, to 'demystify' of 'deconstruct'. The 'radicals', after all, require and invite disagreement. And in this they really are provocative of criticism, and not just a futile battle of rival theorising. In their very debate about it, in their heating of the air, they unconsciously 're-centre' literature, making it more, not less, worth arguing about. They do not mean to but they do. That is a practical (and for the radicals themselves unfortunate but inevitable) consequence of radical theory. But 'radical' criticism, and its theory, is only a part of the total modern critical scene. Among the critics who do not espouse 'radical' views, some, while finding popular outlets for criticism, have remained 'professional critics'. They are celebrated and salaried occupants of the chairs of the critical establishment's 'top jobs'. This has prompted its own separate reaction. But efforts to de-professionalise the role and meaning of the modern critic have taken various, if not particularly fashionable, forms. Some, like Mason, have protested their amateur status, or, like Robson, have mastered a style and manner of critical writing in which expertise (other than that of one's informed humanity) is set firmly aside. A further counter to the professional critic has come from creative writers who are also critics. The practitioner's interests may be a critical weakness or a critical strength. They may exist in the same writer as both. And they may give the appearance of novelty and validity in critical writing that on its own terms may not deserve it. It then becomes again necessary to value the peculiar, separate, and in a broader sense 'professional' role for the literary critic. Without this, and an idea of criticism that has somewhere behind it an ideal, critical study becomes not an effort to stimulate independent opinion, arouse dissent or renovate taste, but an exercise in mass pacification based on a sanctification of the unacknowledged standards and attitudes of the present. It may thus be an unwitting effort in knowledge limitation that is élitist in a different way. The ability to offer, to argue for, and encourage tastes and attitudes that are fundamentally at odds with the times is one definition of the critic (social, political or literary at any time). It is a definition that, in this study of modern British critics, is seen to be only occasionally made flesh. But that it is rare in practice does not mean that it may be any the less a modern ideal, or even, for that same reason, a requirement of modern literary theory.

Notes

1. 'Preface and Acknowledgments', *The Novelist at the Crossroads: and other essays on fiction and criticism* (Routledge and Kegan Paul: London, 1971).
2. *The Language of Fiction: essays in criticism and verbal analysis of the English novel* (1966; Routledge and Kegan Paul: London 1979).
3. *op. cit.*, pp. 65, 15, 57.
4. *ibid.*, pp. 65, 72, 87.
5. *ibid.*, pp. 257, 188, 213, 101.
6. *ibid.*, p. 100.
7. Thomas Rymer, *Reflections on Aristotle's Treatise of Poesie* (1674; reprinted Gregg International, 1979), p. 38.
8. *Language of Fiction*, p. 113.
9. *ibid.*, pp. 115, 122.
10. *ibid.*, pp. 144, 162.
11. *Working with Structuralism: essays and reviews on nineteenth and twentieth-century literature* (1981; Ark Edition: London, 1986), p. 38.
12. *Language of Fiction*, p. 163.
13. *ibid.*, pp. 215, 115, 213.
14. *Novelist at the Crossroads*, pp. 32, 33, 283, 41, 63.
15. *ibid.*, p. 63.
16. *Twentieth Century Literary Criticism: A Reader* (Longman: Harlow, 1972).
17. *op cit.*, p. xviii.
18. *The Modes of Modern Writing: metaphor, metonymy, and typology of modern literature* (Edward Arnold: London, 1977) p. x.
19. *ibid.*, pp. 41, 52.
20. *ibid.*, pp. 71, 109.
21. *ibid.*, pp. 125, 139, 144, 159, 161, 191, 212, 228.
22. 'The Idler', No. 60, *The Yale Edition of the Works of Samuel Johnson*, II (1963) p. 186.

23. *Modes of Modern Writing*, p. 123.
24. *Definition of Literature*, p. 18.
25. *Modes of Modern Writing*, pp. 9, 8.
26. See 'Books, raw and cooked', *Original Copy: Selected Reviews and Journalism 1969–86*, p. 238.
27. *Working with Structuralism*, p. 170.
28. *ibid.*, p. 94.
29. *Language of Fiction*, p. 58.
30. *Novelist at the Crossroads*, p. 277.
31. *Working with Structuralism*, p. 3.
32. *ibid.*, pp. 20–1.
33. *ibid.*, p. 30, 31.
34. *Write On: Occasional Essays 1965–1985* (1986; Penguin: London, 1988), pp. ix, 40.
35. See 'Bourgeois Triangles' and 'Structural Defects', *Write On*, pp. 117, 114.
36. *Modern Criticism and Theory: A Reader* (Longman: London, 1988).
37. *Novelist at the Crossroads*, p. 63.
38. *Working with Structuralism*, pp. 38, 45.
39. *Language of Fiction*, p. 143.
40. *ibid.*, p. 245.
41. *Novelist at the Crossroads*, pp. 49, 18, 67–8.
42. *Modes of Modern Writing*, p. 137.
43. *Novelist at the Crossroads*, p. ix.
44. *Working with Structuralism*, p. 126.
45. *Novelist at the Crossroads*, pp. 281, 266.
46. *Language of Fiction*, pp. 153, 122.
47. *Novelist at the Crossroads*, p. 266.
48. *ibid.*, p. 118.

Index

Abrams, M. H., 232
Adamson, Joy, 195
Addison, Joseph, 24, 35, 122
Adorno, Theodor, 20
Allott, Muriel, 102
Althusser, Louis, 19, 43, 50, 57, 58
Amis, Kingsley, 226
Amis, Martin, 242
Anderson, Charles, 198, 206
Arnold, Matthew, 14, 15, 58, 133, 139, 148, 149, 157, 158, 166, 172, 176, 187, 193
'The Scholar Gypsy', 69
Auden, W. H., 12, 34, 164
Austen, Jane, 33, 224, 249
  Emma, 235
  Mansfield Park, 226–7

Baldwin, Michael, 198
Barthes, Roland, 29, 43, 56, 58, 234, 248
  The Pleasure of the Text, 38
Baskin, Leonard, 237
Baudelaire, Charles, 182
Beckett, Samuel, 115, 230
Beddoes, Thomas Lovell, 118
Beljame, A. J., 36
Belsey, Catherine, 41–71, 73, 77, 79, 97, 104, 121, 126, 165, 180, 194, 244
  'The Case of Hamlet's Conscience', 44–6, 50
  Critical Practice, 42, 43, 46–60
  'Disrupting Sexual Difference', 60, 64

John Milton, 42, 63–5, 105
  'Love and Death in "To his Coy Mistress"', 68
  'Re-Reading English and the Uncommitted Reader', 67
  The Subject of Tragedy, 42, 60–3, 67, 144
  Workshop on Lacan, 43–4, 56
Benjamin, Walter, 19
Benveniste, Emile, 50
Betjeman, John, 93
Blake, William, 33, 172, 177–8, 209
Bogan, Louise, 172
Bogarde, Dirk, 93
Boileau-Déspreaux, Nicolas, 140, 142
Boswell, James, 82, 236
Bowra, Maurice, 90, 198
Brecht, Bertholt, 19, 57
Bridges, Robert, 172
Brontë, Charlotte, 54
  Jane Eyre, 14, 227–8, 245, 248
  Shirley, 14
Brontë, Emily, 33–4
Browning, Robert, 33, 172
  'My Last Duchess', 156
Bunyan, John, 33
Burke, Edmund, 121
Burroughs, William, 230
Byron, George Gordon, Lord, 33, 115, 165, 168–9, 172, 179
  Don Juan, 169, 182
  Lines on Learning that Lady Byron was Ill, 169
  Cambridge Quarterly, The, 16, 132

253

Capote, Truman, 242
Carey, John, 72–99, 101, 102, 103, 104, 106, 107, 119, 120–1, 124, 125, 126, 131, 153, 161, 167, 176, 180, 194, 195, 237
John Donne, 86–9, 97
Original Copy, 89–94
Poems of John Milton, The, 74–5
Thackeray: Prodigal Genius, 82–6, 95, 98
The Violent Effigy, 75–80, 82, 96
'Wording and Re-Wording: Paraphrase in Literary Criticism', 80–2, 90, 119
Carlyle, Thomas, 92, 93
Castenada, Carlos, 200
Caudwell, Christopher, 20
Chaucer, Geoffrey, 33, 34, 65, 111, 115
Cherry-Garrard, Apsley, 197
Chesterton, G. K., 92, 167
Church Now, The, 241
Churchill, Charles, 172
Clare, John, 202
Clarke, C. C., *Romantic Paradox*, 103
Coleridge, Samuel Taylor, 80, 172, 209
Conan Doyle, Arthur, 57–8
Conrad, Joseph, 12, 16, 33, 34, 189
Critical Quarterly, The, 204–6
Cunningham, J. V., 172

Dante, Alighieri, 165
Darwin, Charles, 115
Defoe, Daniel, 33
Derrida, Jacques, 43, 187
Dickens, Charles, 33, 34, 54, 74, 75–80, 81, 89, 94
Dombey and Son, 79
Hard Times, 228–9, 239, 244, 248
Oliver Twist, 78
Pickwick Papers, 182
Dickinson, Emily, 172, 198, 206–8, 213, 214–15
Digger, The, 39
Dinsdale, Tim, 195
Donne, John, 55, 66, 74, 79, 86–9, 95, 96, 97, 111, 117, 126, 140, 157, 159, 172

Anniversaries, 94
'The Comparison', 89
The Courtier's Library, 96
'Death be not Proud', 66, 88
Songs and Sonnets, 86
'What if this present were the world's last night', 88
Douglas, Keith, 198, 204–5, 215, 216
Dröscher, Vitus, 196
Dryden, John, 33, 34, 37, 67, 80, 98, 115, 123, 134, 140, 142, 153, 172, 193, 203, 215
All for Love, 117
Iliad, the, Book I, 148
'The Last Parting of Hector and Andromache', 149–50
Satires of Juvenal, 117, 141
Dylan, Bob, 37, 104, 111, 121, 126

Eagleton, Terry, 7–40, 41, 42, 44, 45, 47, 52, 55, 60, 63, 66, 69, 73, 74, 94, 95, 104, 121, 122, 124, 126, 127, 135, 152, 153, 165, 176, 180, 194, 244
The Body as Language, 10, 28
Criticism and Ideology, 15–18, 19, 20
Exiles and Emigrés, 11, 12, 16, 34
The Function of Criticism, 23–4, 35
Literary Theory, 8, 22–3, 24, 26, 38
Marxism and Literary Criticism, 18
Myths of Power: A Marxist Study of the Brontës, 12–14, 19, 21, 36, 52, 75
The New Left Church, 10
The Rape of Clarissa, 20–1, 22, 24, 34, 35
Shakespeare and Society, 11, 12, 19, 25, 26
Slant, 18
Walter Benjamin, 19–20
William Shakespeare, 25–32, 51, 52, 53, 60, 65, 76
Eliade, Mircea, 199
Eliot, George, 15, 33, 34, 58, 63, 249
The Mill on the Floss, 53–4

Eliot, T. S., 12, 33, 34, 51, 68,
  86–7, 103, 104, 110–13, 116,
  119, 121, 123, 126, 140, 157,
  159, 164, 170, 171, 179, 193,
  234
 'Animula', 122
 critical writings, 174, 175, 179,
  188–9
 Four Quartets, 125
 'Prufrock', 123
Eichmann, Adolph, 29
Empson, William, 14, 80, 119–20,
  168
 Seven Types of Ambiguity, 80, 110,
  122
 Essays in Criticism, 102

Faas, Ekbert, 210, 216, 217
Ferry, David, *The Limits of Mortality*,
  103
Fielding, Henry, 33, 36, 226
Fish, Stanley, 49
Fitzgerald, F. Scott, 242
Fitzgibbon, Constantine, 196
Flaubert, Gustave, 249
Fowler, Alistair, 74
Freud, Sigmund, 26, 43, 45, 58
Froman, Robert, 195
Frost, Robert, 169, 175, 180, 181
 'Design', 123, 186
Frye, Northrop, 49, 188

Galsworthy, John, 238
Gascoigne, George, 172
Godard, J.-L., 37
Golding, William, 242
Goldmann, Lucien, 20
Goudney, Alice, 195
Gower, John, 111, 118
 Confessio Amantis, 111
Grahame, Kenneth, 169
 The Wind in the Willows, 171, 176,
  182, 185
Gray, Thomas, 172
Greenaway, John, 200
Greene, Graham, 12, 34, 230, 241,
  242, 249
 Brighton Rock, 246
Greville, Fulke, 172
Grierson, Herbert, 86

Guardian, the, 200
Guinness Book of Records, The, 91

Hallam, Arthur, 106–7
Hardy, Thomas, 172, 226, 238, 249
 Tess of the d'Urbervilles, 229
 The Woodlanders, 238
Heaney, Seamus, 93
Hegel, Georg Wilhelm Friedrich,
  26
Hemingway, Ernest, 230, 235
 'Cat in the Rain', 239–40
Herbert, George, 172
Herbert of Cherbury, Lord, 173
Hill, Geoffrey, 104, 118, 123
 'September Song', 123
Hitchcock, Alfred, 179
Hodgart, Mathew, 200
Holloway, John, 229
Homer, 22, 60, 147–50, 153, 156,
  158, 165
Hopkins, Gerard Manley, 33, 169,
  172, 186
 Letters, 188
Hughes, Ted, 192–221, 222, 249
 A Choice of Emily Dickinson's Verse,
  206–8
 A Choice of Shakespeare's Verse,
  217–18
 Crow, 216, 237–8
 Oedipus, 200
 Poetry in the Making, 201–4
 Selected Poems of Keith Douglas,
  204–5
 'Ted Hughes Writes', 208
 'Wind', 203

Iser, Wolfgang, 49

Jablow, Alta, 198
Jakobson, Roman, 234
James, Clive, 73, 90, 93
James, Henry, 12, 33, 34, 54, 58,
  134, 135, 157, 182
 The Ambassadors, 226, 229–30,
  245, 248
Jameson, Fredric, 20
Jauss, Hans Robert, 49
Johnson, Pamela Hansford, 197

Johnson, Samuel, 11, 14, 30, 33, 50, 57, 67, 122, 134, 139, 146, 167, 172, 179, 186–8, 193, 236, 246
 'The Battle of the Pygmies and Cranes', 122
 Juvenal imitations, 142
 Life of Cowley, 88, 120
 Life of Dryden, 187
 Life of Milton, 105, 123, 187
 The Preface to Shakespeare, 157
 The Rambler, No. 168, 111
 The Vanity of Human Wishes, 105
Johnson, Sally Patrick, 195
Jones, John, *The Egotistical Sublime*, 103
Jonson, Ben, 33, 140, 144, 159, 172, 236
Joyce, James, 15, 33, 34, 241, 249
 Dubliners, 235
 Finnegans Wake, 235
 Ulysses, 226, 235, 246
Juvenal, 140–3
 'Satire III', 140
 'Satire VI', 141

Kant, Immanuel, 182
Keats, John, 33, 34, 102, 108–10, 114–15, 116, 123, 124, 172
 'Endymion', 109–10
 'Ode to a Nightingale', 69
Kermode, Frank, 248
Kipling, Rudyard, 165, 180, 184–5
Knights, L. C., 146

la Rue, Danny, 179
Lacan, Jacques, 43, 45, 57, 58, 187
Lardner, Ring, 242
Larkin, Philip, 93, 104, 124, 210
 'Like Something Almost Being Said', 117
 'Absences', 117, 210
Lattimore, Richmond, 150
Lawrence, D. H., 12, 15, 33, 34, 134, 165, 235, 238–9, 242
 Women in Love, 185
Leavis, F. R., 12, 14, 15, 17, 23, 33, 34, 54, 57, 67, 75, 85, 86, 105, 114, 119, 122, 125, 131, 132, 133, 152, 155, 157, 158, 159, 164, 166, 178, 188–9, 224, 228, 229, 232, 245, 248
 The Great Tradition, 34
Lerner, Lawrence, 245–6
Lethbridge, T. C., 196
Lewis, C. Day, 200
Lewis, C. S., 81, 164, 166–8, 169, 180, 183
Liddell, Robert, 229
Lilly, J. C., 195
Listener, The, 198–200, 241
Lodge, David, 222–51
 Changing Places, 242
 The Language of Fiction, 223–30, 238, 239, 243
 Modern Criticism and Theory, 244
 The Modes of Modern Writing, 233–7, 242, 243, 246
 The Novelist at the Crossroads, 230–2, 238, 242, 244, 246, 247
 Small World, 242
 Twentieth Century Literary Criticism: A Reader, 232, 244
 Working with Structuralism, 93, 237–41, 243
 Write On, 241–2, 243
London review of Books, the, 241
Loti, Pierre, 135
Lowell, Robert, 117, 121, 198
Lukács, Georg, 20

Macherey, Pierre, 19, 20, 37, 43, 56, 58
MacNeice, Louis, 196
Mailer, Norman, *The Executioner's Song*, 242
Malory, Thomas, 106
Marcuse, Herbert, 20
Marlowe, Christopher, 115
 Tamburlaine, 51
Martial, 141
Martz, Louis, 88
Marvell, Andrew, 66, 111, 140, 172
 'A Dialogue between Soul and Body', 66, 118
 'An Horatian Ode', 67
 'To his Coy Mistress', 68
Marx, Karl, 37, 43, 45
 Grundrisse, 19, 26, 58

Index

Marx, Karl *(continued)*
  Das Kommunistische Manifest, 152
Mason, H. A., 130–60, 161, 168, 176–7, 183, 190, 213, 250
  Editing Wyatt, 154
  To Homer through Pope, 147–50, 155, 158
  Humanism and Poetry in the Early Tudor Period, 133–9
  'Is Juvenal a Classic?', 140–3, 147, 153, 154, 159
  Shakespeare's Tragedies of Love, 143–7, 154
  Sir Thomas Wyatt: A Literary Portrait, 150, 154
  The Tragic Plane, 150–2
Melville, Herman, *Moby Dick*, 37
Miller, Hillis, 248
'Mills and Boon' novels, 33
Milton, John, 37, 63, 64, 66, 69, 79, 81, 105–6, 111, 116, 122, 124, 125, 164, 168, 172
  Comus, 64
  'Minor Poems', 74
  'On the Morning of Christ's Nativity', 65
  Paradise Lost, 63–4, 79, 105, 234
  Paradise Regained, 168
  Samson Agonistes, 74, 81, 105
Moi, Toril, 21
Momaday, N. Scott, 173
More, Thomas, 135
  Utopia, 138, 141
Muir, Kenneth, 138, 154
Muppett show, the, 37

Narayan, R. K., 200
Nation, the, 195
New Society, 241
New Statesman, the, 195–97
New York Review of Books, the, 200
New York Times Book Review, the, 200
Nicholson, Max, 200
Nietzsche, Friedrich, 26
Novel, 231

Observer, the, 200, 241
O'Connor, Philip, 196
Oldham, John, 140

Ong, Walter J., 225
Opie, Iona and Peter, 198
Orwell, George, 12, 34
Owen, Wilfred, 200

Parrinder, Patrick, 15
Parsons, I. M., 199
Pelican Guide to English Literature, the, 55, 66
Penguin Critical Anthologies, 102
Penguin English Poets, 102
Perkins, William, 45
Pilinszky, János, 206
Plath, Sylvia, 205–6, 212–13, 214–15
  Ariel, 209
Plato, 209
Poetry Book Society Bulletin, 208
Popa, Vasko, 202, 213, 216
Pope, Alexander, 14, 33, 34, 35, 49, 67, 92, 93, 98, 101, 120, 140, 142, 153, 158, 159, 172, 183, 246
  'The Art of Sinking in Poetry', 119
  'An Epistle to Arbuthnot', 123
  'An Essay on Criticism', 193, 212
  Homer's *Iliad* and *Odyssey*, 147–50, 158
  'Rape of the Lock', 149
Pound, Ezra, 157, 172
Powys, T. F., 140
Press, John, 196
Pushkin, Alexander, 199, 212

Raine, Craig, 90, 93, 94, 97
  'Arsehole', 94
Ransom, John Crowe, 210
Rapin, René, 227
Re-Reading Literature series, 7, 25
Richards, I. A., 169, 189
Richardson, Samuel, 20, 21, 33, 35
Ricks, Christopher, 81, 101–29, 155, 161, 194, 195
  T. S. Eliot Memorial Lectures, 103
  T. S. Eliot and Prejudice, 103, 110–13, 119, 122, 124, 126
  The Force of Poetry, 102, 103, 107–8, 111, 117–20, 122

Ricks, Christopher *(continued)*
  Keats and Embarrassment, 108–10, 114, 115, 123, 125
  Milton's Grand Style, 103, 104, 110, 114, 116, 119
  The Poems of Tennyson, 102
  The State of the Language, 124
  Tennyson, 106–7, 108, 113–14, 116, 126
  Twentieth Century Views, 102
Riding, Laura, 215, 216
Riffaterre, Michael, 238
Robinson, Edwin Arlington, 172
Robson, W. W., 161–91, 236, 250
  Critical Essays, 163, 164–9, 181
  The Definition of Literature, 163, 165, 169–73, 175
  Modern English Literature, 162, 189
  A Prologue to English Literature, 163
  The Signs Among Us, 161
Rokeach, Milton, 196
Russell, W. H., 92
Rymer, Thomas, 146, 227

Saint-Exupéry, Antoine de, 197
Salinger, J. D., 242
Santayana, G., 168
Sartre, Jean-Paul, 20, 109
Saussure, Ferdinand de, 43, 48, 50
Scrutiny, 16, 17, 27, 33, 34, 53, 57, 63, 124–5, 127, 131, 132, 143, 154, 155, 156, 158, 163, 248
Segal, Clancy, 195
Selden, Raman, 15
Seneca, 93, 139
Shah, Idries, 199
Shakespeare, William, 22, 27, 33, 34, 58, 60, 106, 121, 122, 140, 143–7, 152, 158, 172, 179, 205, 217–18, 236, 246
  Anthony and Cleopatra, 67, 146–7, 158
  Coriolanus, 52
  Hamlet, 44–6, 184, 239
  Julius Caesar, 52, 61
  King Lear, 30–1, 144, 145, 234
  Macbeth, 27–8, 51, 111, 146, 147
  Measure for Measure, 28
  The Merchant of Venice, 28–9
  Othello, 30, 144, 145, 146, 156, 158
  Richard III, 51
  Romeo and Juliet, 144–5, 156
  Troilus and Cressida, 25–6
Shelley, Percy Bysshe, 33, 172
Sidney, Philip, 16, 65, 193
Singer, Isaac Bashevis, 200, 209, 215
Smart, Christopher, 94, 202
Smith, Stevie,
  'Night-Time in the Cemetery', 117
  'Not Waving But Drowning', 119
Sophocles, 154
Spark, Muriel, 230
Spectator, the, 200
Speirs, Logan, 16
Spender, Stephen, 136
Spenser, Edmund, 33, 34, 65, 81
Sphere History of Literature in the English Language, The, 102
Stein, Gertrude, 235
Stendhal, Henri Beyle, 249
Stephen, Leslie, 36
Sterne, Laurence, 33, 35, 122
Stevens, Wallace, 172
Stevenson, Robert Louis, 7, 92, 169, 183, 189
  Kidnapped, 174, 177, 183
  Treasure Island, 174, 180, 181, 182
Studies in Philology, 44, 46, 47
Sturluson, Snorri, 200
Sunday Times, The, 73, 90, 102, 197–8
Superman, 33
Swift, Jonathan, 35, 49
  Gulliver's Travels, 67

Tablet, the, 241
Tennyson, Alfred (Lord), 33, 113–14, 116, 140, 169, 171, 172, 183
  Idylls of the King, 113–14
  In Memoriam, 51, 107, 114, 123, 184

Index

Tennyson, Alfred (Lord) *(continued)*
   'Locksley Hall Sixty Years After', 179
   'The Lord of Burleigh', 174
   Maud, 106, 114, 178
   'Morte d'Arthur', 106
   The Palace of Art, 51
   The Princess, 110, 113
   'St Simeon Stylites', 114
   'Tithonus', 108
Tennyson, Emily, 107
Thackeray, William Makepeace, 74, 82–6, 93, 98
   Henry Esmond, 96
   The Newcomes, 85
   Pendennis, 95
   Vanity Fair, 83
Thomas, Dylan, 196–7, 210, 212, 214, 215
Tibetan Book of the Dead, 211
Times, The, 121
Times Higher Educational Supplement, the, 241
Times Literary Supplement, the, 118
Tolstoy, Leo, 85, 249
   Anna Karenina, 85
   War and Peace, 125
Trilling, Lionel, 188, 226
Turville-Petre, E. O. G., 198
Twain, Mark, *Huckleberry Finn*, 156

Updike, John, 230

Van Ghent, Dorothy, 229
Vaughan, Henry, 172
Verlaine, Paul, 123

Watson, George, 17
Waugh, Evelyn, 12, 34, 247, 249
Wellek, René, 8
Wells, H. G., 197
   Tono Bungay, 229
Wesker, Arnold, 195
White, Patrick, 198, 211
Whiteley, W. H., 199
Whitman, W., 94
Williams, Raymond, 9, 11, 12, 17, 37
Wimsatt, W. K., 225
Winters, Yvor, 169, 178, 181, 184, 186, 189
   Forms of Discovery, 172–3
Wither, George, 45
Wittgenstein, Ludwig, 26
Woode, Nathaniel, 45
Woolf, Virginia, 33, 235
Wordsworth, Jonathan, *The Music of Humanity*, 103
Wordsworth, William, 5, 14, 33, 34, 51, 55, 68, 93, 103, 111, 118, 119, 120, 121, 172, 179, 181, 193, 209
   Michael, 51
   The Prelude, 68
   'Resolution and Independence', 176
Wyatt, Thomas, 111, 135, 137, 138–9, 154, 157, 159
   'Stond who so list', 139
Wykes, Alan, 195

Yeats, W. B., 15, 34, 51, 68, 140, 172, 215